21世纪职业教育教材·财经商贸系列

外贸单证实务

（第三版）

主　编　王群飞　苏定东

副主编　陈　晔　张旺军

主　审　张　琦

内 容 简 介

本书以单证员的主要工作任务为基础进行项目编写,同时以单证工作的流程为线索编排项目顺序。书中单证员的工作任务以某公司的一笔具体业务为载体,涉及信用证落实、出口托运、原产地证申领、出口报关、出口投保、制单结汇等各个环节,内容真实,操作具体,突出职业能力的培养。本书在每个项目中都配备了一定的理论知识,供学生学习单证基础知识及参加单证员职业资格考试用。此外,每个项目中又配备了2套训练实例,以从不同角度培养学生的实际操作能力。

本书可作为高等职业院校、成人高校的外贸类专业教学用书,也可作为初入外贸行业者的参考用书。

图书在版编目(CIP)数据

外贸单证实务/王群飞,苏定东主编. —3版. —北京:北京大学出版社,2021.8
21世纪职业教育教材·财经商贸系列
ISBN 978-7-301-32171-3

Ⅰ.①外… Ⅱ.①王…②苏… Ⅲ.①进出口贸易 – 原始凭证 – 高等职业教育 – 教材 Ⅳ.①F740.44

中国版本图书馆CIP数据核字(2021)第074200号

书　　　名	外贸单证实务(第三版)
	WAIMAO DANZHENG SHIWU(DI-SAN BAN)
著作责任者	王群飞　苏定东　主编
策 划 编 辑	巩佳佳
责 任 编 辑	巩佳佳
标 准 书 号	ISBN 978-7-301-32171-3
出 版 发 行	北京大学出版社
地　　　址	北京市海淀区成府路205号　100871
网　　　址	http://www.pup.cn　新浪微博:@北京大学出版社
电 子 邮 箱	编辑部 zyjy@pup.cn　总编室 zpup@pup.cn
电　　　话	邮购部 010-62752015　发行部 010-62750672　编辑部 010-62704142
印 刷 者	北京溢漾印刷有限公司
经 销 者	新华书店
	787毫米×1092毫米　16开本　11.75印张　311千字
	2011年12月第1版　2016年6月第2版
	2021年8月第3版　2023年11月第3次印刷
定　　　价	38.00元

未经许可,不得以任何方式复制或抄袭本书之部分或全部内容。
版权所有,侵权必究
举报电话:010-62752024　电子邮箱:fd@pup.cn
图书如有印装质量问题,请与出版部联系,电话:010-62756370

前　言

课程简介

党的二十大报告提出，要推进高水平对外开放，加快建设贸易强国，截至2022年年底，我国已成为140多个国家和地区的主要贸易伙伴，货物贸易总额居世界第一。因此，外贸人才的需求日益增加。在复杂多变的国际经济形势下，只有具备扎实的专业知识、较强的操作技能、良好的综合素质，才能在外贸工作中得心应手，处理各种突发性问题，顺利地完成各笔业务。

外贸单证工作是外贸工作中的核心工作，单证工作的好坏直接影响外贸业务能否顺利完成，因此，单证员素质的高低将直接影响企业的经济效益。为培养具备外贸单证操作能力的应用型人才，我们编写了这本教材。通过学习和训练，学生能够了解外贸业务中各种单证的流转过程，能够缮制各种单证并完成交单手续，能处理在制单和交单过程中的各种问题。

本书对单证员的工作任务进行归纳整合，并以单证员的工作任务为基础编写各项目。同时，本书以单证员的工作流程为线索，编排项目顺序，这有利于学生对单证工作的流程形成更加直观的认识，也有利于教师组织教学时项目的前后衔接。本书在进行项目编写时注重以学生为主体，每个项目都是先提出工作任务，引导学生操作，然后再进行操作示范，让学生对存在的问题进行分析。每个项目都有"能力训练"模块，以训练学生的单证制作能力。同时，本书还打破其他单证教材单纯注重单证缮制这一局限，在教材中加入了"岗位拓展"模块，更有利于培养学生分析问题和解决问题的能力，不断提高学生的岗位协调能力。

使用本书教学时，教师可以先导入项目"工作任务"，让学生尝试着独立完成。然后，教师根据学生完成工作任务的情况进行操作示范，并针对性地讲解，在讲解的过程中引入"知识链接"中的内容。最后，给学生布置相关"能力训练"项目，进一步训练和提升其外贸单证操作能力，并通过"能力训练"对学生进行项目评价。课后要求学生分组讨论，自行查找资料，合作完成"岗位拓展"模块的讨论，教师对讨论结果进行点评。

参加本书编写工作的人员有：湖州职业技术学院王群飞（导论、项目一、项目二、项目五、附录）、沙洲职业工学院苏定东（项目三、项目四）、湖州职业技术学院陈晔（项目六）、湖州职业技术学院张旺军（项目七、项目八）。全书由王群飞、苏定东主编，负责提供编写框架并统稿，陈晔、张旺军担任副主编，张琦教授担任本书的主审。

　　本书在编写过程中得到了学校、学院领导的悉心指导和帮助，还得到了浙江久立集团褚震波先生、湖州佰业进出口有限公司章彦岚女士的大力支持，湖州翔顺工贸有限公司孙晓羽女士、安吉慧峰医用敷料有限公司徐琰丽女士给本书编写提供了大量的资料。同时，编者还借鉴了不少专家学者的研究成果和著作，在此一并表示衷心的感谢。

　　此次修订，主要因国家区域经济一体化、关检合一改革的发展，所以重点对申领原产地证书、办理出口货物报关两个项目进行了修订。另外，这次修订，我们在教材中增加了相关知识点的微课视频，供学生课前课后学习使用。与本教材配套建设的"外贸单证实务"课程是浙江省第二批精品在线开放课程，相关课件、习题等配套资料可以在浙江省高等学校在线开放课程共享平台下载。

　　由于编者水平有限，且本书在描述单证操作时难免有疏漏及不足之处，敬请各位专家、同人和读者批评指正，以便重印或再版时进行修正，不胜感激。

编者

2023 年 11 月

目　录

导论 ·· (1)
　　一、学习目标 ··· (1)
　　二、学习内容 ··· (1)
项目一　审核与修改信用证 ··· (7)
　　一、学习目标 ··· (7)
　　二、工作任务 ··· (7)
　　三、知识链接 ·· (14)
　　四、能力训练 ·· (21)
　　五、岗位拓展 ·· (27)
项目二　缮制商业发票和装箱单 ··· (29)
　　一、学习目标 ·· (29)
　　二、工作任务 ·· (29)
　　三、知识链接 ·· (37)
　　四、能力训练 ·· (39)
　　五、岗位拓展 ·· (43)
项目三　办理出口货物托运 ·· (45)
　　一、学习目标 ·· (45)
　　二、工作任务 ·· (45)
　　三、知识链接 ·· (49)
　　四、能力训练 ·· (55)
　　五、岗位拓展 ·· (58)
项目四　申领原产地证书 ·· (59)
　　一、学习目标 ·· (59)
　　二、工作任务 ·· (59)
　　三、知识链接 ·· (63)
　　四、能力训练 ·· (74)
　　五、岗位拓展 ·· (75)
项目五　办理出口货物报关 ·· (77)
　　一、学习目标 ·· (77)
　　二、工作任务 ·· (77)
　　三、知识链接 ·· (93)
　　四、能力训练 ·· (96)

五、岗位拓展 …………………………………………………………………………（98）
项目六　办理出口货物投保 …………………………………………………………（99）
　　一、学习目标 …………………………………………………………………………（99）
　　二、工作任务 …………………………………………………………………………（99）
　　三、知识链接 …………………………………………………………………………（104）
　　四、能力训练 …………………………………………………………………………（109）
　　五、岗位拓展 …………………………………………………………………………（113）
项目七　缮制其他结汇单证 …………………………………………………………（115）
　　一、学习目标 …………………………………………………………………………（115）
　　二、工作任务 …………………………………………………………………………（115）
　　三、知识链接 …………………………………………………………………………（123）
　　四、能力训练 …………………………………………………………………………（129）
　　五、岗位拓展 …………………………………………………………………………（131）
项目八　交单收汇 ……………………………………………………………………（133）
　　一、学习目标 …………………………………………………………………………（133）
　　二、工作任务 …………………………………………………………………………（133）
　　三、知识链接 …………………………………………………………………………（144）
　　四、能力训练 …………………………………………………………………………（146）
　　五、岗位拓展 …………………………………………………………………………（152）
附录一　企业单证实例 ………………………………………………………………（155）
附录二　常用外贸单证术语 …………………………………………………………（171）
参考文献 ………………………………………………………………………………（179）

导 论

一、学习目标

能力目标： 能分析一笔外贸业务的单证流程。
知识目标： 识记外贸单证的含义，明确外贸单证工作的基本要求。

二、学习内容

(一) 外贸单证的含义及分类

1. 外贸单证的含义

外贸单证(Foreign Trade Documents)，是指在外贸业务中应用的单据与证书，相关人员凭借这些单据与证书来处理国际货物的支付、运输、保险、商检、结汇等。

狭义的单证是指在合同履行过程中应用的单据和信用证，广义的单证则是指外贸业务中的各种文件和凭证。

就出口贸易而言，出口单证是出口货物推定交付的证明，是结算的工具。单证作为一种贸易文件，它的流转环节构成了贸易程序。单证工作贯穿于企业的外销、进货、运输、收汇的全过程，工作量大，时间性强，涉及面广，除了外贸企业内部各部门之间的协作配合外，还必须与银行、海关、交通运输部门、保险公司以及有关的行政管理机关等保持多方面的联系，环环相扣，互有影响，也互为条件。

2. 外贸单证的分类

根据不同的分类标准，外贸单证可以划分为不同的种类。

(1) 根据外贸单证的性质划分。

根据性质不同，外贸单证可以分为金融单据和商业单据。

① 金融单据：指汇票、本票、支票及其他用于取得款项的凭证。
② 商业单据：指发票、运输单证、保险单证、装箱单证以及其他类似单据。

(2) 根据外贸单证的流向划分。

根据流向不同，外贸单证可以分为进口单证和出口单证。

① 进口单证：指进口地的企业及有关部门涉及的单证，包括进口许可证、进口报关单等。
② 出口单证：指出口地的企业及有关部门涉及的单证，如出口许可证、出口报关单、包装单据、运输单据、商业发票、汇票、检验检疫证书、原产地证书、保险单等。

（3）根据外贸单证的用途划分。

根据用途不同，外贸单证可以分为资金单据、商业单据、货运单据、保险单据、公务单据和其他单证。

① 资金单据：如汇票、本票和支票等。
② 商业单据：如商业发票、装箱单等。
③ 货运单据：如海运提单、租船提单、多式运输单据、航空运单、铁路运单、邮政收据等。
④ 保险单据：如保险单、预约保单、保险证明等。
⑤ 公务单据：如海关发票、领事发票、原产地证书、检验检疫证书等。
⑥ 其他单证：如寄单证明、寄样证明、装运通知、船龄证明等。

（二）外贸单证工作的流程

在国际贸易销售合同的履行过程中，信用证落实、托运、报关、保险等各个环节，都是通过各种单证进行操作的，应该说外贸单证是履行销售合同的必要手段和证明。在合同履行的不同阶段都会有相应的单证出立、组合和流通。外贸单证工作的流程如图0-1所示。

教学视频

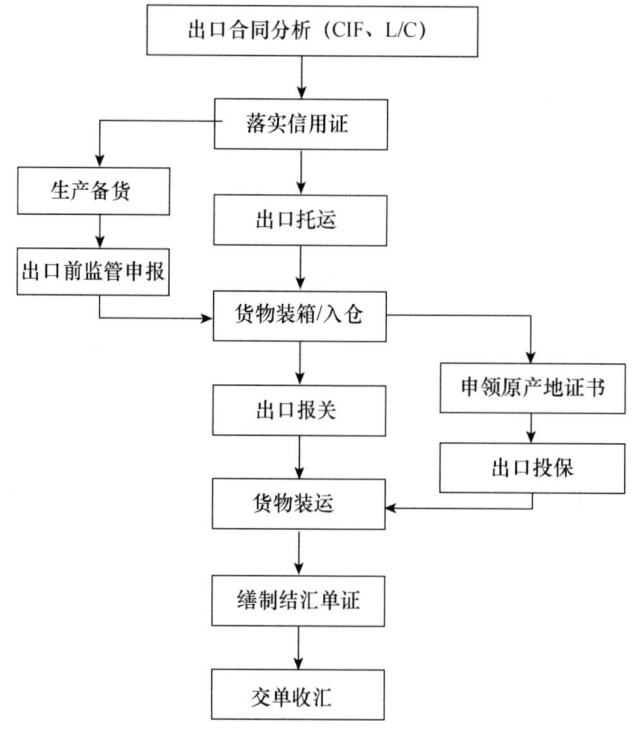

图0-1 外贸单证工作的流程

1．落实信用证

在以信用证方式结算的出口业务中，出口商能否及时取得进口商开立的符合合同要求的信用证，既关系能否安全收汇，又关系出口商能否交货。因此，落实信用证的工作对出口商来说至关重要。落实信用证的工作具体包括催证、审证和改证三个环节。

（1）催证。

一般在签订销售合同时，最好在合同条款中规定进口商开立信用证的最迟期限。如果到了最迟开证时间，进口商还未开立信用证，则出口商应提示对方及时开证，以免影响备货的进度。在具体操作时,出口商应在对方信用证开到以后再进行备货,以免节外生枝,让自己陷入被动。

(2) 审证。

信用证的开立以销售合同为依据,其主要条款也应与销售合同条款相符合。因此,在收到进口商开来的信用证后,通知行应对信用证的真伪、开证行的资信情况、付款责任等进行审核,而出口商则要以销售合同为基础,对信用证的具体内容进行审核。

(3) 改证。

出口商在改证过程中要考虑全局,对一些与销售合同条款不一致又损害自己利益的条款应坚决要求修改;对一些虽与销售合同内容不相符,但是对自己利益影响不大的条款可不要求修改。若有必须要修改的内容,则出口商向进口商提出修改意见,要求对方到原开证行办理改证。出口商收到对方的信用证修改书后,若接受修改,要将修改后的内容和原信用证的内容整合在一起。

2. 出口托运

在 CIF 出口合同项下,出口托运工作由出口商负责。出口商落实信用证后,在进行备货的同时要办理出口货物的托运工作。

单证员要与生产部门沟通好,根据销售合同和信用证的要求以及实际的出货时间来确定大致的船期。确定船期后,出口商缮制订舱委托书向货代公司办理托运。货代公司收到订舱委托书后,缮制托运单向船公司订舱。船公司根据配载原则,结合货物的毛重、尺码、装运港、目的港等情况,安排舱位,并签订配舱回单、装货单等给货代公司。货代公司收到配舱信息后,根据货物的交接形式给出口商发入仓通知或装箱通知等文件。至此,出口商收到了货物出口的船名、航次、货物交接地点与时间等信息,出口托运工作完成。

3. 申领原产地证书

原产地证书是出口商应进口商要求而提供的,是贸易关系人交接货物、结算货款、索赔理赔、进口国通关验收、征收关税的有效凭证,它还是出口国享受配额待遇、进口国对不同出口国实行不同贸易政策的凭证。一般情况下,销售合同或信用证中会规定提供哪种原产地证书。出口商根据进口商的要求申请原产地证书,使进口商享受到优惠的进口关税。

原产地证书一般在报关前申领,根据不同的原产地证书的申领要求,出口商通过网络向当地海关或国际贸易促进委员会申领。

4. 出口报关

海关对进出口货物实行报检报关整合申报。对需要实施出口检验检疫的货物,企业应在报关前向产地/组货地海关进行出口前监管申报。海关实施检验检疫监管后建立电子底账,向企业反馈电子底账数据号。对符合要求的货物,海关会按规定签发检验检疫证书。企业报关时应填写电子底账数据号,办理出口通关手续。

出口企业在货物装运的前几天,应把相关的报关委托书、报关单、商业发票、装箱单等报关单证寄交报关代理人,由报关代理人(报关员)在货物运抵海关监管区后、装货的 24 小时以前向海关进行如实申报。如果海关决定现场查验,报关代理人应到现场配合查验。在完成现场查验、缴纳税费后,海关放行,工作人员便可装运货物。

5. 出口投保

在 CIF 出口合同项下,由出口商办理货物的投保手续。在 CFR 或 FOB 的出口合同项下,出口商也可以根据进口商的要求,代为办理投保,但保险费要单独列支。

出口商应在备妥货物并收到配舱信息后,根据销售合同或信用证的要求,及时向保险公司办理投保手续。投保时,由出口商填制投保单,向保险公司办理投保,保险公司在审核相关资料后,签发保险单或保险凭证,以确认承保。

6. 缮制结汇单证

货物装运完成后,出口商应按照销售合同和信用证的要求,缮制和整理相关结汇单证,在信用证规定的交单有效期内,向银行办理交单手续。常用的结汇单证包括商业发票、装箱单、提单、保险单、原产地证书等,具体视信用证的规定而定。

信用证结算方式下,银行审单的标准是"单证一致、单单一致"。单证的质量将直接影响到安全收汇,因此,出口商必须严格按照信用证中的单据条款缮制单据,单据的种类、内容、份数等都应符合信用证的规定,并应做到正确、完整、及时、简明、整洁。

7. 交单收汇

出口商在缮制完结汇单证后,根据信用证要求交单给指定的银行。在交单之前,出口商要认真审核相关单证,发现不符点要及时修改,避免交单后陷入被动。银行在审核单证确认无误后,就将整套单证寄往国外付款银行索取货款。等国外付款银行付款后,出口商在电子口岸提交数据申请结汇。

(三) 外贸单证工作的基本要求

教学视频

外贸单证工作总的要求是"四个一致",即证同一致,单证一致,单单一致,单货一致。证同一致是指信用证与销售合同保持一致;单证一致是指外贸单据与信用证保持一致;单单一致是指各种单据之间保持一致;单货一致是指单据中所描述的货物与实物保持一致。

单证制作原则上应做到正确、完整、及时、简明和整洁。

1. 正确

正确是外贸单证工作的前提和核心。所谓正确,是指单证制作要符合以下两个方面的要求:一是要做到上面所述的"四个一致",例如,在信用证中规定所有的单据要显示信用证的号码,如果在提单或保险单等结汇单据上不显示信用证号码,就单证不一致了;二是各种单证必须符合有关国际惯例和进出口双方所在国家的相关法律和规定。在实际业务中,由于单证中存在几个不符点而遭对方拒付的情况时有发生。因此,制单必须要把正确放在首位。

2. 完整

所谓完整,是指单证制作必须符合以下两个方面的规定。

(1) 单据份数齐全、成套。

单据份数齐全,是指每一种单证的正本份数、副本份数需按规定的份数要求制作,不能随意减少。单据成套,是指一笔交易中,出口商应按信用证规定制作或取得所有种类的单证。

在信用证业务下,进口商需要哪些单据,每种单据各需多少份,一般都在信用证中标明,出口商只有按规定提交全部合格单据,开证行才能保证付款。例如,提单上显示正本是3份,信用证中要求提交全套正本提单,就必须提交3份正本,否则就视为不完整。因此,在制单审单的过程中相关工作人员必须密切关注,及时催办,以防遗漏或误期,以保证全套单据的完整。

(2) 单据本身内容完整。

任何单据都有其特定的作用,而这些特定的作用又是通过其特定的格式、项目、内容、文字、签章等表现出来的。如果格式使用不当、项目漏填、文字不通、签章不全,就不能构成一份有效的文件,也就不能被银行接受。例如,进口国海关需用进口国本国制定的固定格式的海关发票,而出口商没有用,单据上需要背书的没有背书,需要手签的没有加手签等,都属于单据本身内容不完整的情况。

3．及时

单证工作的时间性强,主要表现在以下两个方面。

(1) 每一种单证的出单日期要及时、有序、合理。

要做到单证出单日期的及时、有序、合理,既要使单证符合一般商业习惯和要求,又要在信用证或销售合同规定的有效期内。例如,保险单的出单日期不得迟于提单的签发日期,提单日期不得迟于装运日期。出单不及时、无序、不合理会造成单证不符、单单不符。此外,各种单证之间的日期不能相互矛盾。

(2) 及时交单议付。

全套结汇单证缮制完成后,应及时到议付行交单议付。《跟单信用证统一惯例(UCP600)》(以下简称"UCP600")第十四条规定:正本运输单据,则须由受益人或其代表在不迟于本惯例所指的发运日之后的二十一个日历日内交单,但是在任何情况下都不得迟于信用证的截止日。如果超过交单期或信用证的有效期交单,银行将拒绝接受单据。

4．简明

所谓简明,是指单据内容应按信用证规定和国际贸易惯例填制,力求简明,力戒烦琐,避免画蛇添足、弄巧成拙。简化单证不仅可以减少工作量和提高工作效率,而且也有利于提高单证质量和减少单证的差错。为简化单证,UCP600第十四条规定:除商业发票外,其他单据中的货物、服务或履约行为的描述,如果有的话,可使用与信用证中的描述不矛盾的概括性用语。

5．整洁

所谓整洁,是指单据的布局要美观、大方,其格式的设计和缮制应力求标准化和规范化。如果说正确和完整是单证的内在质量,那么整洁就是单证的外观质量。单证的外观质量在一定程度上反映了一个国家的科技水平和一个企业的业务水平。单证是否整洁,不但反映出制单人制单的熟练程度和工作态度,而且还会直接影响出单的效果。当单据需要做更改时,每更改一处,就一定要在更改的位置加盖校对章或简签;如果可以重做的,就尽量重新缮制单证。

项目一
审核与修改信用证

一、学习目标

能力目标：能分析信用证的基本内容，能根据外贸销售合同审核信用证并进行修改。

知识目标：识记信用证的基本条款，掌握落实信用证的业务流程，明确信用证审核与修改的要点。

二、工作任务

（一）任务描述

湖州正昌贸易有限公司成立于1992年，注册资本人民币2 000万元，主要从事竹木制品等产品的进出口业务。公司拥有多家下属工厂，产品主要销往欧洲、美国、日本、韩国等。

公司在2019年2月11日与韩国MAIJER公司签订了一份销售藤帘的合同。2019年3月7日，单证员张洁从中国银行湖州市分行处拿到韩国MAIJER公司通过大邱银行开过来的信用证（L/C No.：M51145160747856）。按照惯例，张洁从业务员处拿来与韩国MAIJER公司签订的销售合同（S/C No.：ZC190211），对信用证进行审核，以便后期能顺利交货、交单。

（二）任务分析

总体任务	根据销售合同（S/C No.：ZC190211）审核并修改信用证（L/C No.：M51145160747856）
任务分解	任务一：分析销售合同条款
	任务二：分析信用证条款
	任务三：审核信用证，找出问题条款
	任务四：提出修改意见

（三）操作示范

第一步：分析销售合同条款。

张洁找出与韩国MAIJER公司签订的销售合同（见样单1-1），先对销售合同进行分析。

教学视频

样单1-1 销售合同

湖州正昌贸易有限公司
HUZHOU ZHENGCHANG TRADING CO., LTD.
42 HONGQI ROAD, HUZHOU, CHINA
TEL：＋86-0572-2365×××　FAX：＋86-0572-2365×××

销售确认书
SALES CONFIRMATION

号码：
No.：ZC190211

日期：
Date：FEB. 11, 2019

签约地点：
Signed at：HUZHOU

买方：
Buyers：MAIJER FISTRTION INC

地址：　　　　　　　　　　　　　　　　电传/传真：
Address：3214, WALKER, NAKAGYO-KU,　　Telex/Fax：0082-54-8545×××
　　　　　KYUNG-BUK, KOREA REP.

兹买卖双方同意成交下列商品，订立条款如下：
The undersigned Sellers and Buyers have agreed to close the following transactions according to the terms and conditions stipulated below：

（1）货号 Article No.	（2）商品名称及规格 Name of Commodity and Specification	（3）数量 Quantity	（4）单价 Unit Price	（5）金额 Amount
L-2331	RATTAN CURTAIN	14 408PCS	CIF BUSAN USD2.61/PC	USD37 604.88

1. 数量与金额允许增或减5%
   More or Less：5% MORE OR LESS IN AMOUNT AND QUANTITY IS ALLOWED.
2. 包装：
   Packing：IN CARTONS OF 8PCS EACH
3. 装运期：
   Time of Shipment：NOT LATER THAN MAR. 30, 2019
4. 装运口岸和目的港：
   Port of Loading and Destination：FROM SHANGHAI, CHINA TO BUSAN, KOREA REP.
   TRANSSHIPMENT IS ALLOWED AND PARTIAL SHIPMENT IS PROHIBITED.
5. 付款条件：
   Terms of Payment：BY IRREVOCABLE LETTER OF CREDIT AT SIGHT
6. 保险：由卖方按发票金额110%投保_____险
   Insurance：TO BE EFFECTED BY SELLERS FOR 110% OF FULL INVOICE VALUE COVERING ALL RISKS AND WAR RISK.
7. 备注：
   Remarks：

买方　　　　　　　　　　　　　　　卖方：湖州正昌贸易有限公司
THE BUYER：MAIJER FISTRTION INC.　　THE SELLER：HUZHOU ZHENGCHANG TRADING
　　　　　　　　　　　　　　　　　　　　　　　　　CO., LTD.
ADAM　　　　　　　　　　　　　　　　陈强

张洁仔细地分析了合同各个条款,这是一份与韩国 MAIJER 公司签订的销售藤帘的合同,有溢短装条款,采用即期信用证付款,装运期不迟于3月底,要求卖方办理托运和保险。

第二步:分析信用证条款。

张洁拿出中国银行的出口信用证通知书(见样单 1-2)和信用证(见样单 1-3),对信用证的条款进行初步分析。

样单 1-2　出口信用证通知书

 **湖州市分行**

出口信用证通知书

我行编号:LA92G3120/03		通知日期:2019-03-07
致:HUZHOU ZHENGCHANG TRADING CO.,LTD.		
开证行:DAEGU BANK,LTD.,THE DAEGU		
信用证号:M51145160747856		开证日期:2019-03-05
金　额:USD37 604.88		来证方式:FULL L/C
☒此证一切银行费用均由你司负担,如不同意,请径洽开证申请人。 □此证尚未生效,待收到授权或生效通知后,方可凭以议付。 □此证印押不符,请在出运前与我行联系。 □此证限制我行议付。		
注意事项: 1.请将来证条款与所签合同核对,如有不符或需修改处,请径洽开证申请人。 2.简电通知或未生效的信用证,请在收到证实书或生效通知后再发货。 3.如不接受此证,请自通知日起三日内备函加盖公章连同该证一并退我行。 4.请注意我行对来证中某些条款的提示。 5.提交单据时,请将正本信用证连同该通知书一并交与我行。 6.我行根据 UCP600(2007 REVISION)受理信用证通知。		

样单 1-3　信用证

```
MT S700               ISSUE OF A DOCUMENTARY CREDIT
APPLICATION HEADER    * DAEGU BANK,LTD.,THE
                      * DAEGU
SEQUENCE OF TOTAL      * 27:1/1
FORM OF DOC. CREDIT    * 40A:IRREVOCABLE
DOC. CREDIT NUMBER     * 20:M51145160747856
DATE OF ISSUE           31C:190305
APPLICABLE RULES       * 40E:UCP LATEST VERSION
EXPIRY                 * 31D:DATE 190421 PLACE AT KOREA REP
```

APPLICANT	*50: MAIJER FISTRTION INC.
	3214,WALKER, NAKAGYO-KU,KYUNG-BUK,
	KOREA REP.
BENEFICIARY	*59: HUZHOU ZHENGCHAN TRADING CO. ,LTD.
	42 HONGQI ROAD,
	HUZHOU,
	CHINA
AMOUNT	*32B: CURRENCY USD AMOUNT 37 604.88
AVAILABLE WITH/BY	*41A: ANY BANK
	BY NEGOTIATION
DRAFTS AT...	42C: AT 30 DAYS AFTER SIGHT FOR 100 PERCENT OF INVOICE VALUE
DRAWEE	*42A: *DAEGU BANK, LTD. , THE DAEGU
PARTIAL SHIPMENT	43P: NOT ALLOWED
TRANSSHIPMENT	43T: NOT ALLOWED
PORT OF LOADING	44E: CHINESE MAIN PORT
PORT OF DISCHARGE	44F: BUSAN PORT, KOREA REP.
LATEST DATE OF SHIP.	44C: 190330
DESCRIPT. OF GOODS	45A:
	14 408PCS RATTAN CURTAIN AS PER SALES CONFIRMATION NO. ZC190211
	USD 2.81/PC CIF BUSAN
DOCUMENTS REQUIRED	46A:

+ SIGNED COMMERCIAL INVOICE IN 3 FOLDS CERTIFIED THE GOODS ARE OF CHINESE ORIGIN.
+ PACKING LIST IN 3 FOLDS
+ FULL SET OF ORIGINAL CLEAN ON BOARD MARINE BILL OF LADING MADE OUT TO SHIPPER'S ORDER AND BLANK ENDORSED, MARKED FREIGHT PREPAID AND NOTIFY APPLICANT QUOTING FULL NAME AND ADDRESS.
+ MARINE INSURANCE POLICY FOR 110PCT OF INVOICE VALUE, BLANK ENDORSED, COVERING FPA CLAIMS PAYABLE AT DESTINATION.
+ ORIGINAL CERTIFICATE OF ORIGIN ASIA-PACIFIC TRADE AGREEMENT PLUS ONE COPY ISSUED BY CIQ.
+ SHIPMENT ADVICE WITH FULL DETAILS INCLUDING SHIPPING MARKS, CARTON NUMBERS, VESSEL'S NAME,BILL OF LADING NUMBER,VALUE AND QUANTITY OF GOODS MUST BE SENT WITHIN 3 DAYS OF THE DATE OF SHIPMENT TO US.
+ BENEFICIARY SIGNED STATEMENT CERTIFYING THAT COPIES OF INVOICE, BILL OF LADING AND PACKING LIST HAVE BEEN FAXED TO APPLICANT ON FAX NO. 0082-54-8545×× × WITHIN 3 DAYS OF BILL OF LADING DATE.

ADDITIONAL COND.   47A:

+ A FEE OF USD 80 IS TO BE DEDUCTED FROM EACH DRAWING FOR THE ACCOUNT OF BENEFICIARY. IF DOCUMENTS ARE PRESENTED WITH DISCREPANCY(IES).

	+ UNLESS OTHERWISE EXPRESSLY STATE, ALL DOCUMENTS MUST BE IN ENGLISH.
DETAILS OF CHARGES	71B：ALL BANKING COMMISSIONS AND CHARGES INCLUDING REIMBURSEMENT COMMISSIONS OUTSIDE KOREA REP. ARE FOR BENEFICIARY'S ACCOUNT.
PRESENTATION PERIOD	48：DOCUMENTS MUST BE PRESENTED FOR NEGOTIATION WITHIN 21 DAYS AFTER THE DATE OF SHIPMENT BUT WITHIN THE VALIDITY OF THE CREDIT.
CONFIRMATION INSTRUCTION	*49：WITHOUT
	78：
	+ PLEASE REIMBURSE YOURSELVES BY PRESENTING BENEFICIARY'S DRAFT TO THE DRAWEE BANK.
	+ ALL DOCUMENTS MUST BE MAILED TO DAEGU BANK, LTD. BUSINESS PROCESS SUPPORT DEPT 17FL, 118, SUSEONG-2-GA, SUSEONG-GU, DAEGU, 706-712 KOREA REP. IN ONE LOT BY COURIER MAIL.
"ADVISE THROUGH"	57A：BKCHCNBJ92G
	* BANK OF CHINA
	* HUZHOU
	*（HUZHOU BRANCH）

张洁对信用证的各个条款进行了初步分析后填制了信用证分析单（见样单1-4）。

样单1-4　信用证分析单

信用证分析单

银行编号		合约		受益人		是否生效	
信用证号						银行是否加具保兑	
开证日期						密押/印鉴是否相符	
开证行				开证人		※※唛头※※	
金额				启运口岸			
价格条款				目的地			
汇票付款人				可否转运			
				可否分批			
汇票注意事项				装运期限	最早		
					最晚		
				有效期			
银行费用承担		不符点费		到期地点		提单日____天内议付	____天内寄单

续表

货物描述：				
提单	抬头：		通知人：	保险条款：
	运费及提单要注明条款：			
运输条款：				
单证名称				

教学视频

第三步：审核信用证，找出问题条款。

张洁根据销售合同和 UCP600，对信用证进行逐条审核，发现如下问题条款。

(1) *31D：信用证规定到期地点在韩国，这样受益人必须要在信用证有效期内交单到韩国。但受益人难以掌握单据邮递的时间，容易造成交单逾期，而收汇无保障，对受益人交单不利。

(2) *59：受益人名称中"ZHENGCHAN"拼写错误，应为"ZHENGCHANG"。这是一个非常严重的问题，如果不修改，将错就错，会影响到后面制单时单证章上的拼写和公司名称的拼写不一致，造成单证表面不一致。

(3) 42C：汇票条款中付款期限是"AT 30 DAYS AFTER SIGHT"，而销售合同中规定是即期信用证，会影响收款时间。

(4) 43T：销售合同中转运是允许的，而信用证中转运是不允许的。在本业务中，货物是从上海装运至韩国釜山的，因为距离近，能不能转运不受影响，因此这样的不符条款可以不修改。

(5) 44E：信用证装运港为"CHINESE MAIN PORT"，而销售合同中装运港为"SHNAGHAI, CHINA"，信用证中的规定范围比合同要大，对受益人来讲更为有利，可以不修改。

(6) 45A：产品单价在销售合同中表述为 USD2.61/PC，而信用证中货物描述条款中的表述是 USD2.81/PC。

(7) 46A：信用证中保险单据条款中险别为"FPA"，销售合同中为"ALL RISKS AND WAR RISK"。

(8) 销售合同中有溢短装条款，而信用证中没有，这样对受益人来讲备货时就缺乏弹性，容易造成违约。

第四步：提出修改意见。

张洁本着只要对受益人有利就尽量少改动的原则，对上述审出的问题条款提出最终的修改意见如下。

(1) *31D：信用证规定到期地点在韩国，改为在中国境内到期。

(2) *59:受益人名称中"ZHENGCHAN"拼写错误,改为"ZHENGCHANG"。

(3) 42C:汇票条款中付款期限"AT 30 DAYS AFTER SIGHT",应改为"AT SIGHT"。

(4) 45A:货物描述条款中产品单价应由原来的USD2.81/PC改为USD2.61/PC。

(5) 46A:将信用证中保险单据条款中的险别"FPA"改为"ALL RISKS AND WAR RISK"。

(6) 在信用证中增加溢短装条款"MORE OR LESS 5% IN AMOUNT AND QUANTITY IS ALLOWED"。

(四)任务解决

张洁把最终的修改意见交给业务员,业务员发改证函给客户,再由客户向开证行提出改证申请。信用证修改流程如图1-1所示。

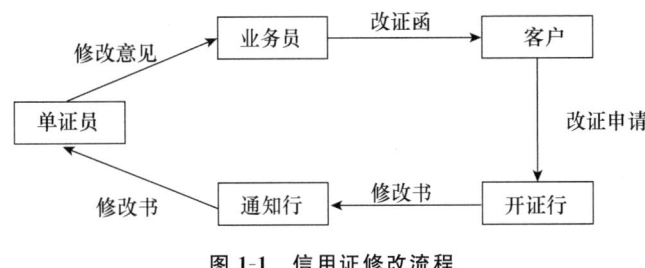

图1-1 信用证修改流程

2019年3月18日,张洁从中国银行湖州市分行处拿到韩国大邱银行发来的信用证修改书(见样单1-5)。

样单1-5 信用证修改书

MT S707	AMENDMENT TO A DOCUMENTARY CREDIT
APPLICATION HEADER	*DAEGU BANK,LTD.,THE
	*DAEGU
SENDER'S REF.	*20:M511145160747856
RECEIVER'S REF.	*21:NONREF
DATE OF ISSUE	31C:190305
DATE OF AMENDMENT	30:190318
BENEFICIARY	*59:HUZHOU ZHENGCHAN TRADING CO.,LTD.
	(BEFORE THIS AMENDMENT) 42 HONGQI ROAD,
	HUZHOU,
	CHINA
NEW DATE OF EXPIRY	31E:190501
LATEST DATE OF SHIP.	44C:190415
NARRATIVE	79:+ IN FIELD 31D EXPIRY PLACE AMEND TO:IN CHINA
	+ IN FIELD 59 AMEND TO:HUZHOU ZHENGCHANG TRADING CO.,LTD.
	42 HONGQI ROAD, HUZHOU, CHINA
	+ IN FIELD 42C AMEND TO:AT SIGHT FOR 100 PERCENT OF INVOICE VALUE
	+ IN FIELD 45A UNIT PRICE AMEND TO:USD2.61/PC

+ IN FIELD 46A AMEND TO: INSURANCE POLICY COVERING ALL RISKS AND WAR RISK

+ IN FIELD 47A, INCREASE THE CLAUSE: MORE OR LESS 5% IN AMOUNT AND QUANTITY IS ALLOWED.

ALL OTHER TERMS AND CONDITIONS REMAIN UNCHANGED.

张洁拿到信用证修改书后,与业务员进行商量,接受此修改书的内容。张洁通知中国银行湖州市分行接受信用证修改,这样,这份信用证修改书就成为原信用证的一部分,具有法律效力。

三、知识链接

(一)信用证的含义及特点

1. 信用证的含义

信用证(Letter of Credit,L/C)是一种银行开立的有条件的承诺付款的书面文件,即开证行根据进口商(开证申请人)的请求和指示向出口商(受益人)开立的一定金额的,并在一定的期限内凭规定的单据承诺付款的书面文件。

UCP600 第二条对信用证的含义也做了明确规定:信用证意指一项不可撤销的安排,无论其名称或描述如何,该项安排构成开证行对相符交单予以承付的确定承诺。

承付是指:① 对于即期付款信用证即期付款;② 对于延期付款信用证发出延期付款承诺并到期付款;③ 对于承兑信用证承兑由受益人出具的汇票并到期付款。

2. 信用证的特点

信用证主要有以下三个特点。

(1) 开证行承担第一性的付款责任。

信用证支付是由开证行以自己的信用做保证进行的,所以,作为一种银行保证文件的信用证,开证行对之负第一性的付款责任。信用证开证行的付款责任,不仅是首要的,而且是独立的、终局的,即使进口商在开证后失去偿付能力,只要出口商提交的单据符合信用证的条款,开证行也要负责付款,付款后如发现有误,也不能向受益人和索偿行进行追索。

(2) 信用证是一项自足文件。

信用证虽然是根据销售合同开立的,但一经开立,信用证就成为独立于销售合同以外的约定。UCP600 第四条明确规定:信用证与可能作为其开立基础的销售合同或其他合同是相互独立的交易,即使信用证中含有对此类合同的任何援引,也与该合同无关,且不受其约束。

(3) 信用证方式是纯单据业务。

银行处理信用证业务时,只凭单据,不问货物,银行只审查受益人所提交的单据是否与信用证条款相符,以决定是否履行付款责任。UCP600 第五条明确规定:银行处理的是单据,而不是单据可能涉及的货物、服务或履约行为。

教学视频

(二)信用证的业务流程

一笔信用证业务要经过申请开立信用证、通知信用证、受益人交单、指定银行垫款、开证行偿付、开证申请人赎单等多个环节。信用证的业务流程如图 1-2 所示。

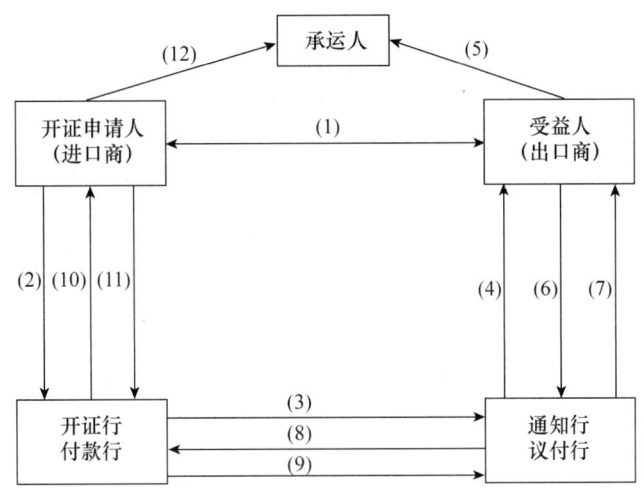

图 1-2　信用证的业务流程

(1) 买卖双方签订销售合同,在销售合同中约定使用信用证方式进行结算。

(2) 开证申请人(进口商)向开证行提出申请,根据销售合同的内容填写开证申请书(见样单 1-6),落实开证保证金,请开证行开证。

(3) 开证行根据开证申请书的内容,向受益人(出口商)开出信用证,并传递给通知行,指示其通知受益人(出口商)。

(4) 通知行核对密押或印鉴无误后,将信用证通知受益人(出口商)。

(5) 受益人(出口商)对信用证进行审核后,按信用证规定装运货物。

(6) 受益人(出口商)备齐各种货运单据,开出汇票,在信用证有效期和交单期内,将所有单据和汇票交给议付行议付。

(7) 议付行按照信用证条款审核单据无误后,按照汇票金额扣除利息,把货款垫付给受益人(出口商)。

(8) 寄单索汇,即议付行将汇票和货运单据按照信用证的要求寄给开证行(或其指定的付款行)并索偿。

(9) 开证行(或其指定的付款行)核对单据无误后,付款给议付行,同时通知开证申请人(进口商)备款赎单。

(10) 开证行向开证申请人(进口商)提示单据。

(11) 开证申请人(进口商)付款赎单,如发现不符,可拒付款项并退单。

(12) 开证申请人(进口商)凭货运单据向承运人提货。

样单 1-6　开证申请书

IRREVOCABLE DOCUMENTARY CREDIT APPLICATION

To:　　　　　　　　　　L/C No.　　　　　　　　　　Date:

Applicant		Beneficiary (full name, address and tel etc.)
Partial shipments (　) allowed (　) not allowed	Transshipment (　) allowed (　) not allowed	Issued by (　) teletransmission 　　　　　(　) express delivery

续表

Loading on board/dispatch/taking in charge at/from Not later than For transportation to	Contract No.: Credit Amount (both in figures and words): Trade Term: ( ) FOB( ) CFR( ) CIF( ) Others:
Description of goods:	Date and place of expiry
	Credit available with ( ) by sight payment ( ) by acceptance ( ) by negotiation ( ) by deferred payment at against the documents detailed herein ( ) and beneficiary's draft for 100% of invoice value at on

Documents required: (marked with X)
1. ( ) Signed commercial invoice in 3 copies indicating L/C No. and Contract No.
2. ( ) Full set of clean on board Bills of Lading made out 〔 〕 to order/〔 〕 to the order of ____ and blank endorsed, marked "freight 〔 〕 prepaid/〔 〕 to collect showing freight amount" notifying 〔 〕the applicant/〔 〕
3. ( ) Air Waybills showing "freight 〔 〕prepaid/〔 〕 to collect indicating freight amount" and consigned to
4. ( ) Insurance Policy/Certificate in 3 copies for 110% of the invoice value showing claims payable in China in currency of the draft, blank endorsed, covering (〔 〕 Ocean Marine Transportation/〔 〕 Air Transportation/〔 〕 Over Land Transportation) All Risks, War Risks. /〔 〕
5. ( ) Packing list/Weight Memo in 3 copies indicating
6. ( ) Certificate of Quantity/Weight in 3 copies issued by 〔 〕 manufacturer/〔 〕 Seller/〔 〕 independent surveyor at the loading port, indicating the actual surveyed quantity/weight of shipped goods as well as the packing condition.
7. ( ) Certificate of Quality in 3 copies issued by 〔 〕 manufacturer/〔 〕 public recognized surveyor/ 〔 〕
8. ( ) Beneficiary's Certified copy of fax dispatched to the applicant within 2 days after shipment advising the contract number, name of commodity, quantity, invoice value, bill of loading, bill of loading date, the ETA date and shipping Co.
9. ( ) Beneficiary's Certificate certifying that extra copies of the documents have been dispatched to the 〔 〕 applicant/〔 〕
10. ( ) Certificate of Origin in copies certifying.
11. ( ) Other documents, if any:

Additional instruction: (marked with X)
1. ( ) All banking charges outside the opening bank are for beneficiary's account.
2. ( ) Documents must be presented within 21 days after the date of issuance of the transport documents but within the validity of this credit.
3. ( ) Third party as shipper is not acceptable, Short Form/Blank B/L is not acceptable.
4. ( ) Both quantity and amount % more or less are allowed.
5. ( ) All documents to be forwarded in one lot by express unless otherwise stated above.
6. ( ) Other terms, if any:

(三) 信用证的内容

1. 信用证的基本内容

以上述信用证（L/C No.：M51145160747856）为例，信用证主要包括以下基本内容。

(1) 信用证本身的说明，包括信用证的类型、信用证号码和开证日期。

(2) 信用证的当事人，一般有以下两类：

① 必须记载的当事人，包括申请人、受益人。

② 可以记载的当事人，包括开证行、通知行、保兑行、指定议付行、付款行、偿付行等。

(3) 信用证的金额，包括币别代号、金额、加减百分率等。

(4) 汇票条款，包括汇票的金额、到期日、出票人、付款人等。

(5) 运输条款，包括运输方式、装运地和目的地、最迟装运日期、可否分批装运或转运等。

(6) 货物条款，包括货物名称、规格、数量、包装、单价以及合约号码等。

(7) 单据条款，主要用来说明要求提交的单据种类、份数、内容要求等。单据一般分为两类：基本单据和其他单据。

① 基本单据，包括商业发票、运输单据和保险单。

② 其他单据，包括检验证书、原产地证书、装箱单或重量单等。

(8) 其他规定，包括对交单期的说明、银行费用的说明，以及对议付行寄单方式、议付背书和索偿方法的指示等。

2. SWIFT 跟单信用证 MT700 的代码解读

SWIFT（Society for Worldwide Interbank Financial Telecommunications）又称环球银行金融电信协会，是国际银行间的国际合作组织，成立于 1973 年，目前全球大多数国家的大多数银行已使用 SWIFT 系统。SWIFT 系统的使用，为银行的结算提供了安全、可靠、快捷、标准化、自动化的通信业务，从而大大提高了银行的结算速度。MT700 是 SWIFT 跟单信用证的开证格式，其代码如表 1-1 所示。

(1) M/O 为 Mandatory 与 Optional 的缩写，前者指必要项目，后者为任意项目。

(2) 页次是指本证的发报次数，用分数来表示，分母分子各一位数字，分母表示发报的总次数，分子则表示这是其中的第几次，例如，"1/2"中的"2"指本证总共发报 2 次，"1"指本次为第 1 次发报。

表 1-1　SWIFT 跟单信用证 MT700 代码表

M/O	Tag 代码	Field Name	栏位名称
M	27	Sequence of Total	页次
M	40A	Form of Documentary Credit	跟单信用证类别
M	20	Documentary Credit Number	信用证号码
O	23	Reference to Pre-Advice	预通知的编号
O	31C	Date of Issue	开证日期
M	40E	Applicable Rules	适用的规则
M	31D	Date and Place of Expiry	到期日及地点
O	51a	Applicant Bank	申请人的银行
M	50	Applicant	申请人

续表

M/O	Tag 代码	Field Name	栏位名称
M	59	Beneficiary	受益人
M	32B	Currency Code, Amount	币别代号、金额
O	39A	Percentage Credit Amount Tolerance	信用证金额加减百分率
O	39B	Maximum Credit Amount	最高信用证金额
O	39C	Additional Amounts Covered	可附加金额
M	41a	Available With… By…	向……银行押汇,押汇方式……
O	42C	Drafts at…	汇票期限
O	42a	Drawee	付款人
O	42M	Mixed Payment Details	混合付款指示
O	42P	Deferred Payment Details	延迟付款指示
O	43P	Partial Shipments	分批装运
O	43T	Transshipment	转运
O	44A	in Charge/Dispatch from… /Place of Receipt	货物监管地/发货地/收货地点
O	44E	Port of Loading/Airport of Departure	装货港或装货机场
O	44F	Port of Discharge/Airport of Destination	目的港或到达机场
O	44B	Place of Final Destination/For Transportation to… /Place of Delivery	最后目的地/货物运至地/交货地
O	44C	Latest Date of Shipment	最后装运日
O	44D	Shipment Period	装运期间
O	45A	Description of Goods and/or Services	货物描述及/或交易条件
O	46A	Documents Required	应提交的单据
O	47A	Additional Conditions	附加条件
O	71B	Charges	费用
O	48	Period for Presentation	提示期间
M	49	Confirmation Instructions	保兑指示
O	53a	Reimbursing Bank	清算银行
O	78	Instructions to the Paying/Accepting/Negotiating Bank	对付款/承兑/议付银行之指示
O	57a	"Advise Through" Bank	收讯银行以外的通知银行
O	72	Sender to Receiver Information	银行间的通知

(四)信用证的种类

按照不同的标准,信用证可以分为不同的种类。

1. 按照信用证项下的汇票是否附有货运单据划分

按照信用证项下的汇票是否附有货运单据,信用证可分为跟单信用证和光票信用证。

(1) 跟单信用证(Documentary Credit),是指凭跟单汇票或仅凭单据付款的信用证。此处的单据指代表货物所有权的单据(如海运提单等),或证明货物已交运的单据(如铁路运单、航空运单、邮包收据等)。

教学视频

(2) 光票信用证(Clean Credit)，是指凭不随附货运单据的光票(Clean Draft)付款的信用证。银行凭光票信用证付款，也可要求受益人附交另一非货运单据，如发票、垫款清单等。

国际贸易的货款结算多数使用跟单信用证。

2．按照开证行所负的责任不同划分

按照开证行所负的责任不同，信用证可分为不可撤销信用证和可撤销信用证。

(1) 不可撤销信用证(Irrevocable Credit)，是指一经开出，在有效期内，未经受益人及有关当事人同意，开证行不能片面修改和撤销的信用证，只要受益人提供的单据符合信用证的规定，开证行必须履行付款义务。

(2) 可撤销信用证(Revocable Credit)，是指开证行不必征得受益人或有关当事人同意而有权随时撤销的信用证。可撤销信用证应注明"可撤销"字样。UCP600中明确规定信用证不可撤销。

3．按照有无另一家银行加以保兑划分

按照有无另一家银行加以保兑，信用证可分为保兑信用证和不保兑信用证。

(1) 保兑信用证(Confirmed Credit)，是指开证行开出的，由另一家银行保证对符合信用证条款规定的单据履行付款义务的信用证。对信用证加以保兑的银行，称为保兑行。

(2) 不保兑信用证(Unconfirmed Credit)，是指开证行开出的，没有经另一家银行保兑的信用证。

如果信用证上没有注明，则认为该信用证是不保兑信用证。

4．按照付款时间不同划分

按照付款时间不同，信用证可分为即期信用证、远期信用证和假远期信用证。

(1) 即期信用证(Sight Credit)，是指开证行或付款行收到符合信用证条款的跟单汇票或装运单据后，立即履行付款义务的信用证。

(2) 远期信用证(Usance Credit)，是指开证行或付款行收到信用证的单据后，在规定期限内履行付款义务的信用证。

(3) 假远期信用证(Usance Credit Payable at Sight)，是指规定受益人开立远期汇票，由付款行负责贴现，并规定一切利息和费用由开证人承担的信用证。对受益人来讲，这种信用证实际上仍属于即期信用证。对申请人来讲，这种信用证与远期信用证类似，如果受益人提交的单证不符，他有权拒付；而在单证相符或虽有不符点但其同意接受的情况下，申请人可先行取单提货，到期偿付开证行。

在假远期信用证项下，开证行即期付款时并不借记申请人账户，而是利用自有资金，实际是为申请人提供了一笔类似于押汇的贸易融资，开证行在远期汇票到期时向申请人收回该笔融资及相应利息。通过开立假远期信用证，受益人即期得到出口款项，申请人远期支付进口款项，各取所需，而开证行则增加了中间业务收入。

5．按照受益人对信用证的权利可否转让划分

按照受益人对信用证的权利可否转让，信用证可分为可转让信用证和不可转让信用证。

(1) 可转让信用证(Transferable Credit)：指信用证的受益人(第一受益人)可以要求授权付款、承担延期付款责任、承兑或议付的银行(统称"转让行")，或者当信用证是自由

议付时,可以要求信用证中特别授权的转让银行,将信用证全部或部分转让给一个或数个受益人(第二受益人)使用的信用证。在可转让信用证中,开证行要明确注明"可转让"字样,可转让信用证只能转让一次。

可转让信用证通常被第一受益人作为从第二受益人出口的货物中获取差价利益的一种支付手段。第一受益人在把信用证转让给第二受益人时,对原信用证的金额、单价、投保比例、有效期、装运期及交单期限可做必要的改动。第二受益人发货后提交的出口单据必须通过转让银行,以便第一受益人换单。

(2) 不可转让信用证(Non-transferable Credit),是指受益人不能将信用证的权利转让给他人的信用证。凡信用证中未注明"可转让"字样的,即是不可转让信用证。

(五) 信用证的审核

许多不符点单据的产生以及提交后被银行退回的情况,大多是对收到的信用证事先审核不仔细造成的,这往往会使一些本来可以纠正的错误由于审核不及时而得不到及时修改。因此,工作人员应在收到信用证的当天,对照有关的销售合同认真仔细地审核信用证,这样可以尽早发现错误并及时采取相应的补救措施。

1. 审证原则

当信用证的条款比销售合同的条款严格时,应当作为信用证中存在的问题提出修改;而当信用证的条款比销售合同的条款宽松时,往往可以不修改。

2. 审核要点

审核信用证时要注意以下几个要点。

(1) 审核信用证条款与销售合同条款是否一致。

信用证中的部分条款在销售合同中有表述,工作人员可以对照销售合同对这些条款进行一一审核。工作人员一般须审核以下内容。

① 开证申请人和受益人的名称、地址;

② 信用证金额、币制及金额增减幅度;

③ 汇票条款,如付款期限、汇票的金额等;

④ 运输条款,如对分批装运、转运、装运港和目的港的相关规定等;

⑤ 货物描述条款,如货物名称、数量、单价等。

(2) 审核信用证开证日期、最迟装运日、到期日等是否合理。

所谓合理,是指开证日期与最迟装运日之间的期限足够工厂备完货物,到期日与最迟装运日之间的间隔不宜太短,以便出口商交货后能有足够的时间完成交单。另外,信用证到期的地点一定要规定在出口商所在地,以便做到及时交单。

(3) 审核单据条款中规定的文件能否提供以及信用证中指定的条款能否做到。

① 审核一些需要认证的单据特别是使馆认证等能否及时办理和提供;

② 审核由其他机构或部门出具的有关文件,如出口许可证、运费收据、检验证明等,能否提供或能否及时提供;

③ 审核信用证中指定的船龄、船籍、船公司或不准在某港口转船等条款能否做到。

（4）审核信用证中有无软条款。

① 审核有无 1/3 正本提单直接寄送进口商的条款。若有此条款，并且接受此条款，则出口商将随时面临货、款两空的危险。

② 审核有无将客检证作为议付文件的条款。若有此条款，并且接受此条款，则受益人正常处理信用证业务的主动权很大程度上掌握在对方手里，影响安全收汇。

（5）审核信用证中有无矛盾之处。

① 审核是否有在空运的运输方式下，要求提供海运提单的情况；

② 审核是否有价格条款是 FOB，在提单中显示"运费预付"的情况；

③ 审核是否有价格条款是 FOB 或 CFR，在信用证中要求提供保险单的情况。

（六）信用证的修改

对信用证进行全面审核后，如发现问题，受益人（出口商）应分情况及时处理。对于影响安全收汇、难以接受或做不到的信用证条款，受益人（出口商）必须要求开证申请人进行修改。

1. 信用证修改的规则

（1）只有开证申请人（进口商）有权决定是否接受修改信用证。

（2）只有受益人（出口商）有权决定是否接受信用证修改。

2. 修改信用证应注意的几点

（1）凡是需要修改的内容，应做到一次性提出，避免出现多次修改信用证的情况。

（2）对于不可撤销信用证中任何条款的修改，都必须取得当事人的同意后才能生效。对信用证修改内容的接受或拒绝有两种表示形式：一是受益人做出接受或拒绝信用证修改的通知；二是受益人按照信用证的内容办事。

（3）收到信用证修改后，受益人（出口商）应及时检查修改内容是否符合要求。

（4）对于信用证的修改内容，要么全部接受，要么全部拒绝，接受修改中的部分内容是无效的。

（5）有关信用证修改，必须通过原信用证通知行方为真实、有效；进口商直接寄送修改申请书或修改书复印件不是有效的修改。

（6）应明确修改费用由谁承担，一般按照责任归属来确定修改费用由谁承担。

四、能力训练

（一）安吉林木饰品有限公司操作案例

安吉林木饰品有限公司于 2019 年 4 月 15 日与西班牙 JEWTS 公司签订销售合同（见样单 1-7），4 月 22 日从中国银行湖州市分行拿到客户通过 CAJA DE AHORROS YM.P. DE NAVARRA 银行开来的信用证（见样单 1-8），同时客户电汇的 10% 预付款也已到账。

样单 1-7　销售合同

安吉林木饰品有限公司
ANJI LINMU DECORATION CO., LTD.
ANJI ECONOMIC DEVELOPING DISTRICT, HUZHOU CITY, ZHEJIANG, CHINA
TEL：+86-0572-5544×××　　FAX：+86-0572-5544×××

售货合约
SALES CONTRACT

合约编码：
S/C NO.：Y024562
日期：
DATE：APR. 15, 2019

买方：
BUYERS：JEWTS HAMAN INC 860
地址：
ADDRESS：ADVA COSEP TARRADELLAS 00243 BARCELONA, SPAIN
电传/传真：
TELEX/FAX：+34-93-4320×××

买卖双方同意按下列条款由买方购进卖方售出下列产品：
THE BUYERS AGREE TO BUY AND THE SELLERS AGREE TO SELL THE FOLLOWING GOODS ON TERMS AND CONDITIONS STATED BELOW：

(1) 商品名称及规格 NAME OF COMMODITY AND SPECIFICATION	(2) 数量 QUANTITY	(3) 单价 UNIT PRICE	(4) 金额 AMOUNT
LADIES' 96% POLYESTER 4% ELASTANE WOVEN GARMENTS DRESS ART. NO. ZC14502 ART. NO. ZC14533	8 820PCS 8 820PCS	CIF BARCELONA USD7.25/PC USD7.55/PC	USD63 945.00 USD66 591.00
(5) TOTAL	17 640PCS		USD130 536.00

(6) 包装：
　　PACKING：IN CARTONS
(7) 装运期：
　　TIME OF SHIPMENT：NOT LATER THAN MAY 19, 2019
(8) 装运口岸：
　　PORT OF SHIPMENT：SHANGHAI, CHINA
(9) 目的港：
　　PORT OF DESTINATION：BARCELONA, SPAIN
　　WITH PARTIAL SHIPMENT AND TRANSSHIPMENT NOT ALLOWED.
(10) 支付方式：
　　TERMS OF PAYMENT：10% OF THE AMOUNT ADVANCED PAYMENT BY T/T, THE BALANCE BY L/C AT 30 DAYS AFTER SIGHT
(11) 保险：
　　INSURANCE：FPA

卖方：　　　　　　　　　　　　　　　　买方：
THE SELLER：　　　　　　　　　　　　THE BUYER：
ANJI LINMU DECORATION CO., LTD.　　　JEWTS HAMAN INC 860
　　　李之浩　　　　　　　　　　　　　　　ZAMEE

样单 1-8 信用证

MT S700	ISSUE OF A DOCUMENTARY CREDIT
APPLICATION HEADER	* CAJA DE AHORROS YM.P. DE NAVARRA
	* PAMPLONA
SEQUENCE OF TOTAL	*27：1/1
FORM OF DOC. CREDIT	*40A：IRREVOCABLE
DOC. CREDIT NUMBER	*20：046CDI577402456
DATE OF ISSUE	31C：190420
APPLICABLE RULES	*40E：UCP LATEST VERSION
EXPIRY	*31D：DATE 190530 PLACE AT NEGOTIATING BANK
APPLICANT	*50：JEWTS HAMAN INC 860
	ADVA COSEP TARRADELLAS
	00243 BARCELONA
	SPAIN
BENEFICIARY	*59：ANJI LINMU DECORATION CO., LTD.
	ANJI ECONOMIC DEVELOPING DISTRICT,
	HUZHOU CITY,
	ZHEJIANG, CHINA
AMOUNT	*32B：CURRENCY GBP AMOUNT 130 536.00
AVAILABLE WITH/BY	*41D：ANY BANK
	BY NEGOTIATION
DRAFT AT...	42C：AT 30 DAYS AFTER SIGHT FOR 80 PERCENT OF INVOICE
	VALUE
DRAWEE	*42A：* CAJA DE AHORROS YM.P. DE NAVARRA
	* PAMPLONA
PARTIAL SHIPMENT	43P：NOT ALLOWED
TRANSSHIPMENT	43T：NOT ALLOWED
PORT OF LOADING	44E：NINGBO PORT, CHINA
PORT OF DISCHARGE	44F：BARCELONA PORT, SPAIN
LATEST DATE OF SHIP.	44C：190510
DESCRIPT OF GOODS	45A：
	LADIES' 96% POLYESTER 4% ELASTANE WOVEN GARMENTS DRESS
	ART. NO. ZC14502　8 820PCS　　USD7.25/PC
	ART. NO. ZC14533　8 820PCS　　USD7.35/PC
	CIF BARCELONA
DOCUMENTS REQUIRED	46A：
	+ SIGNED AND STAMPED COMMERCIAL INVOICE IN 2 FOLDS
	+ SIGNED PACKING LIST IN 2 FOLDS
	+ FULL SET OF ORIGINAL CLEAN ON BOARD MARINE BILL OF LADING MADE OUT TO THE ORDER OF CAJA DE AHORROS YM.P. DE NAVARRA AND BLANK ENDORSED, MARKED FREIGHT PREPAID AND NOTIFY APPLICANT.

+ INSURANCE POLICY OR CERTIFICATE ISSUED FOR 110 PCT OF INVOICE VALUE, MADE OUT TO THE ORDER OF CAJA DE AHORROS YM. P. DE NAVARRA COVERING 'FPA', 'FROM WAREHOUSE TO WAREHOUSE' AND STATING 'CLAIMS, IF ANY, PAYABLE IN SPAIN', IN 1 ORIGINAL AND 1 COPY.

+ ORIGINAL CERTIFICATE OF ORIGIN PLUS ONE COPY ISSUED BY CCPIT.

+ BENEFICIARY'S CERTIFICATE CERTIFYING THAT 1 COMMERCIAL INVOICE, 1 PACKING LIST, 1 WEIGHT CERTIFICATE AND 1 NON NEGOTIABLE COPY OF B/L HAVE BEEN FORWARDED TO APPLICANT WITHIN 48 HOURS AFTER SHIPMENT.

ADDITIONAL COND.   47A:

+ A HANDLING CHARGE OF USD 90 WILL BE DEDUCTED FROM THE PROCEEDS OF EACH SET OF DOCUMENTS WITH DISCREPANCIES.

DETAILS OF CHARGES   71B: ALL BANKING CHARGES AND COMMISSIONS OUTSIDE ISSUING BANK INCLUDING REIMBURSEMENT CHARGES ARE FOR BENEFICIARY'S ACCOUNT.

PRESENTATION PERIOD   48: 21 DAYS AFTER SHIPMEN DATE BUT WITHIN L/C VALIDITY

CONFIRMATION   *49: WITHOUT
INSTRUCTION   78:

REIMBURSEMENT: AT MATURITY DATE AND AFTER RECEIPT OF DOCUMENTS IN STRICT COMPLIANCE WITH L/C TERMS, WE WILL CREDIT THE NEGOTIATING BANK'S INSTRUCTIONS.

DOCUMENTS TO BE SENT TO CAJA DE AHORROS Y M. P. DE NAVARRA, LETTER OF CREDIT PROCESSING AGENT, 3/F CITYPLAZA FOUR, 14 TAIKOO WAN ROAD, PAMPLONA IN ONE LOT BY COURIER MAIL.

"ADVISE THROUGH"   57A: BKCHCNBJ92G

* BANK OF CHINA
* HUZHOU
* (HUZHOU BRANCH)

工作任务：

(1) 分析销售合同内容(S/C No.：Y024562)；

(2) 分析信用证条款(L/C No.：046CDI577402456)；

(3) 审核与修改信用证。

(二) 湖州兴业进出口有限公司操作案例

湖州兴业进出口有限公司于 2019 年 3 月 29 日与突尼斯 TUFFCO 签订销售合同(见样单 1-9)，4 月 6 日从美联银行上海分行拿到客户通过 AMEM 银行开来的信用证(见样单 1-10)。请根据湖州兴业进出口有限公司与客户签订的销售合同，完成对相应信用证的审核与修改。

样单1-9 销售合同

湖州兴业进出口有限公司
HUZHOU XINGYE INDUSTRY CO., LTD.
18TH FLOOR, MEIXIN BUILDING, HUZHOU, ZHEJIANG, CHINA

No.: 2019TU02
Date: MAR. 29, 2019

销售确认书
SALES CONFIRMATION

THE BUYERS: TUFFCO
　　　　　　3052 SFAX TUNISIE

兹买卖双方同意成交下列商品，订立条款如下：
THE UNDERSIGNED SELLERS AND BUYERS HAVE AGREED TO CLOSE THE FOLLOWING TRANSACTIONS ACCORDING TO THE TERMS AND CONDITIONS STIPULATED BELOW：

MARKS	QUANTITIES & GOODS	UNIT PRICE	AMOUNT
TU (PRODUCT'S NAME) QTY： C/NO.：	FIRE EXTINGUISHER 1) 6KG DRY POWDER FIRE EXTINGUISHER 　　　　　　　　　　　　5 000PCS 2) 9LT FOAM EXTINGUISHER COMPLETE EMPTY 　　　　　　　　　　　　200PCS 3) 5KG CO_2 FIRE EXTINGUISHER　3 000PCS 4) 2KG CO_2 FIRE EXTINGUISHER　500PCS 　　　　　　　TOTAL　　8 700PCS	CFR SFAX BY SEA USD18.390/PC USD17.650/PC USD21.067/PC USD11.177/PC	 USD91 950.00 USD3 530.00 USD63 201.00 USD5 588.50 USD164 269.50

PACKING: IN CARTONS
SHIPMENT: ON OR BEFORE JUN. 10, 2019
DELIVERY: FROM SHANGHAI TO SFAX PARTIAL SHIPMENT AND TRANSSHIPMENT IS ALLOWED.
INSURANCE: TO BE EFFECTED BY THE BUYERS
PAYMENT: BY 100 PCT IRREVOCABLE L/C AVAILABLE BY DRAFT AT SIGHT

Buyer Signature　　　　　　　　　　Seller Signature
JPM　　　　　　　　　　　　　　蒋一

样单1-10 信用证

MT S700	ISSUE OF A DOCUMENTARY CREDIT
SEQUENCE OF TOTAL	*27: 1/1
FORM OF DOC. CREDIT	*40A: IRREVOCABLE
DOC. CREDIT NUMBER	*20: CDI702/8053/2019
DATE OF ISSUE	31C: 190405
APPLICABLE RULES	*40E: UCP LATEST VERSION
EXPIRY	*31D: DATE 190630 PLACE CHINA

APPLICANT BANK	51A:	AMEM BANK
		AVENUE MOHAMED V
		TUNIS, TUNISIA
APPLICANT	*50:	TUFFCO
		3052 SFAX TUNISIE
BENEFICIARY	*59:	HUZHOU XINGYE INDUSTRY CO., LTD.
		18TH FLOOR, MEIXING BUILDING, HUZHOU, ZHEJIANG, CHINA
AMOUNT	*32B:	CURRENCY USD AMOUNT 16 429.50
AVAILABLE WITH/BY	*41D:	WACHOVIA BANK, NA, SHANGHAI BRANCH
		BY PAYMENT
PARTIAL SHIPMENT	43P:	ALLOWED
TRANSSHIPMENT	43T:	NOT ALLOWED
PORT OF LOADING	44E:	SHANG PORT
PORT OF DISCHARGE	44F:	SFAX PORT, TUNISIA
LATEST DATE OF SHIP.	44C:	190601
DESCRIPT. OF GOODS	45A:	
		FIRE EXTINGUISHER PER SALES CONFIRMATION NO. 2019TU20 DTD 29/03/2019
DOCUMENTS REQUIRED	46A:	

+ SIGNED COMMERCIAL INVOICE IN 7 FOLDS
+ WEIGHT NOTE AND PACKING LIST IN 3 FOLDS
+ FULL SET OF ORIGINAL CLEAN ON BOARD MARINE BILL OF LADING MADE OUT TO SHIPPER'S ORDER AND BLANK ENDORSED, MARKED FREIGHT PREPAID AND NOTIFY APPLICANT QUOTING FULL NAME AND ADDRESS.
+ ORIGINAL CERTIFICATE OF ORIGIN PLUS ONE COPY ISSUED BY CIQ.
+ SHIPMENT ADVICE WITH FULL DETAILS INCLUDING SHIPPING MARKS, CARTON NUMBERS, VESSEL'S NAME, BILL OF LADING NUMBER, VALUE AND QUANTITY OF GOODS MUST BE SENT WITHIN 3 DAYS OF THE DATE OF SHIPMENT TO US.
+ INSURANCE POLICY IN THREE COPIES.
+ TECHNICAL FILE OF EXTINGUISHER.
+ BENEFICIARY SIGNED STATEMENT CERTIFYING THAT COPIES OF INVOICE, BILL OF LADING AND PACKING LIST HAVE BEEN FAXED TO APPLICANT ON FAX NO. +82-54-8545××× WITHIN 3 DAYS OF BILL OF LADING DATE.
+ SHIPPING ADVICE WITH FULL DETAIL INCLUGING SHIPPING MARKS, CARTON NUMBERS, VESSEL'S NAME, BILL OF LADING NUMBER, VALUE AND QUANTITY OF GOODS MUST BE SENT ON THE DATE OF SHIPMENT TO US.

ADDITIONAL COND.   47A:

+ HOUSE B/L UNACCEPTED.
+ A FEE OF USD 80 IS TO BE DEDUCTED FROM EACH DRAWING FOR THE ACCOUNT OF BENEFICIARY. IF DOCUMENTS ARE PRESENTED WITH DISCREPANCY(IES).

	+ ALL DOCUMENTS MUST BEAR NUMBER OF L/C.
DETAILS OF CHARGES	71B：ALL BANKING COMMISSIONS AND CHARGES INCLUDING REIMBURSEMENT COMMISSIONS OUTSIDE TUNISIA ARE FOR BENEFICIARY'S ACCOUNT.
PRESENTATION PERIOD	48：DOCUMENTS MUST BE PRESENTED FOR NEGOTIATION WITHIN 21 DAYS AFTER THE DATE OF SHIPMENT BUT WITHIN THE VALIDITY OF THE CREDIT.
CONFIRMATION	*49：WITHOUT
INSTRUCTION	78：
	+ PLEASE REIMBURSE YOURSELVES BY PRESENTING BENEFICIARY'S DRAFT TO THE DRAWEE BANK.
	+ WACHOVIA BANK SHANGHAI HOLDS SPECIAL INSTRUCTION REGARDING DOCUMENTS DISPOSAL AND REIMBURSEMENT OF THIS L/C.
"ADVISE THROUGH"	57A：BKCHCNBJ92G
	*BANK OF CHINA
	*HUZHOU
	*（HUZHOU BRANCH）

工作任务：

(1) 分析销售合同的内容（S/C No.：2019TU02）；

(2) 分析信用证条款（L/C No.：CDI702/8053/2019）；

(3) 审核与修改信用证。

五、岗位拓展

讨论话题：信用证修改问题。

2019年10月14日，湖州正昌贸易有限公司收到一份来自韩国客户的信用证，单证员在审核后发现存在以下两个不符点。

(1) 信用证中LATEST DATE OF SHIPMENT：191030，而合同中最迟装运期为2019年11月10日。

(2) 信用证中受益人名称、地址：HUZHOU ZHENGCHANG TRADING CO., LTD.
43 HONGQI ROAD, HUZHOU, CHINA

而合同中名称、地址：HUZHOU ZHENGCHANG TRADING CO., LTD.
42 HONGQI ROAD, HUZHOU, CHINA

即信用证打错了地址，将"42"错打为"43"。

讨论引导：

(1) 分组讨论，综合各方面因素权衡利弊，这个信用证要不要修改？应考虑哪些因素？

(2) 如果不修改，应该如何操作？应与哪些当事人及时沟通？

项目二
缮制商业发票和装箱单

一、学习目标

能力目标：能进行装箱资料的核算，能根据销售合同和信用证缮制商业发票和装箱单。

知识目标：明确商业发票和装箱单的缮制要点，了解不同种类的发票和包装单据。

二、工作任务

（一）任务描述

2019年3月18日，单证员张洁在收到信用证修改书后，为了操作方便，将修改书的内容与原信用证进行了整合，重新做了一份完整的信用证（见样单2-1）。

样单2-1　信用证

MT S700	ISSUE OF A DOCUMENTARY CREDIT
APPLICATION HEADER	*DAEGU BANK, LTD., THE
	*DAEGU
SEQUENCE OF TOTAL	*27：1/1
FORM OF DOC. CREDIT	*40A：IRREVOCABLE
DOC. CREDIT NUMBER	*20：M51145160747856
DATE OF ISSUE	31C：190305
APPLICABLE RULES	*40E：UCP LATEST VERSION
EXPIRY	*31D：DATE 190501 PLACE IN CHINA
APPLICANT	*50：MAIJER FISTRTION INC.
	3214, WALKER, NAKAGYO-KU, KYUNG-BUK,
	KOREA REP.
BENEFICIARY	*59：HUZHOU ZHENGCHANG TRADING CO., LTD.
	42 HONGQI ROAD,
	HUZHOU,
	CHINA
AMOUNT	*32B：CURRENCY USD AMOUNT 37 604.88
AVAILABLE WITH/BY	*41A：ANY BANK

	BY NEGOTIATION
DRAFTS AT...	42C: AT SIGHT FOR 100 PERCENT OF INVOICE VALUE
DRAWEE	*42A: *DAEGU BANK, LTD., THE DAEGU
PARTIAL SHIPMENT	43P: NOT ALLOWED
TRANSSHIPMENT	43T: NOT ALLOWED
PORT OF LOADING	44E: CHINESE MAIN PORT
PORT OF DISCHARGE	44F: BUSAN PORT, KOREA REP.
LATEST DATE OF SHIP.	44C: 190415
DESCRIPT. OF GOODS	45A:

    14 408PCS RATTAN CURTAIN AS PER SALES CONFIRMATION NO. ZC190211
    USD 2.61/PC CIF BUSAN

DOCUMENTS REQUIRED   46A:

+ SIGNED COMMERCIAL INVOICE IN 3 FOLDS CERTIFIED THE GOODS ARE OF CHINESE ORIGIN.
+ PACKING LIST IN 3 FOLDS
+ FULL SET OF ORIGINAL CLEAN ON BOARD MARINE BILL OF LADING MADE OUT TO SHIPPER'S ORDER AND BLANK ENDORSED, MARKED FREIGHT PREPAID AND NOTIFY APPLICANT QUOTING FULL NAME AND ADDRESS.
+ MARINE INSURANCE POLICY FOR 110PCT OF INVOICE VALUE, BLANK ENDORSED, COVERING ALL RISKS AND WAR RISK, CLAIMS PAYABLE AT DESTINATION.
+ ORIGINAL CERTIFICATE OF ORIGIN ASIA-PACIFIC TRADE AGREEMENT PLUS ONE COPY ISSUED BY CIQ.
+ SHIPMENT ADVICE WITH FULL DETAILS INCLUDING SHIPPING MARKS, CARTON NUMBERS, VESSEL'S NAME, BILL OF LADING NUMBER, VALUE AND QUANTITY OF GOODS MUST BE SENT WITHIN 3 DAYS OF THE DATE OF SHIPMENT TO US.
+ BENEFICIARY SIGNED STATEMENT CERTIFYING THAT COPIES OF INVOICE, BILL OF LADING AND PACKING LIST HAVE BEEN FAXED TO APPLICANT ON FAX NO. 0082-54-8545××× WITHIN 3 DAYS OF BILL OF LADING DATE.

ADDITIONAL COND.   47A:

+ A FEE OF USD 80 IS TO BE DEDUCTED FROM EACH DRAWING FOR THE ACCOUNT OF BENEFICIARY. IF DOCUMENTS ARE PRESENTED WITH DISCREPANCY(IES).
+ UNLESS OTHERWISE EXPRESSLY STATE, ALL DOCUMENTS MUST BE IN ENGLISH.
+ MORE OR LESS 5% IN AMOUNT AND QUANTITY IS ALLOWED.

DETAILS OF CHARGES   71B: ALL BANKING COMMISSIONS AND CHARGES INCLUDING REIMBURSEMENT COMMISSIONS OUTSIDE KOREA REP. ARE FOR BENEFICIARY'S ACCOUNT.

PRESENTATION PERIOD	48：DOCUMENTS MUST BE PRESENTED FOR NEGOTIATION WITHIN 21 DAYS AFTER THE DATE OF SHIPMENT BUT WITHIN THE VALIDITY OF THE CREDIT.
CONFIRMATION INSTRUCTION	*49：WITHOUT
	78：
	+ PLEASE REIMBURSE YOURSELVES BY PRESENTING BENEFICIARY'S DRAFT TO THE DRAWEE BANK.
	+ ALL DOCUMENTS MUST BE MAILED TO DAEGU BANK, LTD. BUSINESS PROCESS SUPPORT DEPT 17FL, 118, SUSEONG-2-GA, SUSEONG-GU, DAEGU,706-712 KOREA REP. IN ONE LOT BY COURIER MAIL.
"ADVISE THROUGH"	57A：BKCHCNBJ92G
	*BANK OF CHINA
	*HUZHOU
	*（HUZHOU BRANCH）

3月25日张洁联系公司生产部门,确认本批单子的出货信息。生产部门传来的出仓单如表2-1所示。

表2-1 出仓单

销售合同号	货号	品名规格	数量	装箱	纸箱尺寸(cm)	纸箱毛重/净重(KG)
ZC190211	L-2331	藤帘	14 408 张	8 张/箱	25×50×25	12.5/10.5

然后,张洁按照销售合同和信用证的要求,进行装箱资料核算,并完成商业发票和装箱单的缮制。

（二）任务分析

总体任务	根据销售合同和信用证缮制商业发票和装箱单
任务分解	任务一：核算装箱资料
	任务二：缮制商业发票
	任务三：缮制装箱单

（三）操作示范

第一步：核算装箱资料。

张洁根据生产部门传过来的出货信息,先对照销售合同及信用证核算装箱资料。

(1) 出货数量：货号L-2331,14 408张,与销售合同、信用证规定数量一致,没有溢短装。

(2) 箱数核算：14 408/8＝1 801(箱)。

(3) 重量核算：

  毛重 1 801×12.5＝22 512.5（kg）；

  净重 1 801×10.5＝18 910.5（kg）。

(4) 体积核算：$25×50×25×10^{-6}×1\,801=56.28(m^3)$。

核算后张洁发现，按照以前的出货经验，本次出货正好可以装一个12.192米（40英尺）的集装箱。

销售合同中没有规定本批货的唛头，为了操作方便，张洁按标准化运输标志的要求设计了唛头：

  MAIJER   ——客户简称
  ZC190211   ——合同号
  BUSAN   ——目的港
  C/NO.1-1801   ——箱数

第二步：缮制商业发票。

张洁根据销售合同、装箱资料的核算结果及信用证中的商业发票条款缮制商业发票（见样单2-2）。

信用证中的商业发票条款为：

+ SIGNED COMMERCIAL INVOICE IN 3 FOLDS CERTIFIED THE GOODS ARE OF CHINESE ORIGIN.

条款分析：信用证要求商业发票加注证明条款"CERTIFIED THE GOODS ARE OF CHINESE ORIGIN."。这一点需要在商业发票中显示出来。

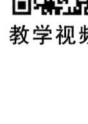
教学视频

样单2-2 商业发票

COMMERCIAL INVOICE

TO: INVOICE NO.：_____
                  INVOICE DATE：_____
                  S/C NO.：_____
                  S/C DATE：_____

FROM：_____   TO：_____
LETTER OF CREDIT NO.：_____ ISSUED BY：_____

MARKS AND NUMBERS	NUMBER AND KIND OF PACKAGE DESCRIPTION OF GOODS	QUANTITY	UNIT PRICE	AMOUNT

        TOTAL：
SAY TOTAL：

商业发票的缮制要点如下。

（1）出口商名称和地址（Exporter's Name and Address）。

一般在印制商业发票时，在其正上方已经事先印妥出口商名称和地址或标明由出口商出具。在信用证支付方式下，本栏须填写信用证受益人名称和地址，除非信用证另有规定。

(2) 发票名称(Name of Invoice)。

发票应在明显位置上标明"Invoice"(发票)或"Commercial Invoice"(商业发票)字样。

(3) 发票编号(Invoice No.)。

发票编号由各公司统一编号。发票作为中心票据,其他票据的号码(如装箱单号码)可与发票编号相一致。

(4) 发票日期(Invoice Date)。

在全套单据中,发票是签发日最早的单据。发票日期只要不早于销售合同的签订日期,不迟于提单的签发日期即可。

(5) 销售合同号及信用证号(S/C No. & L/C No.)。

商业发票上的销售合同号应与信用证上列明的销售合同号一致,一笔交易牵涉几个销售合同的,应在发票上标明。当采用信用证支付货款时,商业发票上还应填写信用证号。当采用其他支付方式时,可不填信用证号。

(6) 收货人/抬头人(Consignee)。

本栏前通常印有"To""Sold to Messrs""For Account and Risk of Messrs."等。收货人/抬头人即进口商,名称应与信用证中所规定的严格一致。如果信用证中没有特别的规定,即将信用证的申请人或收货人的名称、地址填入本栏。

(7) 启运地及目的地(From... To...)。

本栏要填上货物自装运地(港)至目的地(港)的地名,如果货物需要转运,还应注明转运地。这些内容应与提单上的相关部分一致。

(8) 唛头(Marks and Numbers)。

商业发票中的唛头应与提单上的唛头相一致,如果无唛头,必须打上 N/M(No Mark);如果信用证规定了唛头的相关内容,应按照信用证中的规定进行缮制。

(9) 数量及货物描述(Quantity and Description)。

当采用信用证支付货款时,商业发票中对货物的描述应与信用证中的描述一致。如属托收方式的,商业发票中对货物的描述可参照销售合同的规定并结合实际情况进行。

应当注意的是,商品名称必须按信用证原词填列,不得使用统称,除非信用证另有规定。如果信用证中的商品名称以英语以外的第三国语言表示,则商业发票(包括其他单据)亦应按信用证规定的第三国语言表示。如果货物有各种不同规格或各规格价格不同,则各种规格的数量、重量应分别列出。货物重量要与运输单据中的货物重量一致,货物规格要与信用证中的货物规格一致。货物的包装情况既要与实货相符,又要与信用证中的描述相符。

(10) 单价(Unit Price)。

单价一般包括计价货币、计价单位、单位价格金额和贸易术语四部分内容,如果信用证中有具体规定,则应与信用证一致。

(11) 总值(Amount)。

除非信用证中另有规定,否则货物总值不能超过信用证金额。

实际制单时,若来证要求在发票中扣除佣金,则必须扣除。折扣的处理方法与佣金的处理方法相同。

有时,信用证要求在成交价格为 CIF 时,分别列出运费、保险费,并显示 FOB 的价格,制单时则应按要求分别列出。

（12）声明文句及其他内容（Declaration and Other Contents）。

若信用证要求在发票内特别加列船名、原产地、进口许可证号码等声明文句,单证员制单时必须一一详列。常用的声明字句有:证明所到货物与销售合同或订单所列货物相符;We hereby certify that the goods named have been supplied in conformity with Order No. ×××。

（13）出单人签名或盖章及其他（Signature and Others）。

发票一般都由出口商签章,在信用证项下其名称必须与信用证的受益人名称一致。虽然 UCP600 第十八条规定发票无须签字。但是,若信用证中有"Signed invoice"等类似词语,则发票必须签章,若信用证中规定"Manually signed…",则还必须由发票授权人手签。

第三步:缮制装箱单。

张洁根据核算出来的装箱信息、商业发票及信用证中的装箱单条款缮制了装箱单(见样单 2-3)。

教学视频

信用证中的装箱单条款如下:

+ PACKING LIST IN 3 FOLDS

样单 2-3　装箱单

PACKING LIST

TO:　　　　　　　　　　　　　　　　　　INVOICE NO.:＿＿＿＿＿＿＿

　　　　　　　　　　　　　　　　　　　　INVOICE DATE:＿＿＿＿＿＿＿

　　　　　　　　　　　　　　　　　　　　S/C NO.:＿＿＿＿＿＿＿＿＿＿

FROM:＿＿＿＿＿＿＿＿＿＿＿＿　　　　TO:＿＿＿＿＿＿＿＿＿＿＿＿＿

LETTER OF CREDIT NO.:＿＿＿＿＿＿＿＿＿＿＿＿

MARKS AND NUMBERS	DESCRIPTION OF GOODS	QUANTITY	PACKAGE	G.W	N.W	MEAS.

　　　　　　　　　　TOTAL:

SAY TOTAL:

装箱单的缮制要点如下。

（1）单据名称（Name of Documents）。

单据名称应按照信用证规定缮制,通常用"Packing List""Packing Specification" "Detailed Packing List"等。如果信用证要求用中性装箱单（Neutral Packing List）,则装箱单名称打"Packing List",且装箱单内不打出口商的名称,不能签章。

（2）单据号码（No.）。

单据号码应与发票号码一致。

(3) 销售合同号或销售确认书号(S/C No.)。

此项填写这批货物的销售合同号码或者销售确认书的号码。

(4) 唛头(Shipping Mark)。

唛头应与发票一致,有时注实际唛头,有时也可以只注"as Per Invoice No. ×××"。

(5) 箱号(Case No.)。

箱号又称包装件号码,在单位包装货量或品种不固定的情况下,需注明每个包装件内的包装情况,因此,包装件应编号。有的信用证要求此处注明"Case No.1—UP",UP是指总箱数。

(6) 货描(Description of Goods;Specification)。

货描应与发票一致,货名如有总称,应先注总称,然后逐项列明详细货名、规格、品种。

(7) 数量(Quantity)。

此项应注明此箱内每件货物的包装件数。

(8) 毛重(Gross Weight)。

此项一般应注明每个包装件的毛重和此包装件内不同规格、品种、花色货物各自的总毛重,最后在合计栏处注明总货量。信用证或销售合同中如果没有明确要求,此项也可以只写总毛重;信用证或销售合同中如果有"Detailed Packing List"字样,则此项应逐项列明。

(9) 净重(Net Weight)。

此项一般应注明每个包装件的净重和此包装件内不同规格、品种、花色货物各自的总净重,最后在合计栏处注明总货量。信用证或销售合同中如果没有明确要求,此项也可以只写总净重;信用证或销售合同中如果有"Detailed Packing List"字样,则此项应逐项列明。

(10) 尺码(Measurement)。

此项应注明每个包装件的尺码和总尺码。

(11) 出票人签章(Signature)。

出票人签章应与发票相同。若信用证有"Signed Packing List"等类似规定,则装箱单必须签章;若信用证规定"Manually Signed…",还必须由装箱单授权人手签;若信用证规定装箱单为"Neutral Packing List",则装箱单内不应出现出口商的名称,不能签章。

(四) 任务解决

完成商业发票(见样单2-4)和装箱单(见样单2-5)的缮制工作后,张洁联系业务员,确认本批货物可以备妥的时间。在确认3月31日前生产部门能完成备货后,张洁开始准备托运资料,向货代公司订舱。

样单2-4 商业发票

湖州正昌贸易有限公司
HUZHOU ZHENGCHANG TRADING CO., LTD.
42 HONGQI ROAD, HUZHOU, CHINA
TEL:+86-0572-2365×××   FAX:+86-0572-2365×××

COMMERCIAL INVOICE

TO:MAIJER FISTRTION INC.   INVOICE NO.:ZC19311
3214,WALKER, NAKAGYO-KU,   INVOICE DATE:MAR. 25,2019

KYUNG-BUK, KOREA REP.   S/C NO.: ZC190211
FROM: SHANGHAI, CHINA   TO: BUSAN PORT, KOREA REP.
LETTER OF CREDIT NO.: M51145160747856   ISSUED BY: DAEGU BANK, LTD., THE DAEGU

MARKS AND NUMBERS	NUMBER AND KIND OF PACKAGE DESCRIPTION OF GOODS	QUANTITY	UNIT PRICE	AMOUNT
MAIJER ZC190211 BUSAN C/NO. 1-1801	ART. NO.: L-2331 RATTAN CURTAIN AS PER SALES CONFIRMATION NO. ZC190211	14 408PCS	CIF BUSAN USD2.61/PC	USD37 604.88

SAY TOTAL: SAY U.S. DOLLARS THIRTY-SEVEN THOUSAND SIX HUNDRED AND FOUR AND POINT EIGHTY EIGHT

WE HEREBY CERTIFIED THE GOODS ARE OF CHINESE ORIGIN.

湖州正昌贸易有限公司

HUZHOU ZHENGCHANG TRADING CO., LTD.

陈强

样单2-5 装箱单

湖州正昌贸易有限公司

HUZHOU ZHENGCHANG TRADING CO., LTD.

42 HONGQI ROAD, HUZHOU, CHINA

TEL: +86-0572-2365×××   FAX: +86-0572-2365×××

PACKING LIST

TO: MAIJER FISTRTION INC.   INVOICE NO.: ZC19311
3214, WALKER, NAKAGYO-KU,   INVOICE DATE: MAR. 25, 2019
KYUNG-BUK, KOREA REP.   S/C NO.: ZC190211
FROM: SHANGHAI, CHINA   TO: BUSAN PORT, KOREA REP.
LETTER OF CREDIT NO.: M51145160747856

MARKS AND NUMBERS	DESCRIPTION OF GOODS	QUANTITY	PACKAGE	G.W	N.W	MEAS.
MAIJER ZC190211 BUSAN C/NO. 1-1801	ART. NO.: L-2331 RATTAN CURTAIN AS PER SALES CONFIRMATION NO. ZC190211	14 408PCS	1 801CTNS	22 512.5KGS	18 910.5KGS	56.28CBM
	TOTAL	14 408PCS	1 801CTNS	22 512.5KGS	18 910.5KGS	56.28CBM

SAY TOTAL: SAY ONE THOUSAND EIGHT HUNDRED AND ONE CARTONS ONLY.

湖州正昌贸易有限公司

HUZHOU ZHENGCHANG TRADING CO., LTD.

陈强

三、知识链接

(一) 商业发票

1. 商业发票的定义

商业发票(Commercial Invoice)是出口商向进口商开列的发货价目清单,是买卖双方记账的依据,也是进出口报关交税的总说明。商业发票的内容包括商品的名称、规格、价格、数量、金额、包装等。商业发票是一笔业务的全面反映,同时也是进口商办理进口报关不可缺少的文件。因此,商业发票是全套出口单据的核心,在单据制作过程中,其余单据均需参照商业发票缮制。

2. 商业发票的作用

商业发票主要有以下几个方面的作用。

(1) 可供进口商了解和掌握装运货物的全面情况。

商业发票是一笔交易的全面叙述,详细列明了装运货物的名称、商品规格、装运数量、价格条款、商品单价、商品总值等信息。进口商可根据商业发票识别该批货物属于哪一批订单项,核对签订销售合同的项目,了解和掌握销售合同的履约情况,并进行验收。

(2) 可作为进口商记账、进口报关以及海关核算、统计的依据。

商业发票是销售货物的凭证。进口商需要根据商业发票逐笔登记记账,按时结算货款。同时,商业发票是海关核算税金、验关放行和统计的凭证之一。进口商在清关时需要向当地海关当局递交出口商提供的商业发票。

(3) 可作为出口商记账、出口报关的依据。

出口商凭商业发票的内容,逐笔登记入账。在货物装运前,出口商需要向海关递交商业发票进行报关。

(4) 在不用汇票的情况下,商业发票可以代替汇票作为付款依据。

在即期付款不出具汇票的情况下,商业发票可作为进口商支付货款的依据,替代汇票参与核算。

3. 其他种类的发票

外贸单证中除常用的商业发票外,还包括一些其他种类的发票,主要有银行发票、海关发票、领事发票、形式发票等。

教学视频

(1) 银行发票(Banker's Invoice),是指出口商为办理议付和结汇,以适应议付行和开证行需要而提供的发票。

(2) 海关发票(Customs Invoice),是指某些国家规定在进口货物时,出口商必须提供其海关规定的一种固定格式和内容的发票。

(3) 领事发票(Consular Invoice),又称签证发票,是指按某些国家法令规定,出口商向进口国输入货物时,必须取得进口国在出口国或其邻近地区的领事签证的,作为装运单据一部分和货物进口报关的前提条件之一的特殊发票。

(4) 形式发票(Proforma Invoice),也称预开发票或估价发票,是进口商为了向其本国当局申请进口许可证或请求核批外汇,在未成交之前,要求出口商开立的包括拟出售成交的商品名称、单价、规格等条件的一份参考性发票。

（二）包装单据

包装单据(Packing Documents)，是指一切记载或描述商品包装情况的单据，是商业发票内容的补充。包装单据一般包括商品的包装件数、规格、唛头、重量等，明确阐明商品的包装情况。包装单据便于进口商了解和掌握进口商品的包装及其数量、重量等，当货物到达目的港时，也便于海关检查和核对货物。有些商品不需要包装，如谷物、矿砂、煤炭等，我们称之为"散装货物"(Packed in Bulk)。大多数商品必须进行适当的包装后才能装运出口，以保护该商品的安全。

1. 几种主要的包装单据

包装单据主要包括装箱单、重量单、尺码单等。实际操作中，根据客户的要求和产品的特性，可以使用不同形式、不同种类的包装单据。

（1）装箱单(Packing List/Packing Slip)。

装箱单又称包装单，重点说明每件商品包装的详细情况，标明货物名称、规格、数量、唛头、箱号、件数和重量，以及包装情况。对于不定量包装的商品，会逐件列出每件包装的详细情况；对于定量箱装，每件商品都是统一的重量的情况，则只需说明总件数多少、每箱多少重量、合计重量多少即可。如果信用证条款要求提供详细的包装单，则必须提供尽可能详细的装箱内容，描述每件包装的细节，包括商品的货号、色号、尺寸搭配、毛重、净重及包装的尺寸等。

（2）重量单(Weight List/Weight Note)。

重量单一般是针对按照装货重量成交的货物开具的单据，应尽量详细地标明商品每箱毛重、净重及总重量的情况，供买方安排运输、存仓时参考。重量单一般起码要具备编号、日期、商品名称、唛头、毛重、净重、皮重、总件数等内容。

（3）尺码单(Measurement List)。

尺码单偏重于说明每件货物的尺码和总尺码，即在装箱单内容的基础上再重点说明每件不同规格包装的尺码和总尺码。

除上述三种包装单据外，其他包装单据还有花色搭配单(Assortment List)、包装说明(Packing Specification)、详细装箱单(Detailed Packing List)、包装提要(Packing Summary)、重量证书(Weight Certificate/Certificate of Weight)、磅码单(Weight Memo)等。

2. 包装单据缮制注意事项

缮制包装单据时主要应注意以下几点。

（1）单据的名称必须与信用证要求相符。例如，信用证规定为"Weight Memo"，则单据名称不能用"Weight List"。有的出口商将两种单据的名称印在一起，当信用证仅要求出具其中一种单据时，应将另外一种单据的名称删去。

（2）当提供两种单据时，两种单据的各项内容应与发票和其他单据的内容一致。例如，装箱单上的总件数和重量单上的总重量，应与发票、提单上的总件数或总重量相一致。

（3）包装单据所列的情况，应与货物的包装内容完全相符。

（4）当信用证要求提供"中性包装清单"(Neutral Packing List)时，应由第三方填制，不要注明受益人的名称。这主要是由于进口商在转让单据时，不愿将原始出口商暴露给其买主。例如，当信用证要求用"空白纸张"(Plain Paper)填制时，在单据内一般不要表现出受益人及开证行名称，也不要加盖任何签章。

四、能力训练

(一) 安吉林木饰品有限公司操作案例

接"项目一 审核与修改信用证""能力训练"部分安吉林木饰品有限公司操作案例。安吉林木饰品有限公司的单证员在审核出信用证中的不符点后,通过业务员把不符点告知买方进行修改。2019年4月25日,中国银行湖州市分行接到开证行发过来的信用证修改书,安吉林木饰品有限公司的单证员把信用证内容进行了重新整合,方便以后操作。单证员按照销售合同(见样单1-7)和修改后的信用证(见样单2-6)内容缮制商业发票和装箱单。

样单2-6 信用证

MT S700	ISSUE OF A DOCUMENTARY CREDIT
APPLICATION HEADER	＊CAJA DE AHORROS YM. P. DE NAVARRA
	＊PAMPLONA
SEQUENCE OF TOTAL	＊27:1/1
FORM OF DOC. CREDIT	＊40A:IRREVOCABLE
DOC. CREDIT NUMBER	＊20:046CDI577402456
DATE OF ISSUE	31C:190420
APPLICABLE RULES	＊40E:UCP LATEST VERSION
EXPIRY	＊31D:DATE 190530 PLACE AT NEGOTIATING BANK
APPLICANT	＊50:JEWTS HAMAN INC 860
	ADVA COSEP TARRADELLAS
	00243 BARCELONA
	SPAIN
BENEFICIARY	＊59:ANJI LINMU DECORATION CO., LTD.
	ANJI ECONOMIC DEVELOPING DISTRICT,
	HUZHOU CITY,
	ZHEJIANG, CHINA
AMOUNT	＊32B:CURRENCY USD AMOUNT 130,536.00
AVAILABLE WITH/BY	＊41D:ANY BANK
	BY NEGOTIATION
DRAFT AT…	42C:AT 30 DAYS AFTER SIGHT FOR 90 PERCENT OF INVOICE VALUE
DRAWEE	＊42A:＊CAJA DE AHORROS YM. P. DE NAVARRA
	＊PAMPLONA
PARTIAL SHIPMENT	43P:NOT ALLOWED
TRANSSHIPMENT	43T:NOT ALLOWED
PORT OF LOADING	44E:SHANGHAI PORT, CHINA
PORT OF DISCHARGE	44F:BARCELONA PORT, SPAIN
LATEST DATE OF SHIP.	44C:190519
DESCRIPT OF GOODS	45A:
	LADIES' 96% POLYESTER 4% ELASTANE WOVEN GARMENTS DRESS

ART. NO. ZC14502 8 820PCS USD7.25/PC
ART. NO. ZC14533 8 820PCS USD7.55/PC
CIF BARCELONA PORT

DOCUMENTS REQUIRED 46A:
+ SIGNED AND STAMPED COMMERCIAL INVOICE IN 2 FOLDS
+ SIGNED PACKING LIST IN 2 FOLDS
+ FULL SET OF ORIGINAL CLEAN ON BOARD MARINE BILL OF LADING MADE OUT TO THE ORDER OF CAJA DE AHORROS YM. P. DE NAVARRA AND BLANK ENDORSED, MARKED FREIGHT PREPAID AND NOTIFY APPLICANT.
+ INSURANCE POLICY OR CERTIFICATE ISSUED FOR 110 PCT OF INVOICE VALUE, MADE OUT TO THE ORDER OF CAJA DE AHORROS YM. P. DE NAVARRA COVERING 'FPA', 'FROM WAREHOUSE TO WAREHOUSE' AND STATING 'CLAIMS, IF ANY, PAYABLE IN SPAIN', IN 1 ORIGINAL AND 1 COPY.
+ ORIGINAL CERTIFICATE OF ORIGIN PLUS ONE COPY ISSUED BY CCPIT.
+ BENEFICIARY'S CERTIFICATE CERTIFYING THAT 1 COMMERCIAL INVOICE, 1 PACKING LIST, 1 WEIGHT CERTIFICATE AND 1 NON NEGOTIABLE COPY OF B/L HAVE BEEN FORWARDED TO APPLICANT WITHIN 48 HOURS AFTER SHIPMENT.

ADDITIONAL COND. 47A:
+ A HANDLING CHARGE OF USD 90 WILL BE DEDUCTED FROM THE PROCEEDS OF EACH SET OF DOCUMENTS WITH DISCREPANCIES.

DETAILS OF CHARGES 71B: ALL BANKING CHARGES AND COMMISSIONS OUTSIDE ISSUING BANK INCLUDING REIMBURSEMENT CHARGES ARE FOR BENEFICIARY'S ACCOUNT.

PRESENTATION PERIOD 48: 21 DAYS AFTER SHIPMEN DATE BUT WITHIN L/C VALIDITY

CONFIRMATION *49: WITHOUT

INSTRUCTION 78:
REIMBURSEMENT: AT MATURITY DATE AND AFTER RECEIPT OF DOCUMENTS IN STRICT COMPLIANCE WITH L/C TERMS, WE WILL PER THE NEGOTIATING BANK'S INSTRUCTIONS.
DOCUMENTS TO BE SENT TO CAJA DE AHORROS Y M. P. DE NAVARRA, LETTER OF CREDIT PROCESSING AGENT, 3/F CITYPLAZA FOUR, 14 TAIKOO WAN ROAD, PAMPLONA IN ONE LOT BY COURIER MAIL.

"ADVISE THROUGH" 57A: BKCHCNBJ92G
* BANK OF CHINA
* HUZHOU
* (HUZHOU BRANCH)

4月26日,安吉林木饰品有限公司单证员从公司业务员处拿到了本批货物的出货信息,并开始缮制商业发票和装箱单。生产部门传来的出仓单如表2-2所示。

表 2-2 出仓单

销售合同号	货号	品名规格	数量	装箱	纸箱尺寸(cm)	毛重/净重(KG/每箱)
Y024562	ZC14502	96%涤 4%弹力女连衣裙	8 820 件	42 件/箱	50×50×25	14.5/12.5
	ZC14533		8 820 件	42 件/箱	50×50×25	14.5/12.5

补充资料：

Invoice No.：LM2019001；

Marks：N/M。

工作任务：

1. 核算装箱资料；

2. 缮制商业发票和装箱单。

（二）湖州兴业进出口有限公司操作案例

接"项目一 审核与修改信用证""能力训练"部分湖州兴业进出口有限公司操作案例。2019年4月25日，湖州兴业进出口有限公司单证员拿到信用证修改书，对照原信用证进行了整合。5月15日单证员拿到生产部门的出货箱单，如表2-3所示。他先进行装箱资料的核算，然后根据销售合同（见样单1-9）和信用证（见样单2-7）的内容缮制商业发票和装箱单。

表 2-3 出货箱单

品名(Article)	数量(PCS)	数量/箱(PCS/CTN)	箱数(CTNS)	毛重/箱(KG)	净重/箱(KG)	纸箱规格(cm)
6KG 干粉灭火器	5 000	10	500	@22	@20	40×30×30
9L 泡沫灭火器	200	10	20	@22	@20	40×30×30
5KG CO_2 灭火器	3 000	10	300	@22	@20	40×30×30
2KG CO_2 灭火器	500	10	50	@22	@20	40×30×30

样单 2-7 信用证

```
MT S700                    ISSUE OF A DOCUMENTARY CREDIT
SEQUENCE OF TOTAL          *27：1/1
FORM OF DOC. CREDIT        *40A：IRREVOCABLE
DOC. CREDIT NUMBER         *20：CDI702/8053/2019
DATE OF ISSUE              31C：190405
APPLICABLE RULES           *40E：UCP LATEST VERSION
EXPIRY                     *31D：DATE 190630 PLACE CHINA
APPLICANT BANK             51A：AMEM BANK
                               AVENUE MOHAMED V
                               TUNIS，TUNISIA
APPLICANT                  *50：TUFFCO
                               3052 SFAX TUNISIE
BENEFICIARY                *59：HUZHOU XINGYE INDUSTRY CO.，LTD.
                               18TH FLOOR，MEIXIN BUILDING，HUZHOU，
                               ZHEJIANG，CHINA
```

AMOUNT		*32B: CURRENCY USD AMOUNT 164 269.50
AVAILABLE WITH/BY		*41D: WACHOVIA BANK,NA,SHANGHAI BRANCH BY PAYMENT
PARTIAL SHIPMENT		43P: ALLOWED
TRANSSHIPMENT		43T: ALLOWED
PORT OF LOADING		44E: SHANGHAI PORT
PORT OF DISCHARGE		44F: SFAX PORT, TUNISIN
LATEST DATE OF SHIP.		44C: 190610
DESCRIPT. OF GOODS		45A:

FIRE EXTINGUISHER PER SALES CONFIRMATION NO. 2019TU02 DTD 29/03/2019

DOCUMENTS REQUIRED   46A:

+ SIGNED COMMERCIAL INVOICE IN 7 FOLDS
+ WEIGHT NOTE AND PACKING LIST IN 3 FOLDS
+ FULL SET OF ORIGINAL CLEAN ON BOARD MARINE BILL OF LADING MADE OUT TO SHIPPER'S ORDER AND BLANK ENDORSED, MARKED FREIGHT PREPAID AND NOTIFY APPLICANT QUOTING FULL NAME AND ADDRESS.
+ ORIGINAL CERTIFICATE OF ORIGIN PLUS ONE COPY ISSUED BY CIQ.
+ SHIPMENT ADVICE WITH FULL DETAILS INCLUDING SHIPPING MARKS, CARTON NUMBERS, VESSEL'S NAME, BILL OF LADING NUMBER, VALUE AND QUANTITY OF GOODS MUST BE SENT WITHIN 3 DAYS OF THE DATE OF SHIPMENT TO US.
+ BENEFICIARY SIGNED STATEMENT CERTIFYING THAT COPIES OF INVOICE, BILL OF LADING AND PACKING LIST HAVE BEEN FAXED TO APPLICANT ON FAX NO. +82-54-8545××× WITHIN 3 DAYS OF BILL OF LADING DATE.
+ SHIPPING ADVICE WITH FULL DETAIL INCLUING SHIPPING MARKS, CARTON NUMBERS, VESSEL'S NAME, BILL OF LADING NUMBER, VALUE AND QUANTITY OF GOODS MUST BE SENT ON THE DATE OF SHIPMENT TO US.

ADDITIONAL COND.   47A:

+ HOUSE B/L UNACCEPTED.
+ A FEE OF USD 80 IS TO BE DEDUCTED FROM EACH DRAWING FOR THE ACCOUNT OF BENEFICIARY. IF DOCUMENTS ARE PRESENTED WITH DISCREPANCY(IES).
+ ALL DOCUMENTS MUST BEAR NUMBER OF L/C.

DETAILS OF CHARGES		71B: ALL BANKING COMMISSIONS AND CHARGES INCLUDING REIMBURSEMENT COMMISSIONS OUTSIDE TUNISIA ARE FOR BENEFICIARY'S ACCOUNT.
PRESENTATION PERIOD		48: DOCUMENTS MUST BE PRESENTED FOR NEGOTIATION WITHIN 21 DAYS AFTER THE DATE OF SHIPMENT BUT WITHIN THE VALIDITY OF THE CREDIT.
CONFIRMATION		*49: WITHOUT
INSTRUCTION		78:

+ PLEASE REIMBURSE YOURSELVES BY PRESENTING BENEFICIARY'S DRAFT TO THE DRAWEE BANK.
+ WACHOVIA BANK SHANGHAI HOLDS SPECIAL INSTRUCTION REGARDING DOCUMENTS DISPOSAL AND REIMBURSEMENT OF THIS L/C.

"ADVISE THROUGH"   57A：BKCHCNBJ92G
* BANK OF CHINA
* HUZHOU
*（HUZHOU BRANCH）

补充资料：
发票号码：19BY411；
发票日期：2019 年 5 月 15 日。
工作任务：
1. 核算装箱资料；
2. 缮制商业发票和装箱单。

五、岗位拓展

讨论话题：商业发票认证问题。

2019 年 12 月 5 日,湖州正昌贸易有限公司收到一份来自埃及客户的信用证,其中关于商业发票的单据条款如下：

+ BENEFICIAY'S SIGNED COMMERCIAL INVOICE IN 3 ORIGINALS AND 3 COPIED BASED ON QSG(QUALITY SERVICE GROUP) CERTIFICATE OF QUALITY AND WEIGHT AND ONE ORIGINAL TO BE LEGALIZED BY THE EGYPTIAN EMBASSY AND THE CHAMBER OF COMMERCE IN THE COUNTRY OF ORIGIN.

讨论引导：

（1）对于上述商业发票条款,请查询、分析条款含义并了解出口到埃及的货物制单的特殊要求。

（2）分组讨论,给出结论报告,然后分析"BASED ON QSG"是指发票上需要这个机构认证,还是在检测了质量和重量的基础上再出具发票。

（3）根据结论报告设计具体操作流程。

项目三
办理出口货物托运

一、学习目标

能力目标： 能缮制托运委托书，办理出口托运手续。

知识目标： 明确托运委托书的缮制要点，了解出口托运的流程。

二、工作任务

（一）任务描述

2019年3月27日，单证员张洁在完成商业发票（见样单2-4）和装箱单（见样单2-5）的缮制工作后，考虑生产部门的备货时间以及信用证中4月15日的最迟装运期，打算预定4月5日左右去韩国釜山的船。

在这笔业务中，韩国客户没有指定船公司，对船只也没有具体要求，因此张洁就向与公司一直业务往来的湖州中远国际货运有限公司询问配舱事宜，在确定4月6日的具体船期后开始缮制订舱委托书，办理托运手续。

（二）任务分析

总体任务	制作托运委托书并办理托运手续
任务分解	任务一：确认托运细节
	任务二：缮制托运委托书
	任务三：办理托运手续

（三）操作示范

第一步：确认托运细节。

张洁根据销售合同及信用证中的要求以及项目二中核算出来的装箱资料，确认以下托运细节。

1. 确认托运委托书中发货人、收货人、通知人三个当事人

在信用证下要做到单证一致、单单一致。托运委托书是以后制作提单的依据，因此，在缮制托运委托书时要参照信用证中的提单条款，本业务信用证中的提单条款为：

+ FULL SET OF ORIGINAL CLEAN ON BOARD MARINE BILL OF LADING MADE OUT TO SHIPPER'S ORDER AND BLANK ENDORSED, MARKED FREIGHT PREPAID AND NOTIFY APPLICANT QUOTING FULL NAME AND ADDRESS.

（1）托运人(Shipper)：一般为出口商,本业务填写销售合同中出口商的名称和地址。

（2）收货人(Consignee)：也称提单的抬头,分为记名抬头、指示性抬头和不记名抬头三种。记名抬头要具体指明收货人。例如,若提单条款中抬头规定"Consigned to ABC Company",则收货人一栏填写"ABC Company",此提单不能背书转让,且只能由 ABC 公司提货。对卖方而言,这样做风险很大。指示性抬头是外贸单证实务中使用最多的一种抬头,指示性抬头具体又分为空白抬头("To Order")和记名指示性抬头("To Order of ×××")两种。指示性抬头可以背书转让。不记名抬头,收货人一栏空着不填或填"To Bearer",提单无须背书即可转让,风险很大,因此在外贸单证实务中很少使用。本业务中收货人为"TO SHIPPER'S ORDER"。

（3）通知人(Notify Party)：填写信用证规定的提单通知人的名称和地址,通知人没有提货的权利,仅供船方做到货通知用。本业务中通知人处应填写开证申请人(APPLICANT)。

2. 确认运费到付/预付、港口、唛头等

（1）运费：本业务中运费为预付(FREIGHT PREPAID)。

（2）港口：本业务中装运港为上海,目的港为釜山。

（3）唛头：本业务中唛头应为：

MAIJER
ZC190211
BUSAN
C/NO. 1-1801

3. 确认门点装柜还是做内装箱,整柜还是拼箱

张洁与生产部门沟通后,确认本业务为门点装柜,大致装柜时间为 4 月 4 日。

本批货物整柜：$1×40'$。

第二步：缮制托运委托书。

张洁根据确认的订舱细节及商业发票和装箱单的相关内容开始缮制托运委托书(空白托运委托书见样单 3-1)。

样单 3-1　托运委托书

Shipper(托运人)：
Consignee(收货人)：
Notify Party(通知人)：

续表

信用证号码：				合同号码：	
启运港：				目的港：	
装运时间：				运输方式：	
箱型数量：				运费：	
唛头		品名	件数	毛重 KG	体积 CBM
装箱时间、地点及联系方式 装箱地址： 装箱时间：				操作员： 电话： 传真：	

托运委托书主要包括以下内容。

(1) 托运人(Shipper)。

托运人也称发货人，本栏一般填写出口商的名称、地址、联系电话/传真号。

(2) 收货人(Consignee)。

本栏应按照销售合同或信用证对提单收货人的规定来填写。

在信用证支付条件下，对收货人的规定通常有以下两种表示方法。

① 记名收货人：直接写明收货人的名称，一般是销售合同的买方。

② 指示性收货人：在收货人栏内有指示(Order)字样。指示性收货人一般分为记名指示(To Order of ×××)和不记名指示(To Order)两种。

(3) 通知人(Notify Party)。

通知人也称被通知人，本栏应填写信用证中规定的提单通知人的名称和地址。通知人的职责是及时接收船方发出的到货通知，并将该通知转告真实的收货人。通知人不具备提货的权利。

(4) 信用证号码(L/C No.)。

本栏应填写相关交易的信用证号码。

(5) 销售合同号码(S/C No.)。

本栏应填写相关交易的销售合同号码。

(6) 启运港(Port of Loading)。

本栏应填写销售合同或信用证规定的启运港。如果信用证未规定具体的启运港，则填写实际装运港名称。

(7) 目的港(Port of Discharge)。

本栏应填写销售合同或信用证规定的目的港。如果信用证未规定具体的目的港，则填写实际卸货港名称。

(8) 装运时间(Time of Shipment)。

本栏应填写预计的装运时间，这个时间不能超过销售合同或信用证规定的最迟装运期限。

(9) 运费(Freight)。

本栏应根据信用证提单条款的规定填写"FREIGHT PREPAID"(运费预付)或"FREIGHT TO COLLECT"(运费到付)。非信用证支付方式下,工作人员可根据成交的贸易术语确定运费预付或运费到付。

(10) 唛头(Marks)。

本栏应按实际情况填写货物的装运标志。

(11) 品名(Name of Commodity)。

本栏可以只填写货物的统称,但不得与销售合同和信用证中的描述相矛盾。

(12) 件数(Packages)。

本栏应填写货物总的包装数。

(13) 毛重(Gross Weight)。

本栏应填写货物总的毛重。

(14) 尺码(Measurement)。

本栏应填写货物总的体积。

第三步:办理托运手续。

张洁把缮制好的托运委托书(见样单3-2)传给湖州中远国际货运有限公司的小陈,办理托运手续。

样单3-2 托运委托书

Shipper(托运人): HUZHOU ZHENGCHANG TRADING CO., LTD. 42 HONGQI ROAD, HUZHOU, CHINA					
Consignee(收货人): TO SHIPPER'S ORDER					
Notify Party(通知人): MAIJER FISTRTION INC. 3214, WALKER, NAKAGYO-KU, KYUNG-BUK, KOREA REP.					
信用证号码:M51145160747856			合同号码:ZC190211		
启运港:SHANGHAI			目的港:BUSAN PORT, KOREA REP.		
装运时间:APR.4,2019			运输方式:BY SEA		
箱型数量:1×40′			运费:FREIGHT PREPAID		
唛头	品名	件数	毛重 KG	体积
MAIJER ZC190211 BUSAN C/NO. 1-1801	RATTAN CURTAIN	1 801CTNS	22 512.5KGS	56.28CBM
装箱时间、地点及联系方式 装箱地址: 湖州正昌贸易有限公司 湖州市红旗路42号 装箱时间: 4月4日			操作员:张洁 电话:0572-2365××× 传真:0572-2365×××		

(四)任务解决

4月1日,湖州中远国际货运有限公司确认张洁的订舱信息后,传做箱通知(见样单3-3)给湖州正昌贸易有限公司确认。

样单3-3　做箱通知

做箱通知

TO:湖州正昌/张女士

船名/航次:GOLDEN COMPANION 907N
提单号:COSG55896212
目的港:BUSAN PORT,KOREA REP.
做箱地址:湖州市红旗路42号
箱型:1×40'FCL
装箱时间:2019年4月4日上午9点
预计开船日:2019年4月6日

注:预配数据为1 801CTNS,22 512.5KGS,56.28CBM。
请核对并确认数据,如无误,请签OK传回我公司,谢谢配合!

FROM:湖州中远/小陈
2019年4月1日

张洁确认做箱通知各项信息无误后,签"OK"后回传给湖州中远国际货运有限公司。至此,出口托运工作完成。

三、知识链接

(一)海运托运

1. 海运托运委托书

海运托运委托书是指出口商(托运人/发货人)在报关前向船公司或其代理人申请租船订舱的单据,它也是船公司缮制提单的主要背景资料及依据。

出口商一般通过货代公司向船公司订舱,因此,在办理出口托运时,出口商先向货代公司提供托运委托书,由货代公司缮制出口托运单并向船公司订舱。出口托运单是以托运委托书的内容为依据缮制的,两者内容基本相同,只是格式上有所区别。

2. 出口商海运托运的流程

(1)出口商在货、证齐备后,填制托运委托书,可随附商业发票、装箱单等其他必要单据,委托货代公司代为订舱。有时,出口商还可以委托货代公司代理报关及货物储运等事宜。

(2)货代公司接受订舱委托后,缮制集装箱货物托运单(见样单3-4),随同商业发票、装箱单等其他必要单证一同向船公司办理订舱。

教学视频

样单 3-4 集装箱货物托运单

Shipper（托运人）				D/R NO.（编号） **集装箱货物托运单**	
Consignee（收货人）					
Notify Party（通知人）					
Pre-carriage by（前程运输）					
Place of Receipt（收货地点）					
Ocean Vessel（船名） Voy. No.（航次） Port of Loading（装货港）					
Port of Discharge（卸货港） Place of Delivery（交货地点） Final Destination（目的港）					
Container No.（集装箱号）	Seal No.（封志号）Marks & Nos.（标志与号码）	No. of Containers or P'kgs（箱数或件数）	Kind of Packages; Description of Goods（包装种类与货名）	Gross Weight（毛重/千克）	Measurement（尺码/立方米）
Total Number of Containers of Packages(in Words) 集装箱数或件数合计（大写）					
Freight & Charges（运费与附加费）	Revenue Tons（运费吨）	Rate（运费率）	Per（每）	Prepaid（运费预付）	Collect（到付）
Ex Rate（兑换率）	Prepaid at（预付地点）	Payable at（到付地点）	Place of Issue（签发地点）		
	Total Prepaid（预付总额）	No. of Original B(S)L（正本提单份数）			
Service Type on Receiving □-CY □-CFS □-DOOR		Service Type on Delivery □-CY □-CFS □-DOOR	Reefer-Temperature Required（冷藏温度）	°F	℃
Type of Goods（种类）	Ordinary,（普通） Reefer,（冷藏） Dangerous,（危险品） Auto（裸装车辆）			危险品	Class Property
	Liquid,（液体） Live Animal,（活动物） Bulk（散货）				
可否转船		可否分批			
装期		有效期			
金额					
制单日期					

（3）船公司根据具体情况，如果接受订舱，则在托运单的几联单据上编上与海运提单号码一致的编号，填上船名、航次，并签署，即表示已确认货代公司的订舱，同时把配舱回单、装货单(Shipping Order, S/O)等与托运人有关的单据退还给货代公司。

（4）货代公司根据配舱回单和装货单上的相关信息，给托运人发进仓通知书或做箱通知。

（5）托运人按照进仓通知书或做箱通知上的要求备货并准备报关单证。

（6）如果是做门到门，托运人按做箱通知上的时间在工厂仓库备好货，由货代公司前来装货。如果是做场到场，则托运人按进仓通知书上的规定时间联系货代公司并将货物运至指定仓库，同时提供报关资料委托货代公司报关。

（7）货物集中到港区后，货代公司集中报关单证向海关申报出口，海关关员查验合格放行后可将货物装船。

(8)装船完毕,货代公司发提单确认件给托运人进行确认。托运人向收货人发出装船通知,并从船公司或其代理处取得已装船提单。

(二)空运托运

1. 国际货物托运书

国际货物托运书(Shippers Letter of Instruction)是指托运人用于委托承运人或其代理人填开航空货运单的一种表单,表单上列有填制货运单所需的各项内容,并印有授权承运人或其代理人代其在货运单上签字的文字说明。目前,在外贸单证实务操作中,国际货物托运书(见样单3-5)一般都由托运人代理人填制。

样单3-5 国际货物托运书

国际货物托运书
SHIPPER'S LETTER OF INSTRUCTION

托运人姓名、地址及电话号码 Shipper's Name, Address and Telephone	托运人账号 Shipper's Account Number	航空运单号码 Air Waybill Number	
		999-	
		安全检查 Safety Inspection	
收货人姓名、地址及电话号码 Consignee's Name, Address and Telephone	收货人账号 Consignee's Account Number	是否定妥航班日期、吨位 Booked	
		航班/日期 Flight/Date	航班/日期 Flight/Date
		预付 PP	到付 CC
		供运输用的声明价值 Declared Value for Carriage	供海关用的声明价值 Declared Value for Customs
始发机场 Airport of Departure	目的机场 Airport of Destination	保险金额 Amount of Insurance	
填开货运单的代理人名称 Issuing Carrier's Agent Name		另请通知 Also Notify	
储运注意事项及其他 Handing Information and Others		随附文件 Document to Accompany Air Waybill	
件数 No. of PCS 运价组成点 RCP	毛重 (千克) Gross Weight (kg)	运价种类 Rate Class	商品代号 Commodity Item No.	计费重量 (千克) Chargeable Weight(kg)	费率 Rate	货物品名及数量(包括尺寸或体积) Nature and Quantity of Goods (Incl. Dimensions or Volume)
托运人证实以上所填内容全部属实并愿意遵守承运人的一切运输章程。 The Shipper Certifies That the Particulars on the Face Here-of Are Correct and Agrees to the Conditions of Carriage of the Carrier. 托运人或其代理人签字、盖章 Signature of Shipper or His Agent				航空运费和其他费用 Weight Charge and Other Charges 承运人签字 Signature of Issuing Carrier or Its Agent 日期 Date		

2. 国际货物托运书的缮制

(1) 托运人姓名、地址及电话号码(Shipper's Name, Address and Telephone)。

本栏填托运人的全称、街名、城市名称、国名,以及便于联系的电话号码、电传号码或传真号码。在信用证结汇方式下,托运人一般按信用证的受益人内容填写。

采用集中托运时,托运人为货运代理人;采用直接托运时,托运人为货主。托运危险货物时,托运人必须填写实际托运人,航空公司不接受货运代理人托运。

(2) 托运人账号(Shipper's Account Number)。

本栏只在必要时填写。托运人有时被承运人要求在托运单上提供托运人账号,以方便承运人在收货人拒付运费时向托运人索偿。

(3) 收货人姓名、地址及电话号码(Consignee's Name, Address and Telephone)。

本栏填收货人的全称、街名、城市名称、国名(特别是在不同国家内有相同城市名称时,必须要填上国名)以及电话号码、电传号码或传真号码。本栏不得填写"Order"或"To Order of the Shipper(按托运人的指示)"等字样,因为航空货运单不能转让。

采用集中托运时,收货人为货运代理人海外代理;采用直接托运时,收货人为实际收货人。

(4) 收货人账号(Consignee's Account Number)。

本栏仅供承运人使用,除非承运人需要,一般不需要填写。

(5) 始发机场(Airport of Departure)。

本栏填始发机场的全称,用英文全称或三字代码。

(6) 目的机场(Airport of Destination)。

本栏填目的地机场名称或三字代码(不知道机场名称时,可填城市名称),如果某一城市名称用于一个以上国家时,应加上国名。

(7) 填开货运单的代理人名称(Issuing Carrier's Agent Name)。

若货运单由承运人本人签发,本栏可不填;若货运单由承运人的代理人签发,则本栏可填写实际代理人的名称。

(8) 供运输用的声明价值(Declared Value for Carriage)。

本栏填供运输用的声明价值金额,该价值即为承运人负赔偿责任的限额。承运人按有关规定向托运人收取声明价值费,但如果所交运的货物毛重每千克不超过20美元(或其等值货币),无须填写声明价值金额,可在本栏填入"NVD"(No Value Declared 未声明价值)。如果本栏空着未填写,承运人或其代理人可视为货物未声明价值。

(9) 供海关用的声明价值(Declared Value for Customs)。

国际货物通常要受到目的地海关的检查,海关根据此栏所填数额征税。如果托运人不办理此项声明价值,必须在本栏内打上"NCV"(No Customs Value,无声明价值)字样。

(10) 保险金额(Amount of Insurance)。

中国民航各空运企业暂未开展国际航空运输代保险业务,本栏可空着不填。

(11) 另请通知(Also Notify)。

除填收货人之外,如托运人还希望在货物到达的同时通知他人,可另外填写其他被通知人的全名和地址。

(12) 随附文件(Document to Accompany Air Waybill)。

本栏填随附在货运单上发往目的地的文件,应填上所附文件的名称,例如,活体动物托运证明(Shipper's Certification for Live Animals)。

(13) 货物件数和运价组成点(No. of Pieces, Rate Combination Point)。

本栏填货物包装件数,如 10 包即填"10"。当需要组成比例运价或分段相加运价时,本栏填运价组成点机场的 IATA 代码。

(14) 毛重(Gross Weight)。

本栏目应由承运人或其代理人在对货物称重后填写,如果托运人已经填上重量,则承运人或其代理人必须进行复核。

(15) 运价种类(Rate Class)。

本栏可空着不填,由承运人或其代理人填写。

(16) 计费重量(Chargeable Weight)。

本栏应由承运人或其代理人在量过货物的尺寸(以厘米为单位)后,算出计费重量然后填写,如果托运人已经填上,则承运人或其代理人必须进行复核。本栏计费重量的单位为千克。

(17) 费率(Rate)。

本栏可空着不填。

(18) 货物品名及数量(包括尺寸或体积)[Nature and Quantity of Goods(Incl. Dimensions or Volume)]。

本栏填货物的品名和数量,包括填写货物的外包装尺寸或体积。货物中的每一项均须分开填写,并尽量填写详细。本栏内容应与出口报关发票和进口许可证上所列明的内容相符。危险品应填写适用的准确名称及标贴的级别。

(19) 托运人或其代理人签字、盖章(Signature of Shipper or His Agent)。

托运人或其代理人必须在本栏签字、盖章。

(20) 日期(Date)。

本栏填托运人或其代理人交货的日期。

3. 出口商空运托运流程

(1) 托运人委托运输。

在空运托运中,由托运人自己填写货物托运书。托运书的内容应包括:托运人、收货人、始发机场、目的机场、要求的路线/申请订舱、供运输用的声明价值、供海关用的声明价值、保险金额、处理事项、货运单所附文件、实际毛重、运价种类、计费重量、费率、货物品名及数量、托运人签字、日期等。

(2) 航空货运代理公司预配舱和预订舱。

航空货运代理公司汇总所接受的委托和客户的预报,并输入电脑,计算出各航线的件数、重量、体积,然后根据客户的要求、货物的体积、毛重情况,以及各航空公司不同机型对不同板箱的重量和高度要求,制订预配舱方案,并为每票货物配上运单号。航空货运代理公司根据所指定的预配舱方案,按航班、日期打印出总运单号、件数、重量、体积,然后向航空公司预订舱。

(3) 航空货运代理公司接收货物和单证。

航空货运代理公司把即将发运的货物从托运人手中接过来并运送到自己的仓库,接收货物一般与接单同时进行。接收货物时航空货运代理公司应对货物进行过磅和丈量,并根据发票、装箱单或送货单清点货物,核对货物的数量、品名、销售合同号或唛头等是否与货运单上所列一致。

(4) 正式订舱。

接到托运人的发货预报后,航空货运代理公司从航空公司吨控部门领取订舱单并填写,办理正式订舱手续,同时,向航空公司提供相应的信息,包括货物的名称、体积、重量、件数、目的地、要求出运的时间等。航空公司根据实际情况安排舱位和航班。航空货运代理公司在订舱时,可依照托运人的要求选择最佳的航线和承运人,同时为托运人争取最低、最合理的运价。

订舱后,航空公司签发舱位确认书(舱单),同时给出装货集装器领取凭证,以表示舱位已订妥。

(5) 交接发运。

航空货运代理公司在货物报关完成后,向航空公司交单交货,由航空公司安排航空运输。交货前航空货运代理公司必须为货物粘贴或拴挂货物标签,清点、核对货物,并填制货物交接清单。

(6) 签发航空货运单。

航空公司或航空货运代理公司在货物发运后签发航空货运单。航空货运单包括总运单和分运单,填制航空货运单的主要依据是托运人提供的国际货物托运书,托运书上的各项内容都应体现在航空货运单上。航空货运单一般用英文填写。

4. 集中托运

集中托运是指航空货运代理公司将若干批单独发运的货物集中成一批向航空公司办理托运,填写一份总运单,货物被送至同一目的地,然后由航空货运代理公司委托的当地代理人将货物分发给各个实际收货人的托运方式。这种托运方式可降低航空货运的成本。

集中托运的具体做法如下。

(1) 航空货运代理公司为每一票货物分别制定航空运输分运单,即出具货运代理的运单(House Airway Bill,HAWB)。

(2) 航空货运代理公司将所有货物区分方向,按照其目的地相同的同一国家、同一城市来集中,制定出航空公司的总运单(Master Airway Bill,MAWB)。总运单的托运人和收货人均为航空货运代理公司。

(3) 航空货运代理公司打印出总运单项下的货运清单(Manifest),即总运单有几个分运单,号码各是什么,其中件数、重量各是多少,等等。

(4) 货物到达目的机场后,航空货运代理公司委托的当地代理人负责接货、分拨,按不同的分运单制定各自的报关单据并代为报关,同时,为实际收货人办理有关送货事宜。

(5) 实际收货人在分运单上签字后,航空货运代理公司委托的当地代理人向发货的航空货运代理公司反馈到货信息。

集中托运主要有以下三个特点。

(1) 节省运费。航空货运代理公司的集中托运运价一般都低于航空协会的运价,托运人可享受低于航空公司的运价,从而节省运费。

(2) 提供方便。将货物集中托运,可使货物到达航空公司到达地点以外的地方,延伸了航空公司的服务,方便了货主。

(3) 提早结汇。托运人将货物交与航空货运代理公司后,即可取得货物分运单,可持分运单到银行尽早办理结汇。

四、能力训练

(一) 安吉林木饰品有限公司操作案例

接"项目二 缮制商业发票和装箱单"中"能力训练"部分中安吉林木饰品有限公司操作案例。2019 年 4 月 26 日,安吉林木饰品有限公司的单证员根据信用证(见样单 2-6)的要求及缮制好的商业发票(见样单 3-6)和装箱单(见样单 3-7),缮制托运委托书,向上海大洲货代公司办理订舱手续。

样单 3-6 商业发票

安吉林木饰品有限公司
ANJI LINMU DECORATION CO., LTD.
ANJI ECONOMIC DEVELOPING DISTRICT, HUZHOU CITY, ZHEJIANG, CHINA
TEL:+86-0572-5544×××　　FAX:+86-0572-5544×××

COMMERCIAL INVOICE

TO: JEWTS HAMAN INC 860	DATE: APR 26,2019
ADVA COSEP TARRADELLAS	INVOICE NO.: LM2019001
00243 BARCELONA, SPAIN	CONTRACT NO.: Y024562

FROM: SHANGHAI, CHINA　TO: BARCELONA, SPAIN　LETTER OF CREDIT NO.: 046CDI577402456				
ISSUED BY: AHORROS YM.P. DE NAVARRA, PAMPLONA				
MARKS & NUMBERS	QUANTITIES AND DESCRIPTIONS		UNIT PRICE	AMOUNT
N/M	LADIES' 96% POLYESTER 4% ELASTANE WOVEN GARMENTS DRESS		CIF BARCELONA	
	ART. NO. ZC14502	8 820PCS	USD7.25/PC	USD63 945.00
	ART. NO. ZC14533	8 820PCS	USD7.55/PC	USD66 591.00
	TOTAL　17 640PCS			USD130 536.00

安吉林木饰品有限公司
ANJI LINMU DECORATION CO., LTD
李之洁

样单 3-7　装箱单

安吉林木饰品有限公司
ANJI LINMU DECORATION CO., LTD.
ANJI ECONOMIC DEVELOPING DISTRICT, HUZHOU CITY, ZHEJIANG, CHINA
TEL：+86-0572-5544×××　　FAX：+86-0572-5544×××

PACKING LIST

DATE：APR 26, 2019
INVOICE NO.：LM2019001
CONTRACT NO.：Y024562

MARKS AND NUMBERS	DESCRIPTION OF GOODS	QUANTITY	PACKAGE	G.W	N.W	MEAS.
N/M	LADIES' 96% POLYESTER 4% ELASTANE WOVEN GARMENTS DRESS			@14.5KGS	@12.5KGS	50×50×25 (cm)
	ART. NO. ZC14502	8 820PCS	210CTNS	3 045KGS	2 625KGS	13.125CBM
	ART. NO. ZC14533	8 820PCS	210CTNS	3 045KGS	2 625KGS	13.125CBM
	TOTAL：	17 640PCS	420CTNS	6 090KGS	5 250KGS	26.25CBM

SAY TOTAL：SAY FOUR HUNDRED AND TWENTY CARTONS ONLY.

安吉林木饰品有限公司
ANJI LINMU DECORATION CO., LTD
李之洁

补充资料：

安吉林木饰品有限公司的单证员在与生产部门沟通后，确定在 2019 年 5 月 15 日之前能完成出货，然后与上海大洲货代公司接洽后确定预订 5 月 18 日去西班牙的船。

工作任务：

(1) 缮制托运委托书；

(2) 办理托运手续。

（二）湖州兴业进出口有限公司操作案例

接"项目二　缮制商业发票和装箱单"中"能力训练"部分湖州兴业进出口有限公司操作案例。2019 年 5 月 25 日，湖州兴业进出口有限公司的单证员与生产部门进行沟通后，确定交货期大致在 6 月 5 日以后。于是单证员根据信用证（见样单 2-7）的要求及商业发票（见样单 3-8）、装箱单（见样单 3-9）缮制托运委托书，向货代公司办理订舱手续，预订 6 月 8 日直达 SFAX 的船。

样单 3-8　商业发票

湖州兴业进出口有限公司
HUZHOU XINGYE INDUSTRY CO., LTD.
TEL：+86-572-2031×××/2012×××　　FAX：+86-572-2035×××/2612×××

TO：M/S
TUFFCO
3052 SFAX, TUNISIE

商业发票
COMMERCIAL INVOICE

发票号码
INVOICE NO.：<u>19BY411</u>
合约号码
S/C NO.：<u>2019TU02</u>
日期
DATE：<u>MAY. 15, 2019</u>

装船口岸		目的地		信用证号	
FROM: SHANGHAI,CHINA		TO: SFAX,TUNISIA		L/C NO.: CDI702/8053/2019	
开证银行 ISSUED BY: AMEM BANK AVENUE MOHAMED V TUNIS, TUNISIA					
唛头及号码 MARKS & NUMBERS	数量与货品名称 QUANTITIES & DESCRIPTION		单价 UNIT PRICE		总值 AMOUNT

TU
(PRODUCT'S NAME)
QTY:
C/NO.:
	FIRE EXTINGUISHER
	(CFR SFAX PORT) AS PER PROFORMA
	S/C NO. 2019TU02 DTD 29/03/2019
	6KG DRY POWDER FIRE EXTINGUISHER
	    5 000PCS
	9LT FOAM EXTINGUISHER COMPLETE
	EMPTY 200PCS
	5KG CO_2 FIRE EXTINGUISHER
	    3 000PCS
	2KG CO_2 FIRE EXTINGUISHER
	    500PCS
			CFR SFAX
			
			USD18.390/PC
			
			USD17.650/PC
			
			USD21.067/PC
			
			USD11.177/PC
					
					USD91 950.00
					
					USD3 530.00
					
					USD63 201.00
					
					USD5 588.50

	TOTAL:	8 700PCS	USD164 269.50		

湖州兴业进出口有限公司
HUZHOU XINGYE INDUSTRY CO.,LTD.
蒋一

样单3-9 装箱单

湖州兴业进出口有限公司
HUZHOU XINGYE INDUSTRY CO.,LTD.
TEL: +86-572-2031×××/2012×××   FAX: +86-572-2035×××/2612×××

MARKS & NUMBERS AS PER INV. NO.	重量单和装箱单 WEIGHT NOTE AND PACKING LIST	发票号码 INVOICE NO.: 19BY411 合约号码 S/C NO.: 2019TU02 日期 DATE: MAY.15,2019

ART NO.	DESCRIPTION	QUANTITIES	PACKAGES	G.W.	N.W.	MEAS.
FIRE EXTINGUISHER (CFR SFAX PORT) AS PER PROFORMA C/S NO. 2019TU02 DTD 29/03/2019	6KG DRY POWDER FIRE EXTINGUISHER	5 000PCS	10PCS/CTN 500CTNS	@22KGS 11 000KGS	@20KGS 10 000KGS	40×30×30(cm) 18CBM
	9LT FOAM EXTINGUISHER COMPLETE EMPTY	200PCS	20CTNS	440KGS	400KGS	0.72CBM
	5KG CO_2 FIRE EXTINGUISHER	3 000PCS	300CTNS	6 600KGS	6 000KGS	10.8CBM
	2KG CO_2 FIRE EXTINGUISHER	500PCS	50CTNS	1 100KGS	1 000KGS	1.8CBM
TTL:		8 700PCS	870CTNS	19 140KGS	17 400KGS	31.32CBM

NUMBER OF L/C: CDI702/8053/2019

湖州兴业进出口有限公司
HUZHOU XINGYE INDUSTRY CO.,LTD.
蒋一

补充资料:

由于信用证附加条款中有提到不接受货代提单,故不能做拼箱,大于30立方米的货物只能装一个12.192米(40英尺)的集装箱。

工作任务:

(1) 缮制托运委托书;

(2) 办理托运手续。

五、岗位拓展

讨论话题:交货期来不及导致船期延误。

小A是湖州某出口公司的单证员,销售合同要求船期是5月13日,但是小A在5月初办理托运前,生产部门打电话来说,交货期来不及,估计要到5月15日才能备完货,小A该怎么操作?

讨论引导:

(1) 如果这笔业务是T/T或托收项下的,请提出可行性建议。

(2) 如果这笔业务是信用证项下的,信用证中最迟交货期与销售合同一致,请提出可行性建议。

项目四
申领原产地证书

一、学习目标

能力目标：能缮制各种常用的原产地证书，办理原产地证书申领手续。

知识目标：明确各种常用的原产地证书的缮制要点，了解原产地证书的基本知识。

二、工作任务

（一）任务描述

此批货物是出口至韩国的藤帘（4601220000），符合申领《亚太贸易协定》原产地证书的要求。2019年4月2日，单证员张洁按照信用证中原产地证书的条款要求和前面缮制好的商业发票（见样单 2-4）、装箱单（见样单 2-5），缮制原产地证书，并整理好原产地证书申领资料向湖州海关办理原产地证书申领手续。

（二）任务分析

总体任务	办理原产地证书申领手续
任务分解	任务一：缮制原产地证书
	任务二：办理原产地证书申领手续

（三）操作示范

第一步：缮制原产地证书。

张洁根据信用证中原产地证书的条款以及前面缮制好的商业发票、装箱单缮制《亚太贸易协定》原产地证书（见样单 4-1）。

信用证中原产地证书的条款如下：

+ ORIGINAL CERTIFICATE OF ORIGIN ASIA-PACIFIC TRADE AGREEMENT PLUS ONE COPY ISSUED BY CIQ.

样单 4-1 《亚太贸易协定》原产地证书

1. Goods Consigned from (Exporter's Business Name, Address, Country)	Reference No. **CERTIFICATE OF ORIGIN** Asia-Pacific Trade Agreement (Combined Declaration and Certificate) Issued in THE PEOPLE'S REPUBLIC OF CHINA				
2. Goods Consigned to (Consignee's Name, Address, Country)	3. For Official Use				
4. Means of Transport and Route					
5. Tariff Item Number	6. Marks and Number of Packages	7. Number and Kind of Packages/ Description of Goods	8. Origin Criterion (See Notes Overleaf)	9. Gross Weight or Other Quantity	10. Number and Date of Invoices
11. Declaration by the Exporter The undersigned hereby declares that the above details and statements are correct, that all the goods were produced in …………………………………… (Country) and that they comply with the origin requirements specified for these goods in the Asia-Pacific Trade Agreement for goods exported to …………………………………… (Importing Country) …………………………………… Place and date, signature and stamp of authorized signatory	12. Certification It is hereby certified that the declaration by the exporter is correct. …………………………………… Place and date, signature and stamp of certifying authority				

《亚太贸易协定》原产地证书缮制要点如下。

证书号(Reference No.)：证书号共 16 位，第 1 位为字母，代表证书种类，字母"B"代表《亚太贸易协定》原产地证书；第 2、第 3 位为年份，每年年初变为相应年份；第 4～12 位为注册单位 9 位的产地证注册号；第 13～16 位为顺序号码，每年年初须从 0001 开始排列。证书号不能重号，如证书更改或重发，应使用新号码。

第1栏：货物发运自〔Goods Consigned from (Exporter's Business Name, Address, Country)〕。

本栏应注明出口商的名称、地址与国别。出口商的名称须与发票上的出口商名称一致。

第2栏：货物发运到〔Goods Consigned to (Consignee's Name, Address, Country)〕。

本栏应注明进口商的名称、地址与国别，一般应填《亚太贸易协定》成员国最终收货人名称。进口商的名称须与发票上的进口商名称一致。对于第三方贸易，本栏可以注明"待定"（To Order）。

第3栏：供官方使用（For Official Use）。

本栏仅供签证当局使用，由签证当局填写。签证当局可根据实际情况，填写相应的内容。

(1) 如属后发证书，签证当局会在本栏注明"Issued Retrospectively"。

(2) 如属重发证书，签证当局会在本栏注明原发证书的编号和签证日期，并申明原发证书作废。具体内容是：此证书是某月某日签发的某证书（号码为……）的副本，原证书已作废(This Certificate is in Replacement of Certificate of Origin No.... Dated... Which is Cancelled)。同时，本栏还应盖有"副本"（Duplicate）的红色印章。

第4栏：运输方式与路线（Means of Transport and Route）。

本栏应详细注明出口货物的运输方式和路线。如果信用证条款中无此详细要求，则本栏应打上"空运"或"海运"。如果货物途经第三国，可用如下方式表示："空运""经曼谷从上海到马德里"(By air from Shanghai to Madrid via Bangkok.)。

第5栏：税则号（Tariff Item Number）。

本栏应注明货物的6位数HS编码。

第6栏：唛头（Marks and Number of Packages）。

本栏应注明证书所载货物的包装唛头。该信息应与货物包装上的唛头一致。本栏不得留空，货物无唛头时应填"N/M"；如果唛头过多，第6栏填不下的可填写在第7至第10栏的空白处。

第7栏：包装数量与种类/货物描述（Number and Kind of Packages/Description of Goods）。

填写本栏时请勿忘记填写包装数量及种类，并在包装数量的英文数字描述后用括号加上阿拉伯数字。商品名称应填写具体，应详细到可以准确判定该商品的HS编码。如果信用证中品名笼统或拼音错误，必须在括号内加注具体描述或正确的品名。商品名称等项列完后，应在末行加上******（截止线），以防止加塞伪造内容。有时，国外来证要求填写信用证号码等，可加在截止线下方。例如，

Ten (10) drums of frozen peapods

*** *** *** *** ***

L/C No.：348091345

第8栏：原产地标准〔Origin Criterion (See Notes Overleaf)〕。

根据《亚太贸易协定》原产地规则第二条的规定，受惠产品必须是完全原产自出口成员国的产品；若非出口成员国完全原产的产品，必须符合第三条或第四条规定。

(1) 完全原产自出口成员国的产品，在第8栏填写字母"A"。

(2) 含有进口成分的产品，第8栏的填写方法如下。

① 符合第三条规定的原产地标准的产品，第8栏填写字母"B"，字母"B"后应填写原产于非成员国或原产地不明的原料、部件或产品的总货值占出口产品离岸价的百分比（例如，"B"50%）。

② 符合第四条规定的原产地标准的产品,第 8 栏填写字母"C",字母"C"后应填写原产于成员国领土内的累计含量的总值占出口产品离岸价的百分比(例如,"C"60%)。

③ 符合第十条特定原产地标准的产品,第 8 栏填写字母"D"。

④ 如果符合原产地规则第三条(二)规定的原产地标准,则第 8 栏中填写字母"E",字母"E"后应填写原产地标准(例如,"E CTH")。

第 9 栏:毛重或其他数量(Gross Weight or Other Quantity)。

本栏应注明证书所载产品的毛重或其他数量(例如,件数)。以重量计算的产品,本栏填产品的毛重;只有净重的产品,本栏填净重也可,但要标明为净重,即加上"N. W."(Net Weight)。

第 10 栏:发票号码与日期(Number and Date of Invoices)。

本栏应注明发票的号码与日期。发票日期不得迟于证书的签发日期。

第 11 栏:出口商声明(Declaration by the Exporter)。

生产国的横线上应填上"CHINA"(证书上已印制)。进口国的横线上的国名一定要填写正确。进口国必须是《亚太贸易协定》成员国,一般与最终收货人或目的港的国别一致。申报单位的申报员应在本栏签字,并加盖已注册的中英文签证章(印章应清晰),并填上申报地点和时间。

第 12 栏:签证当局的证明(Certification)。

本栏应填签证地址和日期,一般情况下,本栏填写的地址和日期应与出口商申报的地址和日期一致。签证机构授权的签证人员应在本栏手签,并加盖签证当局印章。

第二步:办理原产地证书申领手续。

张洁通过中国国际贸易单一窗口在线申请原产地证书,按界面提示进行原产地证书信息录入,填写完原产地证书详细信息并保存之后,单击"发送"按钮,提交到海关,等待审核。

(四) 任务解决

湖州海关在审核《亚太贸易协定》原产地证书(见样单 4-2)无误后,通过审核。张洁随时关注着中国国际贸易单一窗口已申请原产地证书的状态,当状态变为"已发证"时,即申请成功。

样单 4-2 《亚太贸易协定》原产地证书

1. Goods Consigned from (Exporter's Business Name, Address, Country) HUZHOU ZHENGCHANG TRADING CO. ,LTD. 42 HONGQI ROAD, HUZHOU, CHINA	Reference No. B193333331450008 **CERTIFICATE OF ORIGIN** Asia-Pacific Trade Agreement (Combined Declaration and Certificate) Issued in THE PEOPLE'S REPUBLIC OF CHINA
2. Goods Consigned to (Consignee's Name, Address, Country) MAIJER FISTRTION INC. 3214,WALKER , NAKAGYO-KU,KYUNG-BUK, KOREA REP.	3. For Official Use

续表

4. Means of Transport and Route FROM SHANGHAI TO BUSAN BY SEA					
5. Tariff Item Number	6. Marks and Number of Packages	7. Number and Kind of Packages；Description of Goods	8. Origin Criterion (See Notes Overleaf)	9. Gross Weight or Other Quantity	10. Number and Date of Invoices
460122	MAIJER ZC190211 BUSAN C/NO. 1-1801	1 801(ONE THOUSAND EIGHT HUNDRED AND ONE) CARTONS OF RATTAN CURTAIN ********************	A	14 408PCS	ZC19311 MAR. 25,2019
11. Declaration by the Exporter The undersigned hereby declares that the above details and statements are correct，that all the goods were produced in CHINA ……………… (Country) and that they comply with the origin requirements specified for these goods in the Asia-Pacific Trade Agreement for goods exported to KOREA REP. ……………… (Importing Country) 张洁 HUZHOU, CHINA APR. 2, 2019 Place and date, signature and stamp of authorized signatory		12. Certification It is hereby certified that the declaration by the exporter is correct. HUZHOU, CHINA APR. 2, 2019 Place and date, signature and stamp of certifying authority			

三、知识链接

（一）原产地证书的含义和作用

1. 原产地证书的含义

原产地证书（Certificate of Origin），是指出口国政府主管部门的授权机构、商会或出口商及制造商根据相关的原产地规则签发的证明货物原产地或制造地的一种具有法律效力的证明文件。

2. 原产地证书的作用

原产地证书主要具有以下几个方面的作用。

（1）原产地证书可证明有关出口货物符合出口国货物原产地规则。

（2）原产地证书可供进口国海关掌握进口货物的原产地国别，从而采取不同的国别政策，决定进口税率和确定税别待遇。

教学视频

(3)原产地证书是对某些国家或某种商品采取控制进口额度和进口数量的依据。
(4)原产地证书是进出口通关、结汇和贸易统计的依据。

(二)原产地证书的种类

由于原产地规则的不同,原产地证书可分为优惠原产地证书和非优惠原产地证书。优惠原产地证书主要用于享受关税减免待遇,如普惠制原产地证书、区域性经济集团互惠原产地证书、专用原产地证书等。非优惠原产地证书主要用于征收关税、贸易统计、保障措施、歧视性数量限制、反倾销和反补贴、政府采购等,如一般原产地证书。常见原产地证书及其签发机构和证书形式如表4-1所示。

表4-1 常见原产地证书及其签发机构和证书形式

原产地证书	签发机构	证书形式
一般原产地证书	国际贸易促进委员会(以下简称"贸促会")、海关	C/O原产地证书
普惠制原产地证书	海关	GSP原产地证书(FORM A)
区域性经济集团互惠原产地证书	海关、贸促会(可签发部分证书)	中国-东盟自由贸易区优惠关税原产地证书(FORM E) 《亚太贸易协定》原产地证书(FORM B) 中国-巴基斯坦自由贸易区原产地证书(FORM P) 中国-智利自由贸易区原产地证书(FORM F) 《中国-新西兰自由贸易协定》原产地证书(FORM N) 《中国-秘鲁自由贸易协定》原产地证书(FORM R) 中国-新加坡自由贸易区优惠税率原产地证书(FORM X) 海峡两岸经济合作框架协议原产地证书(ECFA证书) 《中国-哥斯达黎加自由贸易协定》原产地证书(FORM L) 中国-冰岛自由贸易区原产地证书(FORM I) 《中国-韩国自由贸易协定》原产地证书(FORM K) 《中国-澳大利亚自由贸易协定》原产地证书 《中国-格鲁吉亚自由贸易协定》原产地证书 ……
专用原产地证书	海关	输欧盟托考伊葡萄酒原产地名称证书 输欧盟奶酪制品证书 输欧盟烟草真实性证书 输欧盟农产品原产地证书

(三)原产地证书的申领程序

2019年10月15日,对外贸易经营者备案和原产地企业备案"两证合一"系统上线,企业在办理对外贸易经营者备案的同时自动完成原产地企业备案。

1. 企业通过海关申请签证

(1)企业网上备案。

已完成对外贸易经营者备案的企业,登录"互联网+海关"全国一体化在线政务服务平台,可凭统一社会信用代码查看原产地企业备案信息。对于不申请对外贸易经营者备案的生产型企业,可直接登录"互联网+海关"全国一体化在线政务服务平台向海关备案。

(2) 企业网上申请。

已备案企业可根据各类原产地证书的要求,通过国际贸易单一窗口或通过九城、榕基等软件发送原产地证书的电子数据,提交海关审核。

(3) 企业现场签证或自助打印。

① 企业通过网络平台申请的原产地证书的信息经海关审核通过后,企业便可自行打印原产地证,并到海关现场签证。

② 对于审核结果为缓证的情况,企业须携带空白原产地证书和相应材料到海关现场审核、打印、签证。

③ 对于符合自助打印的原产地证书,经海关审核通过后,企业可直接在国际贸易单一窗口打印证书,无须到海关现场签证。

2. 企业通过贸促会申请签证

(1) 企业网上注册。

企业完成对外贸易经营者备案后,用统一社会信用代码登录贸促会原产地证书申报系统,上传手签员签名图片和企业印章图片。若未按要求上传印章图片,企业到贸促会领取原产地证书时需携带印章并在现场加盖。

(2) 企业网上申请。

企业登录贸促会原产地证书申报系统,进行原产地证书的信息录入、保存操作,然后单击"发送"按钮,提交到贸促会,等待审核。

(3) 企业取证或自助打印。

提交申请后,企业要及时查看原产地证书的状态。当状态变为"已发证"时,说明贸促会审核通过了企业提交的申请,企业即可到当地贸促会取证。

企业如果申请了原产地证的自助打印服务,审核通过后便可自助打印原产地证。

(四) 一般原产地证书

教学视频

一般原产地证书是证明货物原产于某一特定国家或地区,享受进口国正常关税(最惠国)待遇的证明文件。

根据我国有关原产地证书申领的相关规定,出口商应在货物出运前向当地海关或贸促会申请办理原产地证书。

一般原产地证书共有12栏(见样单4-3)。

样单4-3 一般原产地证书

1. Exporter	Certificate No.
2. Consignee	CERTIFICATE OF ORIGIN OF THE PEOPLE'S REPUBLIC OF CHINA
3. Means of Transport and Route	5. For Certifying Authority Use Only
4. Country/Region of Destination	

续表

6. Marks and Numbers	7. Number and Kind of Packages; Description of Goods	8. HS Code	9. Quantity	10. Number and Date of Invoices
11. Declaration by the Exporter The undersigned hereby declares that the above details and statements are correct, that all the goods were produced in China and that they comply with the Rules of Origin of the People's Republic of CHINA. …………………………………………………… Place and date, signature and stamp of authorized signatory			12. Certification It is hereby certified that the declaration by the exporter is correct. …………………………………… Place and date, signature and stamp of certifying authority	

一般原产地证书缮制要点如下。

证书号(Certificate No.)：证书号共16位，第1位为字母，代表证书的种类，一般原产地证书的第1位为字母"C"；第2、第3位为年份，每年年初变为相应年份；第4～12位为注册单位的9位原产地证书注册号；第13～16位为顺序号码，每年年初须从0001开始排列。证书号不能重号，如证书更改或重发，须用新号码。例如，证书号C193800000050045是注册号为380000005的单位2019年办理的第45票一般原产地证书。

第1栏：出口商(Exporter)。

出口商栏必须填写，应填明在中国境内的出口商的详细地址，包括街道名、门牌号码等。出口商必须是已办理原产地证书注册的企业，且公司英文名称应与在当地海关备案的英文名称一致。若在贸易过程中中间商要求显示其名称，可将其填在这一栏，格式为"出口商名称VIA中间商名称"。

第2栏：收货人(Consignee)。

本栏一般应填写销售合同中的买方、信用证上规定的提单通知人或特别声明的收货人，如果最终收货人不明确，可填发票抬头人。为方便外贸工作，本栏也可按信用证上的要求填上"TO ORDER"或"TO WHOM IT MAY CONCERN"。

第3栏：运输方式及路线(Means of Transport and Route)。

运输方式有海运、陆运、空运、海空联运等。运输路线中始发地应填中国大陆最后一道离境地，如系转运货物，应加上转运港。本栏还可填明预定自中国出口的日期，日期必须真实，不得捏造。

第4栏：目的地国家(地区)(Country/Region of Destination)。

本栏应填写货物最终运抵目的地的国家或地区，即最终进口国(地区)，一般与最终收货人所在国家(地区)一致，不能填写中间商国家名称。

第5栏：供签证当局使用(For Certifying Authority Use Only)。

本栏由签证当局填写，申请单位应将本栏留空。签证当局可根据实际情况，填写相应内容。

(1) 如属后发证书，签证当局会在本栏加打"Issued Retrospectively"。

(2) 如属签发复本(重发证书)，签证当局会在本栏注明原发证书的编号和签证日期，并声明原发证书作废，具体内容是：This Certificate is in Replacement of Certificate of Origin No.... Dated... Which is Cancelled，并加打"Duplicate"。

第6栏：唛头及包装号(Marks and Numbers)。

本栏应按实际货物和发票上的唛头，填写完整的图案文字标记及包装号。唛头中处于同一行的内容不要换行打印。

需要注意的是：

(1) 唛头不得出现"HONG KONG""MACAO""TAIWAN""R. O. C."等产地制造字样。

(2) 本栏不得留空。货物无唛头时，应填"N/M"。如果唛头内容过多，第6栏填不下的可填在第7~10栏的空白处。唛头为图文等较复杂的内容或内容过多时，也可在该栏填上"See Attachment"，并另加附页。附页需一式四份，附页上方应填上"Attachment to the Certificate of Origin No....（证书号码）"，参照一般原产地证书，附页下方左右两边应分别打上申报地点、申报日期、签证地点和签证日期，左下方盖上申报单位签证章并由申报单位申报员签名。附页应与一般原产地证书大小一致。

(3) 本栏的内容及格式必须与实际货物外包装箱上所标的内容一致。

第7栏：包装数量及种类；商品名称(Number and Kind of Packages; Description of Goods)。

本栏填写商品名称、包装数量及种类，包装数量的英文数字描述后应用括号标注对应的阿拉伯数字。如果信用证中品名笼统或拼写错误，必须在括号内加注具体描述或正确品名。商品名称等项列完后，本栏末行应加上截止线，以防止有人加填伪造内容。国外信用证有时要求填写销售合同号、信用证号码等，可加填在本栏截止线下方。

例如：FIVE HUNDRED (500)CTNS OF SHRIMPS

   *** *** *** *** ***

   L/C：2846905067640

第8栏：HS编码(HS Code)。

本栏应准确填打商品的四位数HS编码。如果同一份证书包含几种不同的商品，应将相应的编码全部填写上。本栏不得留空。

第9栏：数量(Quantity)。

本栏应以商品的正常计量单位填制，如"只""件""匹""双""台""打"等。以重量计算的商品，可填毛重，也可填净重。如果填写毛重，须加注"G. W."(Gross Weight)；如填写净重，则须加注"N. W."(Net Weight)。

第10栏：发票号及日期(Number and Date of Invoices)。

本栏不得留空，且所填写的内容必须与正式商业发票一致。为避免误解，月份一般用英文缩写形式表示，如JAN.、FEB.、MAR.等，年份要填4位数字，如"2006"不能填"06"。发票号太长需换行时，应使用折行符"-"。发票日期不能迟于提单日期和申报日期。

第11栏：出口商声明(Declaration by the Exporter)

申请单位的申报员应在本栏手签，并填上申报地点、时间，加盖已注册的中英文签证章，印章应清晰。本栏的日期不得早于发票日期。

第12栏：签证当局证明(Certification)。

本栏应填打签证地址和日期，一般情况下应与出口商申报的地址、日期一致，同时，签证机构授权的签证人员应在本栏手签，并加盖签证当局印章。签发日期不能早于发票日期和申请日期。

注意：签证当局一般只在证书正本上加盖印章，如客户要求，也可在副本上加盖印章。

（五）普惠制原产地证书

普惠制原产地证书是指依据给惠国的要求而出具的能证明出口货物原产自受惠国的证明文件。该证书具有法律效力，并能使出口货物在给惠国享受普惠制优惠关税待遇，在最惠国税率基础上进一步减免进口关税。

我国普惠制原产地证书的签证工作由海关总署负责统一管理，由设在各地的直属海关负责签发。普惠制原产地证书限于给惠国已公布法令并正式通知对我国实行普惠制待遇的国家所给予关税优惠的商品。这些商品必须符合给惠国原产地规则及直运规则。

之前给予我国普惠制待遇的国家共39个：欧盟26国(比利时、丹麦、德国、法国、爱尔兰、意大利、卢森堡、荷兰、希腊、葡萄牙、西班牙、奥地利、芬兰、瑞典、波兰、捷克、斯洛伐克、拉脱维亚、爱沙尼亚、立陶宛、匈牙利、马耳他、塞浦路斯、斯洛文尼亚、罗马尼亚、保加利亚)、英国、挪威、瑞士、土耳其、俄罗斯、白俄罗斯、乌克兰、哈萨克斯坦、日本、加拿大、澳大利亚、新西兰和列支敦士登公国。

随着我国经济实力的增强，自2014年以来，我国相继从欧盟、加拿大等国的普惠制名单中"毕业"，2019年4月1日，日本正式终结对中国的普惠制待遇之后，给予中国普惠制待遇的国家仅剩俄罗斯、白俄罗斯、哈萨克斯坦、乌克兰、挪威。也就是说，对我国出口到俄罗斯、白俄罗斯、哈萨克斯坦、乌克兰、挪威的商品，企业可以办理普惠制原产地证书，进口商清关时还可以享受到关税优惠待遇。

根据我国海关总署相关规定，出口商应在货物出运前，向当地海关申请办理普惠制原产地证书。

普惠制原产地证书共有12栏(见样单4-4)。

样单4-4 普惠制原产地证书

1. Goods Consigned from (Exporter's Business Name, Address, Country)	Reference No. **GENERALIZED SYSTEM OF PREFERENCES CERTIFICATE OF ORIGIN** (Combined declaration and certificate) FORM A Issued in THE PEOPLE'S REPPUBLIC OF CHINA (country) See Notes Overleaf
2. Goods Consigned to (Consignee's Name, Address, Country)	
3. Means of Transport and Route (as Far as Known)	4. For Official Use

续表

5. Item Number	6. Marks and Numbers of Packages	7. Number and Kind of Packages; Description of Goods	8. Origin Criterion (See Notes Overleaf)	9. Gross Weight or Other Quantity	10. Number and Date of Invoices

11. Certification It is hereby certified, on the basis of control carried out, that the declaration by the exporter is correct. .... Place and date, signature and stamp of certifying authority	12. Declaration by the Exporter The undersigned hereby declares that the above details and statements are correct, that all the goods were produced in CHINA .... （country） and that they comply with the origin requirements specified for those goods in the Generalized System of Preferences for goods exported to .... Place and date, signature and stamp of authorized signatory

普惠制原产地证书的缮制要点如下（与一般原产地证书相同的栏目此处不再重复讲述）。

证书号（Reference No.）：证书号共16位，第1位为字母，代表证书的种类，普惠制原产地证书的第1位为字母"G"；第2、3位为年份，每年年初变为相应年份；第4～12位为注册单位9位的产地证注册号；第13～16位为顺序号码，每年年初须从0001开始排列。证书号不能重号，如证书更改或重发，要用新号码。例如，证书号G193800000050045是注册号为380000005的单位2019年办理的第45票普惠制原产地证书。

第4栏：供签证当局使用（For Official Use）。

本栏由签证当局填写，申请单位应将本栏留空。签证当局可根据实际情况，填写相应内容。

(1) 如属后发证书，签证当局会在本栏加打"Issued Retrospectively"。

(2) 如属签发复本（重发证书），签证当局会在本栏注明原发证书的编号和签证日期，并声明原发证书作废，具体内容是：This Certificate is in Replacement of Certificate of Origin No... Dated... Which is Cancelled，并加打"Duplicate"。

第5栏：项目编号（Item Number）

在收货人、运输条件相同的情况下，如同批出口货物有不同品种，则可按不同品种分列"1""2""3"……进行填报。

第8栏：原产地标准（Origin Criterion）

本栏用字最少，但却是国外海关审证的核心项目。对含有进口成分的商品，因情况复杂，容易出错，国外要求严格，极易造成退证。因此，工作人员应认真审核本栏内容。现将一般情况说明如下。

（1）对完全原产于出口国的商品，本栏应填写字母"P"。

（2）含有进口成分，但符合原产地标准的商品，输往下列国家时，本栏填写要求如下。

① 挪威：填写字母"W"，其后填明出口商品在《商品名称和编码协调制度》中的四位数编号（如"W"9618）；但属于给惠国成分的进口原料可视作本国原料。所以，如果商品的进口成分完全来自给惠国，则该商品的原产地标准仍填写字母"P"；

② 俄罗斯、白俄罗斯、乌克兰、哈萨克斯坦：输往这些国家的商品的进口成分的价值不得超过商品离岸价的50%，符合此要求的，本栏应填写字母"Y"，其后填明进口原料和部件的价值在出口商品离岸价中所占的百分比（如"Y"35%）。

第11栏：签证当局证明（Certification）

本栏应填写签证地点和日期，一般情况下，本栏的地点和日期应与出口商的申报地点和日期一致，同时，签证机构授权的签证人员还应在本栏手签，并加盖签证当局印章。

注意：签证当局只在证书正本加盖印章。

第12栏：出口商声明（Declaration by the Exporter）

本栏生产国的横线上应填上"CHINA"（证书上已印制）。进口国横线上的国名一定要填写正确，进口国必须是给惠国，一般与最终收货人或目的港的国别一致。

申请单位的申报员应在本栏签字，填上申报地点和时间，并加盖已注册的中英文印章，印章应清晰。

注意：申报日期不要填法定休息日，日期不得早于发票日期，一般也不要迟于提单日期。如果迟于提单日期，则要申请后发证书。在证书正本和所有副本上盖章签字时应避免覆盖进口国名称、原产国名称、申报地址和申报时间。更改证书的申报日期一般应与原证书一致，重发证书的申报日期应为实际申报日期。

（六）区域性经济集团互惠原产地证书

教学视频

党的十八大以来，中国积极推进与世界各国的经贸联系。截至2022年年底，我国已经与26个国家和地区签署19个自由贸易协定。2022年年初生效的《区域全面经济伙伴关系协定》，标志着当前世界上人口最多、经贸规模最大、最具发展潜力的自由贸易区正式启航。我国面向全球的自由贸易区网络得到进一步拓展。

区域性经济集团互惠原产地证书目前主要有中国-东盟自由贸易区优惠关税原产地证书、《亚太贸易协定》原产地证书、中国-巴基斯坦自由贸易区原产地证书、中国-智利自由贸易区原产地证书、《中国-新西兰自由贸易协定》原产地证书、中国-新加坡自由贸易区优惠税率原产地证书、《中国-秘鲁自由贸易协定》原产地证书等。区域性经济集团互惠原产地证书是具有法律效力的在协定成员国之间就特定产品享受互惠减免关税待遇的官方凭证。

1. 中国-东盟自由贸易区优惠关税原产地证书

中国-东盟自贸区是我国对外商谈的第一个也是最大的自贸区。2002年双方签署《中国-东盟全面经济合作框架协议》，启动自贸区建设，后陆续签署货物、服务、投资等协议，至2010年全面建成。2015年11月双方在马来西亚首都吉隆坡正式签署《中华人民共和国与东南亚国家联盟关于修订〈中国-东盟全面经济合作框架协议〉及项下部分协议的议定书》（以下简称"升级《议定书》"），2019年8月22日，所有东盟国家均完成了国内核准程序。2019年10月22日，升级《议定书》对所有协定成员全面生效。

自2004年1月1日起,凡出口到东盟的农产品凭中国-东盟自由贸易区优惠关税原产地证书可以享受关税优惠待遇。目前该证书已成为我国证书签发量最大的自由贸易协定证书。原产自我国的部分商品出口到文莱、柬埔寨、印度尼西亚、老挝、马来西亚、缅甸、菲律宾、新加坡、泰国、越南这10个国家可以签发此证书。

中国-东盟自由贸易区优惠关税原产地证书共有13栏(见样单4-5)。

样单4-5　中国-东盟自由贸易区优惠关税原产地证书

1. Products Consigned from (Exporter's Business Name, Address, Country)			Serial No. Reference No. **ASEAN-CHINA FREE TRADE AREA PREFERENTIAL TARIFF CERTIFICATE OF ORIGIN** (Combined Declaration and Certificate) FORM E Issued in THE PEOPOE'S REPUBLIC OF CHINA (Country) See Overleaf Notes		
2. Products Consigned to (Consignee's Name, Address, Country)					
3. Means of Transport and Route(as far as Known) Departure Date Vessel's Name/Aircraft etc. Port of Discharge			4. For Official Use ☐ Preferential Treatment Given ☐ Preferential Treatment Not Given (Please state reasons) .... Signature of Authorized Signatory of the Importing Party		
5. Item Number	6. Marks and Number of Packages	7. Number and Kind of Packages, Description of Products (Including Quantity Where Appropriate and HS Number in Six Digit Code)	8. Origin Criteria (See Overleaf Notes)	9. Gross Weight or Other Quantity and Value (FOB) Only When RVC Criterion is Applied	10. Number, Date of Invoices
11. Declaration by the Exporter The undersigned hereby declares that the above details and statements are correct, that all the products were produced in ....CHINA............ (Country) and that they comply with the origin requirements specified for these products in the rules of origin for the ACFTA for the products exported to .... (Importing Country) Place and date, signature of authorized signatory			12. Certification It is hereby certified, on the basis of control carried out, that the declaration by the exporter is correct. .... Place and date. signature and stamp of certifying authority		
13. ☐ Issued Retroactively　　☐ Exhibition 　　 ☐ Movement Certificate　　☐ Third Party Invoicing					

中国-东盟自由贸易区优惠原产地证书的缮制要点如下。

原产地证书编号包括序列号和证书号两类,二者均为系统自动生成。

该证书的第 1、2、3、5、6、10、11、12 栏的内容和填制要求可参考普惠制原产地证书(Form A)相应各栏的填制要求。

第 4 栏：供官方使用(For Official Use)。

申请单位应将本栏留空，由进口国的海关当局在本栏简要说明根据协定是否给予优惠待遇。

第 7 栏：包装件数及种类、货品描述(包括相应数量及进口国的 HS 编码)[Number and Kind of Packages, Description of Products (Including Quantity Where Appropriate and HS Number in Six Digit Code)]。

其中，货物品名必须详细，以便验货的海关人员可以识别。生产商的名称及任何商标也应列明。

例如：SIX HUNDRED (600)CTNS OF SHRIMPS
　　　　HS 030608
　　　　*** *** *** *** ***

第 8 栏：原产地标准[Origin Criteria(See Overleaf Notes)]。

(1) 完全获得的，本栏填写"WO"。

(2) 在一方境内由取得原产资格的材料生产的，本栏填写"PE"。

(3) 由非原产材料生产的分以下两种情况。

① 符合区域价值成分标准的，即单一国家成分或中国-东盟自由贸易区累计成分大于等于产品离岸价 40％的，本栏应填写增值的百分比，如"40％"(同时第 9 栏需加注货物的 FOB 值)。

② 符合税则归类改变标准的，本栏填写"CTH"。

(4) 符合特定产品规则的分以下三种情况。

① 列入特定原产地规则清单，但采用完全获得原产地规则的，本栏填写"WO"；

② 列入特定原产地规则清单，但采用区域价值成分原产地规则的，本栏填写"PSR"(同时第 9 栏需加注货物的 FOB 值)；

③ 列入特定原产地规则清单，但采用除以上两种原产地规则以外的其他规则的，本栏填写"PSR"。

第 9 栏：毛重或其他数量及价格(FOB)(仅采用区域价值成分标准时填制价格)[Gross Weight or Other Quantity and Value (FOB) Only When RVC Criterion is Applied]。

本栏应以商品的正常计量单位填写，如"只""件""匹""双""台""打"等。以重量计算的商品则填毛重；只有净重的，填净重也可，但要标上"N.W."(NET WEIGHT)。

对于原产地标准采用区域价值成分标准的情况，本栏需显示产品的 FOB 值，其余情况无须填写金额(系统会根据相关要求自动设定)。

2.《亚太贸易协定》原产地证书

《亚太贸易协定》的前身为签订于 1975 年的《曼谷协定》，是在联合国亚太经济和社会委员会主持下，在发展中国家之间达成的一项优惠贸易安排。我国于 2001 年正式加入《亚太贸易协定》，《亚太贸易协定》是我国参加的第一个优惠贸易安排，覆盖近 30 亿人口，也是我国目前唯一涵盖东亚、南亚地区并在实施的优惠贸易协定。

2006 年 9 月 1 日起我国各地检验检疫机构开始签发《亚太贸易协定》原产地证书。2018 年 7 月 1 日，《亚太贸易协定》第四轮关税减让成果文件——《亚太贸易协定第二修正案》正式生效实施。6 个成员国——中国、印度、韩国、斯里兰卡、孟加拉国和老挝将对共计 10 312

个税目的产品削减关税,平均降税幅度为33%。此外,中、韩、印、斯四国还给予协定内最不发达国家孟加拉国共1 259个产品特惠税率安排,给予老挝1 251个产品特惠税率安排,平均降税幅度均为86%。我国的商品出口到韩国、斯里兰卡、印度、孟加拉国、老挝这5个国家可签发《亚太贸易协定》原产地证书,降税幅度从5%到100%不等。

《亚太贸易协定》原产地证书共有12栏,具体样单及缮制方法在前面已有描述,此处不再一一赘述。

3. 中国-巴基斯坦自由贸易区原产地证书

2006年1月1日起中国和巴基斯坦双方先期实施降税的3 000多个税目产品,分别实施零关税和优惠关税。原产于中国的486个8位零关税税目产品的关税在2年内分3次逐步下降,2008年1月1日全部降为零。原产于中国的486个8位零关税税目产品实施优惠关税,平均优惠幅度为22%。给予关税优惠的商品其关税优惠幅度从1%到10%不等。中国-巴基斯坦自由贸易协定第二阶段议定书降税安排于2020年1月1日起实施,降税安排实施后,中巴两国间相互实施零关税产品的税目比例将从之前的35%逐步增加至75%。

中国-巴基斯坦自由贸易区原产地证书共有13栏,各栏的填写方法可参考中国-东盟自由贸易区优惠关税原产地证书相应各栏。

4. 中国-智利自由贸易区原产地证书

《中国-智利自由贸易协定》于2005年签署,2006年生效实施。2016年11月,中智双方启动自贸协定升级谈判,并于2017年11月签署《中华人民共和国政府和智利共和国政府关于修订〈自由贸易协定〉及〈自由贸易协定关于服务贸易的补充协定〉的议定书》。

自2006年10月1日起,各地出入境检验检疫机构开始签发中国-智利自由贸易区原产地证书,对原产于我国的5891个6位税目产品的关税降为零。中国-智利自由贸易区原产地证书采用专用格式。2018年关检合一后,中国-智利自由贸易区原产地证书改为向海关申领。2019年3月1日起,依照《中国-智利自由贸易协定》和我国有关法律规定,申请人可以向贸促会及其地方签证机构申请签发中国-智利自由贸易区原产地证书。

中国-智利自由贸易区原产地证书共有15栏,各栏的填写方法可参考中国-东盟自由贸易区优惠关税原产地证书相应各栏。

5. 《中国-新西兰自由贸易协定》原产地证书

中国-新西兰自由贸易区谈判是2004年11月启动的,也是中国与发达国家启动的第一个自由贸易区谈判。经过3年15轮磋商,双方于2007年12月结束谈判。2008年4月7日,《中华人民共和国政府和新西兰政府自由贸易协定》在两国总理见证下正式签署,并于2008年10月1日正式生效。

为使我国出口到新西兰的产品能够享受该协定项下关税优惠待遇,我国授权签发原产地证书的签证机构已于2008年10月1日起开始签发《中国-新西兰自由贸易协定》原产地证书。

《中国-新西兰自由贸易协定》原产地证书共有15栏,除第11栏外,其他各栏的填写可参考中国-东盟自由贸易区优惠关税原产地证书相应各栏。

第11栏:原产地标准。

(1) 完全原产的,本栏填写"WO"。

(2) 含有进口成分,但符合原产地标准的,本栏填写要求如下。

① 货物是在一方或双方境内,完全由其原产地符合原产地规定的材料生产的,本栏填

写"WP"。

② 货物是在一方或双方境内生产,所使用的非原产材料满足特定原产地规则所规定的税则归类改变、区域价值成分、工序要求及其他要求,且该货物符合其所适用的原产地标准的其他规定,本栏填写"PSR"。

6.《中国-秘鲁自由贸易协定》原产地证书

2009年4月28日,《中国-秘鲁自由贸易协定》在北京签署。该协定于2010年3月1日起开始实施。自2010年3月1日起,我国签证机构开始签发《中国-秘鲁自由贸易协定》原产地证书。

《中国-秘鲁自由贸易协定》原产地证书共有14栏,内容和填制要求可参考中国-东盟自由贸易区优惠关税原产地证书相应各栏。

7. 中国-新加坡自由贸易区优惠税率原产地证书

2008年10月23日,《中国-新加坡自由贸易协定》签署。根据该协定,新方自2009年1月1日起取消全部自我国进口产品关税;我国自2010年1月1日前对97.1%的自新方进口产品实现零关税。双方还在医疗、教育、会计等服务贸易领域做出了高于WTO的承诺。2015年11月中新双方启动升级谈判,2018年11月12日,双方签署《自由贸易协定升级议定书》,该升级议定书已于2019年10月16日生效,其中涉及的原产地规则调整已于2020年1月1日起实施。

中国-新加坡自由贸易区优惠税率原产地证书共有12栏,除第8、第11栏外,其他各栏的内容和填制要求可参考中国-东盟自由贸易区优惠关税原产地证书相应各栏。

第8栏:原产地标准。

(1) 完全原产的,本栏填写"P"。

(2) 含有进口成分,但符合原产地标准的,本栏填写要求如下。

① 货物的区域价值成分大于等于40%时,本栏填写"RVC"。

② 符合产品特定原产地规则的,本栏填写"PSR"。

第11栏:出口商声明。

生产国的横线上应填写"CHINA",进口国横线上的国名应填写"SINGAPORE"。

(七) 专用原产地证书

专用原产地证书是国际组织和国家根据政策和贸易措施的特殊需要,针对某一特殊行业的特定产品规定的原产地证书,主要有输欧盟托考伊葡萄酒原产地名称证书、输欧盟奶酪制品证书、输欧盟烟草真实性证书、输欧盟农产品原产地证书等。之前还有输欧盟纺织品原产地证书,全称为CERTIFICATE OF ORIGIN TEXTILE PRODUCTS。根据欧盟颁布的2011年第955号法规,自2011年10月24日起,取消对我国输欧盟所有纺织品类别原产地证的核查,因此,输欧盟纺织品原产地证书已停止签发。

四、能力训练

(一) 安吉林木饰品有限公司操作案例

接"项目三 办理出口货物托运"中"能力训练"部分安吉林木饰品有限公司操作案例。

2019年5月16日,安吉林木饰品有限公司的单证员根据信用证的要求,依据商业发票(见样单3-6)和装箱单(见样单3-7)缮制一般原产地证书,向中国国际贸易促进委员会湖州市委员会办理原产地证书申领手续。

信用证中原产地证书条款为:
+ ORIGINAL CERTIFICATE OF ORIGIN PLUS ONE COPY ISSUED BY CCPIT.
补充资料:
产品完全原产自中国,不含任何进口成分;
96％涤4％弹力女连衣裙的HS编码为:6204430090。
工作任务:
(1)缮制一般原产地证书。
(2)办理一般原产地证书申领手续。

(二)湖州兴业进出口有限公司操作案例

接"项目三 办理出口货物托运"中"能力训练"部分湖州兴业进出口有限公司操作案例。2019年6月3日,湖州兴业进出口有限公司的单证员在货代公司确定6月8日的船期后,根据信用证中的原产地证书条款要求,以及商业发票(见样单3-8)和装箱单(见样单3-9)缮制一般原产地证,向中国国际贸易促进委员会湖州市委员会办理原产地证书申请手续。

信用证中原产地证书的条款为:
+ ORIGINAL CERTIFICATE OF ORIGIN PLUS ONE COPY ISSUED BY CIQ.
补充资料:
灭火器的HS编码为:8424100000。
工作任务:
(1)缮制一般原产地证书;
(2)办理一般原产地证书申领手续。

五、岗位拓展

讨论话题:原产地证书的申领问题。

浙江国众贸易有限公司出口一批电子产品到越南,客户要求办一份一般原产地证书。原产地证申领员小何在贸促会原产地证申领系统里输入信息,制作完一般原产地证书后单击"保存"并校验的时候出来一个提示对话框:"所涉商品可能被允许申领优惠原产地证书"。请问小何是进行修改,还是仍旧申领一般原产地证书?

讨论引导:
(1)出口到越南的电子产品可以申领何种原产地证书?
(2)如果此次交易是采用信用证支付的,信用证上要求的是一般原产地证书,也没有其他特殊的规定,应该如何操作?
(3)如果此次交易不是采用信用证支付,应该如何操作?

项目五
办理出口货物报关

一、学习目标

能力目标： 能缮制出口货物报关单，能办理委托报关手续。
知识目标： 明确报关单的缮制要点，了解关检融合的基本知识。

二、工作任务

（一）任务描述

本批出货的藤帘的 HS 编码为 4601220000，其出口监管条件为 B，是法定检验产品，需要申报出口前监管服务（原出口报检）。2019 年 3 月 29 日，单证员张洁联系生产部门，确认货已备好，就根据本批货物的出货信息和相关报检要求，在中国国际贸易单一窗口进行出口前监管申报，生成电子底账数据。

根据湖州中远国际货运有限公司做箱通知（见样单 3-3）的要求，货物将于 2019 年 4 月 4 日进行装箱。因此，2019 年 3 月 31 日，单证员张洁按照本批出货的具体情况，缮制出口货物报关单，然后随附商业发票（见样单 2-4）、装箱单（见样单 2-5），委托湖州中远国际货运有限公司代理报关。

（二）任务分析

总体任务	办理委托报关手续
任务分解	任务一：缮制出口货物报关单
	任务二：办理委托报关手续

（三）操作示范

第一步：缮制出口货物报关单。

张洁根据商业发票、装箱单以及其他相关资料，缮制出口货物报关单（见样单 5-1），供报关员电子报关时参考。

教学视频

样单 5-1 出口货物报关单

中华人民共和国海关出口货物报关单

预录入编号：　　　　海关编号：　　　　　　　　　　　　　　　　　页码/页数：

境内发货人		出境关别		出口日期	申报日期	备案号
境外收货人		运输方式		运输工具名称及航次号	提运单号	
生产销售单位		监管方式		征免性质	许可证号	
合同协议号		贸易国（地区）		运抵国（地区）	指运港	离境口岸
包装种类		件数	毛重（千克）	净重（千克）	成交方式	运费	保费	杂费
随附单证及备注						
标记唛码及备注						
项号	商品编号	商品名称及规格型号	数量及单位	单价/总价/币制	原产国（地区）	最终目的国（地区）	境内货源地	征免
特殊关系确认：		价格影响确认：		支付特许权使用费确认：		自报自缴
报关人员 报关人员证号			电话		海关批注及签章	
兹申明以上内容承担如实申报、依法纳税之法律责任 申报单位			申报单位（签章）			

其他资料:一个12.192米(40英尺)的标准集装箱,从上海到釜山的运费是300美元,投保一切险的费率是0.1%。

出口货物报关单的缮制要点如下。

(1) 预录入编号。

预录入编号是指预录入报关单的编号。一份报关单对应一个预录入编号,由系统自动生成。

(2) 海关编号。

海关编号是指海关接受申报时给予报关单的编号。一份报关单对应一个海关编号,由系统自动生成。

(3) 境内发货人。

本栏应填报在海关备案的对外签订并执行出口贸易合同的中国境内法人、其他组织名称,以及相应的编码。编码应填报法人或其他组织18位统一社会信用代码,没有统一社会信用代码的,填报其在海关的备案编码。

(4) 出境关别。

本栏根据货物实际出境的口岸海关,填报海关规定的"关区代码表"(此表部分内容见表5-1)中相应口岸海关的名称及代码。

表 5-1 关区代码表(部分内容)

关区代码	关区名称	关区代码	关区名称	关区代码	关区名称
2248	洋山港区	2202	吴淞海关	2203	沪机场关
2900	杭州关区	2901	杭州海关	2903	温州海关
2904	舟山海关	2905	台州海关	2906	绍兴海关
2907	湖州海关	2908	嘉兴海关	2909	杭经开关
2910	杭州机场	2911	杭关邮办	2912	杭关萧办
2915	丽水海关	2916	杭州快件	2917	衢州海关
2918	杭关余办	2919	杭富阳办	2920	金华海关
2921	金关义办	2922	金关永办	2931	温关邮办
2932	温经开关	2933	温关机办	2934	温关鳌办
2935	温关瑞办	2936	温关乐办	2941	舟关嵊办
2951	台关临办	2952	台关温办	2961	绍关虞办
2962	绍关诸办	2981	嘉关乍办	2982	嘉关善办
2983	嘉兴加工	2984	嘉关宁办	2991	杭加工区
3100	宁波关区	3101	宁波海关	3102	镇海海关
3103	甬开发区	3104	北仑海关	3105	甬保税区
3106	大榭海关	3107	甬驻余办	3108	甬驻慈办
3109	甬机场办	3110	象山海关	3111	甬加工区

(5) 出口日期。

出口日期是指运载出口货物的运输工具办结出境手续的日期,为8位数字,顺序为年(4位)、月(2位)、日(2位)。出口日期在申报时免予填报。无实际进出境的货物,填报海关接受申报的日期。

(6) 申报日期。

申报日期是指海关接受出口货物收发货人、受委托的报关企业申报数据的日期,为 8 位数字,顺序为年(4 位)、月(2 位)、日(2 位)。以电子数据报关单方式申报的,申报日期为海关计算机系统接受申报数据时记录的日期。以纸质报关单方式申报的,申报日期为海关接受纸质报关单并对报关单进行登记处理的日期。本栏在申报时免予填报。

(7) 备案号。

本栏应填报出口货物发货人、生产销售单位在海关办理加工贸易合同备案或征、减、免税审核确认等手续时,海关核发的《加工贸易手册》、海关特殊监管区域和保税监管场所保税账册、《征免税证明》或其他备案审批文件的编号。一份报关单只允许填报一个备案号。

(8) 境外收货人。

境外收货人通常是指签订并执行出口贸易合同中的买方或合同指定的收货人。

本栏应填报境外收货人的名称及编码。名称一般填报英文名称,检验检疫要求填报其他外文名称的,在英文名称后填报,以半角括号分隔。对于 AEO(经认证的经营者,Authorized Economic Operator)互认国家(地区)企业,编码填报 AEO 编码,填报样式为:"国别(地区)代码+海关企业编码",例如,当境外收货人为新加坡 AEO 企业 SG123456789012 时,填报新加坡国别代码+12 位企业编码;非 AEO 互认国家(地区)企业等其他情形,编码免予填报。

特殊情况下无境外收货人的,本栏填报"NO"。

(9) 运输方式。

本栏应根据货物实际出境的运输方式,按照海关规定的"运输方式代码表"(见表 5-2)选择填报相应的运输方式。

表 5-2 运输方式代码表

运输方式代码	运输方式名称
0	非保税区
1	监管仓库
2	水路运输
3	铁路运输
4	公路运输
5	航空运输
6	邮件运输
7	保税区
8	保税仓库
9	其他方式运输
H	边境特殊海关作业区
T	综合实验区
W	物流中心
X	物流园区
Y	保税港区
Z	出口加工区
L	旅客携带
G	固定设施运输

(10) 运输工具名称及航次号。

本栏应填报载运货物出境的运输工具名称或编号及航次号。填报内容应与运输部门向海关申报的舱单(载货清单)所列相应内容一致。

水路运输填报船舶编号(来往港澳小型船舶为监管簿编号)或者船舶英文名称,同时,后面应加上船舶的航次号,两者之间用"/"分隔。航空运输填报航班号。

(11) 提运单号。

本栏应填报出口货物提单或运单的编号。一份报关单只允许填报一个提单或运单号,一票货物对应多个提单或运单时,应分单填报。

(12) 生产销售单位。

本栏应填报出口货物在境内的生产或销售单位的名称,包括:

① 自行出口货物的单位;

② 委托进出口企业出口货物的单位;

③ 免税品经营单位经营出口退税国产商品的,填报该免税品经营单位统一管理的免税店。

本栏还应填报相应代码:

① 填报18位法人和其他组织统一社会信用代码;

② 无18位统一社会信用代码的,填报"NO"。

(13) 监管方式。

监管方式是指以国际贸易中出口货物的交易方式为基础,结合海关对进出口货物的征税、统计及监管条件综合设定的海关对出口货物的管理方式。其代码由4位数字构成,前两位是按照海关监管要求和计算机管理需要划分的分类代码,后两位是参照国际标准编制的贸易方式代码。

本栏应根据实际对外贸易情况,按海关规定的"监管方式代码表"(此表部分内容见表5-3)选择填报相应的监管方式简称及代码。一份报关单只允许填报一种监管方式。

表5-3 监管方式代码表(部分内容)

代码	简称	全称
0110	一般贸易	一般贸易
0130	易货贸易	易货贸易
0139	旅游购物商品	用于旅游者5万美元以下的出口小批量订货
0200	料件放弃	主动放弃交由海关处理的来料或进料加工料件
0214	来料加工	来料加工装配贸易进口料件及加工出口货物
0245	来料料件内销	来料加工料件转内销
0255	来料深加工	来料深加工结转货物
0258	来料余料结转	来料加工余料结转
0265	来料料件复出	来料加工复运出境的原进口料件
0300	来料料件退换	来料加工料件退换
0314	加工专用油	国营贸易企业代理来料加工企业进口柴油
0320	不作价设备	加工贸易外商提供的不作价进口设备
0345	来料成品减免	来料加工成品凭征免税证明转减免税
0400	成品放弃	主动放弃交由海关处理的来料及进料加工成品

续表

代码	简称	全称
0420	加工贸易设备	加工贸易项下外商提供的进口设备
0444	保区进料成品	按成品征税的保税区进料加工成品转内销货物
0445	保区来料成品	按成品征税的保税区来料加工成品转内销货物
0446	加工设备内销	加工贸易免税进口设备转内销
0456	加工设备结转	加工贸易免税进口设备结转
0466	加工设备退运	加工贸易免税进口设备退运出境
0500	减免设备结转	用于监管年限内减免税设备的结转
0513	补偿贸易	补偿贸易
0544	保区进料料件	按料件征税的保税区进料加工成品转内销货物
0545	保区来料料件	按料件征税的保税区来料加工成品转内销货物
0615	进料对口	进料加工（对口合同）
0642	进料以产顶进	进料加工成品以产顶进
0644	进料料件内销	进料加工料件转内销
0654	进料深加工	进料深加工结转货物
0657	进料余料结转	进料加工余料结转
0664	进料料件复出	进料加工复运出境的原进口料件

(14) 征免性质。

本栏应根据实际情况，按照海关规定的"征免性质代码表"（此表部分内容见表 5-4）选择填报相应的征免性质简称及代码，持有海关核发的《征免税证明》的，按照《征免税证明》中批注的征免性质填报。一份报关单只允许填报一种征免性质。

表 5-4 征免性质代码表（部分内容）

征免性质代码	征免性质简称	征免性质全称
101	一般征税	一般征税进出口货物
118	整车征税	构成整车特征的汽车零部件纳税
119	零部件征税	不构成整车特征的汽车零部件纳税
201	无偿援助	无偿援助进出口物资
299	其他法定	其他法定减免税进出口货物
301	特定区域	特定区域进口自用物资及出口货物
307	保税区	保税区进口自用物资
399	其他地区	其他执行特殊政策地区出口货物
401	科教用品	大专院校及科研机构进口科教用品
403	技术改造	企业技术改造进口货物
406	重大项目	国家重大项目进口货物
408	重大技术装备	生产重大技术装备进口关键零部件及原材料
412	基础设施	通信、港口、铁路、公路、机场建设进口设备
413	残疾人	残疾人组织和企业进出口货物
417	远洋渔业	远洋渔业自捕水产品
418	国产化	国家定点生产小轿车和摄录机企业进口散件
419	整车特征	构成整车特征的汽车零部件进口

续表

征免性质代码	征免性质简称	征免性质全称
420	远洋船舶	远洋船舶及设备部件
421	内销设备	内销远洋船用设备及关键部件
422	集成电路	集成电路生产企业进口货物
423	新型显示器件	新型显示器件生产企业进口物资
499	ITA产品	非全税号信息技术产品
501	加工设备	加工贸易外商提供的不作价进口设备
502	来料加工	来料加工装配和补偿贸易进口料件及出口成品
503	进料加工	进料加工贸易进口料件及出口成品
506	边境小额	边境小额贸易进口货物
510	港澳OPA	港澳在内地加工的纺织品获证出口
601	中外合资	中外合资经营企业进出口货物
602	中外合作	中外合作经营企业进出口货物
603	外资企业	外商独资企业进出口货物

(15)许可证号。

本栏应填报出口许可证、两用物项和技术出口许可证、两用物项和技术出口许可证(定向)、纺织品临时出口许可证、出口许可证(加工贸易)、出口许可证(边境小额贸易)的编号。免税品经营单位经营出口退税国产商品的,免予填报。一份报关单只允许填报一个许可证号。

(16)合同协议号。

本栏应填报出口货物合同(包括协议或订单)编号。未发生商业性交易的免予填报。免税品经营单位经营出口退税国产商品的,免予填报。

(17)贸易国(地区)。

本栏应根据海关规定的"国别(地区)代码表"(此表部分内容见表5-5)选择填报相应的贸易国(地区)的中文名称及代码。

表5-5 国别(地区)代码表(部分内容)

代码	中文名称	英文名称
AFG	阿富汗	Afghanistan
ACB	阿尔巴尼亚	Albania
DZA	阿尔及利亚	Algeria
AND	安道尔	Andorra
AGO	安哥拉	Angola
ATG	安提瓜和巴布达	Antigua and Barbuda
CHL	智利	Chile
CHN	中国	China
FRA	法国	France
JPN	日本	Japan
PRK	朝鲜	Korea (the Democratic People's Republic of)
KOR	韩国	Korea (the Republic of)

续表

代码	中文名称	英文名称
TUN	突尼斯	Tunisia
TUR	土耳其	Turkey
GBR	英国	United Kingdom of Great Britain and Northern Ireland（the）
USA	美国	United States of America（the）
SGP	新加坡	Singapore
THA	泰国	Thailand
VNM	越南	Viet Nam

(18) 运抵国(地区)。

本栏应填报出口货物离开我国关境直接运抵或者在运输中转国(地区)未发生任何商业性交易的情况下最后运抵的国家(地区)。

本栏应根据海关规定的"国别(地区)代码表"选择填报相应的运抵国(地区)的中文名称及代码。

(19) 指运港。

本栏应填报出口货物运往境外的最终目的港,最终目的港不可预知的,按尽可能预知的目的港填报。

本栏应按照实际情况,根据海关规定的"港口代码表"(此表部分内容见表 5-6)选择填报相应港口的名称及代码。

表 5-6 港口代码表(部分内容)

代码	中文名称	英文名称
ARE018	迪拜(阿联酋)	Dubai, United Arab Emirates
ARE006	阿布扎比(阿联酋)	Abudhabi, United Arab Emirates
ARE901	沙迦(阿联酋)	Sharjah, United Arab Emirates
AUS033	布里斯班(澳大利亚)	Brisbane, Australia
AUS036	布鲁姆(澳大利亚)	Broome, Australia
AUS039	班伯里(澳大利亚)	Banbury, Australia
DEU063	汉堡(德国)	Hamburg, Germany
DEU012	布腊克(德国)	Brake, Germany
DEU015	不来梅(德国)	Bremen, Germany
JPN606	枕崎(日本)	Makurazaki, Japan
JPN384	大阪(日本)	Osaka, Japan
JPN501	东京(日本)	Tokyo, Japan
KOR003	釜山(韩国)	Busan, Korea(Republic of)

(20) 离境口岸。

本栏应填报装运出境货物的跨境运输工具离境的第一个境内口岸的中文名称及代码。采取多式联运跨境运输的,本栏填报多式联运货物最初离境的境内口岸中文名称及代码。

离境口岸类型包括港口、码头、机场、机场货运通道、边境口岸、火车站、车辆装卸点、车检场、陆路港、坐落在口岸的海关特殊监管区域等。本栏应根据海关规定的"国内口岸代码表"(此表部分内容见表 5-7)选择填报相应的境内口岸名称及代码。

表 5-7 国内口岸代码表(部分内容)

代码	中文名称	英文名称
310001	上海	Shanghai
310011	中国(上海)自由贸易试验区	China (Shanghai) Pilot Free Trade Zone
311002	洋山港	Yangshan Harbor
311003	洋山保税港区	Yangshan Free Trade Port Zone
311201	上海站	Shanghai Zhan
330001	杭州	Hangzhou
330002	杭州萧山国际机场	Hangzhou Xiaoshan International Airport
330600	浙江省绍兴市	Zhejiang Sheng Shaoxing Shi
330700	浙江省金华市	Zhejiang Sheng Jinhua Shi
330701	嘉兴	Jiaxing
330702	嘉兴港	Jiaxing Harbor
330703	嘉兴出口加工区 A 区	Jiaxing Export Processing Zone Zone A

(21) 包装种类。

本栏应填报出口货物的所有包装材料,包括运输包装和其他包装。运输包装是指提运单所列货物件数单位对应的包装,其他包装包括货物的各类包装,以及植物性铺垫材料等。本栏应根据海关规定的"包装种类代码表"(见表 5-8)选择填报相应的包装种类名称及代码。

表 5-8 包装种类代码表

代码	中文名称
00	散装
01	裸装
22	纸制或纤维板制盒/箱
23	木制或竹藤等植物性材料制盒/箱
29	其他材料制盒/箱
32	纸制或纤维板制桶
33	木制或竹藤等植物性材料制桶
39	其他材料制桶
04	球状罐类
06	包/袋
92	再生木托
93	天然木托
98	植物性铺垫材料
99	其他包装

(22) 件数。

本栏应填报出口货物运输包装的件数(按运输包装计)。特殊情况填报要求如下:

① 舱单件数为集装箱的,填报集装箱个数。

② 舱单件数为托盘的,填报托盘数。

本栏不得填报"0",裸装货物应填报"1"。

(23) 毛重(千克)。

本栏应填报出口货物及其包装材料的重量之和,计量单位为千克,不足 1 千克的填报"1"。

(24) 净重（千克）。

本栏应填报出口货物的毛重减去外包装材料后的重量，即货物本身的实际重量，计量单位为千克，不足1千克的填报"1"。

(25) 成交方式。

本栏应按出口货物实际成交价格条款，根据海关规定的"成交方式代码表"（见表5-9）选择填报相应的成交方式代码。

表5-9 成交方式代码表

成交方式代码	成交方式名称
1	CIF
2	C&F
3	FOB
4	C&I
5	市场价
6	垫仓
7	EXW

(26) 运费。

本栏应填报出口货物运至我国境内输出地点装载后的运输费用。运费可按运费率、运费单价、总价三种方式之一填报，注明运费标记（运费标记"1"表示运费率，"2"表示每吨货物的运费单价，"3"表示运费总价），并根据海关规定的"货币代码表"（见表5-10）选择填报相应的货币代码。

表5-10 货币代码表

货币代码	货币名称	货币代码	货币名称
110	港币	304	德国马克
113	伊朗里亚尔	305	法国法郎
116	日本元	306	爱尔兰镑
118	科威特第纳尔	307	意大利里拉
121	澳门元	309	荷兰盾
122	马来西亚林吉特	312	西班牙比赛塔
127	巴基斯坦卢比	315	奥地利先令
129	菲律宾比索	318	芬兰马克
132	新加坡元	326	挪威克郎
136	泰国铢	330	瑞典克朗
142	人民币	331	瑞士法郎
143	新台币	332	俄罗斯卢布
201	阿尔及利亚第纳尔	398	清算瑞士法郎
300	欧元	501	加拿大元
301	比利时法郎	502	美元
302	丹麦克朗	601	澳大利亚元
303	英镑	609	新西兰元

本栏的填报示例如下：

① 2%的运费率填报为"2/1"；

② 150美元的运费单价填报为"502/150/2"（注：502为美元代码）；

③ 2 000 美元的运费总价填报为"502/2 000/3"。

(27) 保费。

本栏应填报出口货物运至我国境内输出地点装载后的保险费用。

本栏可按保险费率或保险费总价两种方式之一填报，注明保险费标记(保险费标记"1"表示保险费率，"3"表示保险费总价)，并根据海关规定的"货币代码表"选择填报相应的货币代码。

本栏的填报示例如下：

① 0.1%的保险费率填报为"0.1/1"；

② 5 000 港元保险费总价填报为"110/5 000/3"(注：110 为港元的代码)。

(28) 杂费。

本栏应填报成交价格以外的，按照《中华人民共和国进出口关税条例》相关规定应计入完税价格或应从完税价格中扣除的费用。本栏可按杂费率或杂费总价两种方式之一填报，注明杂费标记(杂费标记"1"表示杂费率，"3"表示杂费总价)，并根据海关规定的"货币代码表"选择填报相应的货币代码。

填报本栏时应注意：应计入完税价格的杂费填报为正值或正率；应从完税价格中扣除的杂费填报为负值或负率。

(29) 随附单证及编号。

本栏应根据海关规定的"监管证件代码表"(见表 5-11)和"随附单据代码表"选择填报除许可证件以外的其他出口许可证件或监管证件、随附单据代码及编号。

本栏填报时分为随附单证代码和随附单证编号两栏，其中随附单证代码栏应根据海关规定的"监管证件代码表"和"随附单据代码表"选择填报相应证件代码；随附单证编号栏填报证件编号。

一般贸易出口货物，只能使用原产地证书申请享受协定税率或者特惠税率(以下统称"优惠税率")的(无原产地声明模式)，"随附单证代码"栏填报原产地证书代码"Y"，在"随附单证编号"栏填报"优惠贸易协定代码"和"原产地证书编号"。可以使用原产地证书或者原产地声明申请享受优惠税率的(有原产地声明模式)，"随附单证代码"栏填报"Y"，"随附单证编号"栏填报"优惠贸易协定代码"及"C"(凭原产地证书申报)或"D"(凭原产地声明申报)，以及"原产地证书编号(或者原产地声明序列号)"。一份报关单对应一份原产地证书或原产地声明。各优惠贸易协定代码如下：

"01"代表《亚太贸易协定》；

"02"代表《中国-东盟自由贸易协定》；

"03"代表内地与香港紧密经贸关系安排(香港 CEPA)；

"04"代表内地与澳门紧密经贸关系安排(澳门 CEPA)；

"06"代表台湾农产品零关税措施；

"07"代表《中国-巴基斯坦自由贸易协定》；

"08"代表《中国-智利自由贸易协定》；

"10"代表《中国-新西兰自由贸易协定》；

"11"代表《中国-新加坡自由贸易协定》；

"12"代表《中国-秘鲁自由贸易协定》；

"13"代表最不发达国家特别优惠关税待遇；

"14"代表"海峡两岸经济合作框架协议(ECFA)"；

"15"代表《中国-哥斯达黎加自由贸易协定》；

"16"代表《中国-冰岛自由贸易协定》；
"17"代表《中国-瑞士自由贸易协定》；
"18"代表《中国-澳大利亚自由贸易协定》；
"19"代表《中国-韩国自由贸易协定》；
"20"代表《中国-格鲁吉亚自由贸易协定》。

表 5-11 监管证件代码表

监管证件代码	监管证件名称
1	进口许可证
2	两用物项和技术进口许可证
3	两用物项和技术出口许可证
4	出口许可证
5	纺织品临时出口许可证
6	旧机电产品禁止进口
7	自动进口许可证
8	禁止出口商品
9	禁止进口商品
A	检验检疫
B	电子底账
D	出/入境货物通关单(毛坯钻石用)
E	濒危物种允许出口证明书
F	濒危物种允许进口证明书
G	两用物项和技术出口许可证(定向)
I	麻醉精神药品进出口准许证
J	黄金及黄金制品进出口准许证
L	药品进出口准许证
M	密码产品和设备进口许可证
O	自动进口许可证(新旧机电产品)
P	固体废物进口许可证
Q	进口药品通关单
R	进口兽药通关单
S	进出口农药登记证明
U	合法捕捞产品通关证明
V	人类遗传资源材料出口、出境证明
X	有毒化学品环境管理放行通知单
Z	赴境外加工光盘进口备案证明
b	进口广播电影电视节目带(片)提取单
d	援外项目任务通知函
f	音像制品(成品)进口批准单
g	技术出口合同登记证
i	技术出口许可证
k	民用爆炸物品进出口审批单
m	银行调运人民币现钞进出境证明
n	音像制品(版权引进)批准单
u	钟乳石出口批件
z	古生物化石出境批件

(30) 标记唛码及备注。

本栏应填报标记唛码中除图形以外的文字、数字,无标记唛码的填报"N/M"。

(31) 项号。

此项一般应分两行填报。第一行填报报关单中的商品顺序编号;第二行填报备案序号。专用于加工贸易及保税、减免税等已备案、审批的货物,填报该项货物在《加工贸易手册》或《征免税证明》等备案、审批单证中的顺序编号。有关优惠贸易协定项下报关单的填制要求按照海关总署相关规定执行。

(32) 商品编号。

此项应填报由 10 位数字组成的商品编号。其中,前 8 位为《中华人民共和国进出口税则》和《中华人民共和国海关统计商品目录》确定的编码;第 9、第 10 位为监管附加编号。

(33) 商品名称及规格型号。

此项一般应分两行填报。第一行填报进出口货物规范的中文商品名称,第二行填报商品的规格型号。具体填报要求如下:

① 商品名称及规格型号应据实填报,并应与出口货物发货人或受委托的报关企业所提交的合同、发票等相关单证相符。

② 商品名称应当规范,规格型号应当足够详细,以能满足海关归类、审价及许可证件管理要求为准,可参照《中华人民共和国海关进出口商品规范申报目录》中对商品名称、规格型号的要求进行填报。

(34) 数量及单位。

此项应分三行填报。

① 第一行按进出口货物的法定第一计量单位填报数量及单位,法定计量单位以《中华人民共和国海关统计商品目录》中的计量单位为准。

② 凡列明有法定第二计量单位的,在第二行按照法定第二计量单位填报数量及单位。无法定第二计量单位的,第二行为空。

③ 成交计量单位及数量填报在第三行。

(35) 单价。

此项应填报同一项号下出口货物实际成交的商品单位价格。无实际成交价格的,填报单位货值。

(36) 总价。

此项应填报同一项号下出口货物实际成交的商品总价格。无实际成交价格的,填报货值。

(36) 币制。

此项应按海关规定的"货币代码表"选择填报相应的货币名称及代码,如"货币代码表"中无实际成交币种,需将实际成交货币按申报日外汇折算率折算成"货币代码表"列明的货币,然后进行填报。

(37) 原产国(地区)。

此项应依据《中华人民共和国进出口货物原产地条例 2019 修订》《中华人民共和国海关关于执行〈非优惠原产地规则中实质性改变标准〉的规定》以及海关总署关于各项优惠贸易协定原产地管理规章规定的原产地确定标准填报。同一批出口货物的原产地不同的,应分别填报原产国(地区)。

此项应按海关规定的"国别(地区)代码表"选择填报相应的国家(地区)名称及代码。

(38) 最终目的国(地区)。

此项应填报已知的出口货物的最终实际消费、使用或进一步加工制造国家(地区)。

此项应按海关规定的"国别(地区)代码表"选择填报相应的国家(地区)名称及代码。

(39) 境内货源地。

此项应填报出口货物在国内的产地或原始发货地。出口货物产地难以确定的,填报最早发运该出口货物的单位所在地。

此项应按海关规定的"国内地区代码表"(此表部分内容见表 5-12)选择填报相应的国内地区名称及代码。

表 5-12 国内地区代码表(部分内容)

国内地区代码	国内地区名称	国内地区代码	国内地区名称
33012	杭州经济技术开发区	33089	衢州
33013	杭州高新技术产业开发区	33099	舟山
33015	浙江杭州出口加工区	33109	丽水
33019	杭州其他	33119	台州
33022	宁波经济技术开发区	33129	余姚
33024	宁波北仑港保税区	33139	海宁
33025	浙江宁波出口加工区	33149	兰溪
33026	宁波梅山保税港区	33159	瑞安
33027	宁波保税物流园	33169	萧山
33029	宁波其他	33179	江山
33032	温州经济技术开发区	33189	义乌
33039	温州其他	33199	东阳
33045	浙江嘉兴出口加工区	33205	浙江慈溪出口加工区
33049	嘉兴	33209	慈溪
33059	湖州	33219	奉化
33069	绍兴	33229	诸暨
33072	金华经济技术开发区	33239	黄岩
33079	金华	33909	浙江其他

(40) 征免。

此项应按照海关核发的《征免税证明》或有关政策规定,对报关单所列每项商品选择海关规定的"征减免税方式代码表"中相应的征减免税方式进行填报。

(41) 特殊关系确认。

出口货物免予填报此项。

(42) 价格影响确认。

出口货物免予填报此项。

(43) 支付特许权使用费确认。

出口货物免予填报此项。

(44) 自报自缴。

当出口企业、单位采用"自主申报、自行缴税"(自报自缴)模式向海关申报时,此项应填报"是";反之则此项填报"否"。

(45) 申报单位。

自理报关的,此项应填报出口企业的名称及编码;委托代理报关的,此项应填报报关企业的名称及编码。编码为法人和其他组织的18位统一社会信用代码。

报关人员还应填报在海关备案的姓名、编码、电话,并加盖申报单位印章。

(46) 海关批注及签章。

本栏供海关作业时签注。

第二步:办理委托报关手续。

张洁准备好《代理报关委托书》(见样单5-2)、出口货物报关单(见样单5-3)、商业发票、装箱单及合同等,委托湖州中远国际货运有限公司办理报关手续。

单证员在《代理报关委托书》两处相应位置盖上单位公章和法人章,其余各栏由报关员代为填写。

样单5-2 代理报关委托书

代理报关委托书

编号:□□□□□□□□□□□

我单位现 __A__ (A. 逐票 B. 长期)委托贵公司代理 __A__ (A. 报关查验 B. 垫缴税款 C. 办理海关证明联 D. 审批手册 E. 核销手册 F. 申办减免税手续 G. 其他)等通关事宜,详见《委托报关协议》。

我单位保证遵守《中华人民共和国海关法》和国家有关法规,保证所提供的情况真实、完整、单货相符。否则,愿承担相关法律责任。

本委托书有效期自签字之日起至2019年4月15日止。

委托方(盖章):湖州正昌贸易有限公司

法定代表人或其授权签署《代理报关委托书》的人(签字)

年　月　日

委托报关协议

为明确委托报关具体事项和各自责任,双方经平等协商签订协议如下:

委托方	湖州正昌贸易有限公司	被委托方		
主要货物名称	藤制的帘子	*报关单编码	No.	
HS编码	4601220000	收到单证日期	年　月　日	
出口日期	2019年4月6日	收到单证情况	合同□	发票□
提单号	COSG55896212		装箱清单□	提(运)单□
贸易方式	一般贸易		加工贸易手册□	许可证件□
原产地/货源地	湖州		其他	
传真电话		报关收费	人民币:　　　元	
其他要求:		承诺说明:		
背面所列通用条款是本协议不可分割的一部分,对本协议的签署构成了对背面通用条款的同意。		背面所列通用条款是本协议不可分割的一部分,对本协议的签署构成了对背面通用条款的同意。		
委托方业务签章:		被委托方业务签章:		
经办人签章:		经办报关员签章:		
联系电话:　　　　　　　年　月　日		联系电话:　　　　　　　年　月　日		

(白联:海关留存;黄联:被委托方留存;红联:委托方留存)　　　中国报关协会监制

样单 5-3　出口货物报关单

中华人民共和国海关出口货物报关单

预录入编号：　　　　　　海关编号：　　　　　　页码/页数：

境内发货人 9133059602536 2147 湖州正昌贸易有限公司	出境关别 洋山港区 2248		出口日期		申报日期		备案号
境外收货人 MAIJER FISTRTION INC	运输方式 水路运输 2		运输工具名称及航次号 GOLDEN COMPANION/907N		提运单号 COSG5589 6212		
生产销售单位 9133059602536 2147 湖州正昌贸易有限公司	监管方式 一般贸易 0110		征免性质 一般征税 101		许可证号		
合同协议号 ZC190211	贸易国（地区） 韩国 KOR		运抵国（地区） 韩国 KOR		指运港 釜山 KOR003		离境口岸 洋山港 311002
包装种类 纸制或纤维板制盒/箱	件数 1 801	毛重（千克） 22 512.5	净重（千克） 18 910.5	成交方式 CIF	运费 502/300/3	保费 502/ 143.59/3	杂费 //

随附单证及编号
随附单证1：　随附单证2：Y01

标记唛码及备注 MAIJER/ZC190211/BUSAN/C/NO.1-1801

项号	商品编号	商品名称及规格型号	数量及单位	原产国（地区）	最终目的国（地区）	境内货源地	单价/总价/币制
1	4601220000	藤制的席子	18 910.5 千克 14 408 张	中国 142	韩国 133	湖州 33059	2.61 37 604.88 USD502

特殊关系确认：	价格影响确认：	支付特许权使用费确认：	海关批注及签章
			征免 照章征税
报关人 兹申明以上内容承担如实申报，依法纳税之法律责任 申报单位：	报关人员证号	电话 申报单位（签章）	自报自缴：否

(四)任务解决

2019年4月5日湖州正昌贸易有限公司收到货代公司的通知,该批货物经海关审核放行。

2019年4月6日,货物装船后货代公司发提单确认件(见样单5-4)给张洁进行确认。

样单5-4 提单确认件

湖州中远国际货运有限公司提单确认件

TO：张小姐,烦请确认提单并回传。提单号：COSG55896212

SHIPPER：
HUZHOU ZHENGCHANG TRADING CO., LTD.
42 HONGQI ROAD, HUZHOU, CHINA

CONSIGNEE：
TO SHIPPER'S ORDER

NOTIFY PARTY：
MAIJER FISTRTION INC.
3214,WALKER, NAKAGYO-KU,KYUNG-BUK,
KOREA REP

船名航次：GOLDEN COMPANION 907N
SHANGHAI   BUSAN

MARKS	CARTONS	GOOODS DESCRIPTION	GW.	MEAS.
MAIJER	1 801CTNS	RATTAN CURTAIN	22 512.5KGS	56.28CBM

ZC190211
BUSAN
C/NO. 1-1801

FREIGHT PREPAID
CN/SN：TGHU2187451/2125007

张洁在核对货物相关信息无误后进行回传。

三、知识链接

(一)报检的含义及范围

1. 报检的含义

报检是指有关当事人根据法律、行政法规的规定、对外贸易合同的约定或证明履约的需要,向检验检疫机构申请检验、检疫、鉴定,以获准出入境或取得销售使用的合法凭证及某种公证证明所必须履行的法定程序和手续。

2. 报检的范围

根据国家法律、行政法规的规定和目前我国对外贸易的实际情况,出入境检验检疫的报检范围主要包括四个方面:一是法律、行政法规规定必须由检验检疫机构实施检验检疫的;二是输入国家或地区规定必须凭检验检疫机构出具的证书方准入境的;三是有关国际条约或与我国有协议、协定,规定必须经检验检疫的;四是对外贸易合同约定须凭检验检疫机构签发的证书进行交接、结算的。

根据《中华人民共和国进出口商品商检法》及其实施条例、《中华人民共和国进出境动植物检疫法》及其实施条例、《中华人民共和国国境卫生检疫法》及其实施细则、《中华人民共和国食品安全法》等有关法律、行政法规的规定,以下对象在出入境时必须向检验检疫机构报检,由检验检疫机构实施检验检疫或鉴定工作。

(1) 列入《出入境检验检疫机构实施检验检疫的进出境商品目录》内的货物。

(2) 入境废物、进口旧机电产品。

(3) 出口危险货物包装容器的性能检验和使用鉴定。

(4) 进出境集装箱。

(5) 进境、出境、过境的动植物、动植物产品及其他检疫物。

(6) 装载动植物、动植物产品和其他检疫物的装载容器、包装物、铺垫材料;进境动植物性包装物、铺垫材料。

(7) 来自动植物疫区的运输工具,装载进境、出境、过境的动植物、动植物产品及其他检疫物的运输工具。

(8) 进境拆解的废旧船舶。

(9) 出入境人员、交通工具、运输设备,以及可能传播检疫传染病的行李、货物和邮包等物品。

(10) 旅客携带物(包括微生物、人体组织、生物制品、血液及其制品、骸骨、骨灰、废旧物品和可能传播传染病的物品,以及动植物、动植物产品和其他检疫物)和携带伴侣动物。

(11) 国际邮寄物(包括动植物、动植物产品和其他检疫物、微生物、人体组织、生物制品、血液及其制品,以及其他需要实施检疫的国际邮寄物)。

(12) 其他法律、行政法规规定需经检验检疫机构实施检验检疫的其他应检对象。

(二) 报关的含义及范围

1. 报关的含义

《中华人民共和国海关法》规定:"进出境运输工具、货物、物品,必须通过设立海关的地点进境或者出境。"因此,由设立海关的地点进出境并办理规定的海关手续是运输工具、货物、物品进出境的基本规则,也是进出境运输工具负责人、进出口货物收发货人、进出境物品的所有人应履行的一项基本义务。

报关是指进出口贸易的有关当事人或其代理人、进出境运输工具负责人、进出境物品的所有人在规定的有效期内向海关办理有关货物、运输工具、物品进出境手续的全过程。它强调的是一个过程。

2. 报关的范围

按照报关对象的不同,报关可以分为运输工具报关、物品报关和货物报关三类。其中,运输工具报关的手续较为简单,作为货物、人员及其携带物品的进出境载体,其报关主要是向海关直接交验相关的合法证件、清单和其他运输单证。物品报关由于其非贸易性质,且一般限于自用、合理数量,因此报关手续也较为简单。而货物报关就比较复杂,本节所述的一般贸易下,出口货物报关业务包括:按照规定填制出口货物报关单,如实申报出口货物的商品编码、实际成交价格、目的地等相应内容,并提交相应的报关单证,办理出口货物的查验,申请办理缴纳税费、结关等事宜。

(三) 关检融合改革

党的十八大以来,贸易便利化改革深入发展。2014年,上海国际贸易单一窗口启动试点,2017年年底,国际贸易单一窗口覆盖至全国所有口岸。2018年,关检融合改革启动。2018年3月,第十三届全国人民代表大会第一次会议通过了关于国务院机构改革方案的决定,将国家质量监督检验检疫总局的出入境检验检疫管理职责和队伍划入海关总署。2018年4月20日,出入境检验检疫正式并入中国海关。原出入境检验检疫系统统一以海关名义对外开展工作。关检合一后,通关作业上实现了一次申报、一次查验、一次放行的"三个一"标准。对于广大进出口企业来说,通关费用减少,通关效率提升,贸易便利化程度进一步提高。

教学视频

海关总署从以下几个方面推动关检融合改革工作。

1. 企业报关报检资质整合

2018年4月20日起,海关总署对企业报关报检资质进行了优化整合。

(1) 将检验检疫自理报检企业备案与海关进出口货物收发货人备案,合并为海关进出口货物收发货人备案。企业备案后同时取得报关和报检资质。

(2) 将检验检疫代理报检企业备案与海关报关企业(包括海关特殊监管区域双重身份企业)注册登记或者报关企业分支机构备案,合并为海关报关企业注册登记和报关企业分支机构备案。企业注册登记或者企业分支机构备案后,同时取得报关和报检资质。

(3) 将检验检疫报检人员备案与海关报关人员备案,合并为报关人员备案。报关人员备案后同时取得报关和报检资质。

2. 全面取消通关单

从2018年6月1日起,海关总署全面取消原出入境检验检疫局签发的出入境货物通关单,海关统一向口岸场站发送放行指令。收发货人凭海关放行指令提离货物。涉及法定检验检疫要求的出口商品申报时,企业无须在报关单随附单证栏中填写原通关单代码和编号,应当填写报检电子回执上的企业报检电子底账数据号,并填写代码"B"。

3. 报检单、报关单整合

从2018年8月1日起,海关总署对进出口货物实行报检报关整合申报,报关单、报检单合并为一张横版报关单,原报关、报检共229个申报项目合并精简至105个,统一了国别(地区)、港口、币制等8个原报关、报检共有项的代码。原出入境货物报检单停止使用。

4. "三个一"工程改革

关检合一后,海关通关作业上实现了一次申报、一次查验、一次放行的"三个一"标准。

(1) 一次申报:以前企业要在不同的系统中录入报关、报检信息,现在企业通过国际贸易单一窗口或是互联网+海关的平台,只需要录入一次,上传一次单证,生成一个新版报关单就能完成申报。

(2) 一次查验:海关、检验检疫的查验指令下达保留三个环节,即查验指令、实施查验、查验结果异常处置,不用两次重复查验。

(3) 一次放行:海关统一向口岸场站发送放行指令,收发货人凭海关放行指令提离货物。

(四)出口货物的报关程序

1. 实施出口检验检疫的货物,企业应在报关前向产地/组货地海关提出申请

出口关检可以一次申报,但报关时间会被延长。因为出口检验完后最终出口时间,甚至货物是否实际出口都不确定,如果同时报关,时间会很长,还有可能要撤销报关。所以,工作人员应先办理出口前监管服务,再进行出口报关。

2. 海关实施检验检疫监管后建立电子底账,向企业反馈电子底账数据号

海关对符合要求的出口货物按规定签发检验检疫证书。出境报检单打印界面,将原所需单证"出境货物通关单"改为"出境货物检验检疫工作联系单"。

海关总署对法定检验商品以外的部分进出口商品实施抽查检验。抽查检验的商品范围包括节日灯串、电动剃须刀、电热水龙头、吹风机、器具开关、电烤锅(电烤炉、空气炸锅等)、LED照明光源、仿真饰品、儿童滑板车、电动童车、毛绒玩具、儿童自行车等。

3. 出口企业委托报关代理人出口申报,报关时应填写电子底账数据号

在货物装运的前几天,出口企业把相关的报关委托书、报关单、商业发票、装箱单等报关单证寄交报关代理人,由专门的报关员在货物运抵海关监管区后、装货的 24 小时以前向海关进行如实申报。涉及法定检验检疫要求的出口商品,在申报时企业无须在报关单随附单证栏中填写原通关单代码和编号,应当填写报检电子回执上的企业报检电子底账数据号,并填写代码"B"。

如果海关决定现场查验,报关代理人应到现场配合查验。在完成现场查验、缴纳税费后海关放行,相关工作人员可装运货物。

四、能力训练

(一)安吉林木饰品有限公司操作案例

接"项目四 申领原产地证书"中"能力训练"部分安吉林木饰品有限公司操作案例。2019 年 5 月 12 日,上海大洲货代公司传来进仓通知(见样单 5-5),要求报关资料于 2019 年 5 月 16 日前寄往上海大洲货代公司。安吉林木饰品有限公司的单证员根据进仓通知的要求,依据商业发票(见样单 3-6)和装箱单(见样单 3-7)缮制出口货物报关单,并准备报关资料,委托货代公司办理报关手续。

补充资料:

出口口岸:洋山港区(2248);

安吉林木饰品有限公司统一社会信用代码:913305961235692371;

生产厂家:安吉林木饰品有限公司;

运费总价:4 300 美元;

保险费率:1.2%。

工作任务:

(1)缮制出口货物报关单;

(2)准备报关资料。

样单 5-5　进仓通知

进仓通知

TO：安吉林木

贵司预配货物,品名 96%涤 4%弹力女连衣裙　件数 420CTNS　目的港 BARCELONA

提单号：CNSE094479　现配船名 CMA CGM MOZART V.039　开航日 5月18日

报关资料请于 5月16日10：00　时前送至我司航海路 378号4号楼D座集装箱部

货物请于 5月16日10：00 时前,按此进仓编号 DCF145678A45 送至我司仓库,我司仓库恕不接受除此以外的进仓编号。

电话：021-25687×××　联系人：张明

传真：021-25687×××

进仓地址：上海市海虹路 4046 号海洲储运

联系电话：021-65443×××

联系人：李伟先生

注：请配合我司按规定的时间送报关资料和送货。送报关资料时,请提供经营单位税务登记号(共 15 位)。

（二）湖州兴业进出口有限公司操作案例

接"项目四 申领原产地证书"中"能力训练"部分湖州兴业进出口有限公司操作案例。2019 年 5 月 29 日,湖州兴业进出口有限公司的单证员收到货代公司传过来的做箱通知(见样单 5-6)。2019 年 6 月 4 日,单证员根据商业发票(见样单 3-8)、装箱单(见样单 3-9)缮制出口货物报关单,准备报关资料,要委托货代公司办理报关手续。

样单 5-6　做箱通知

做箱通知

TO：湖州兴业

船名/航次：ITAL FIDUCIA 019W

提单号：COSU6018011491

目的港：SFAX ,TUNISIA

做箱地址：湖州市东大路 59 号

箱型：1×40′FCL

装箱时间：2019 年 6 月 5 日上午 9 点

预计开船日：2019 年 6 月 8 日

注：预配数据为 870CTNS,19 140KGS,31.32CBM。

请确认核对数据,如无误请签 OK 传回我司,谢谢配合！

　　　　　　　　　　　　　　　　　　　　　　FROM：湖州外航

　　　　　　　　　　　　　　　　　　　　　　2019 年 5 月 29 日

补充资料:
出口口岸:吴淞海关(2202);
灭火器的 HS 编码:8424100000;
法定计量单位:个;
湖州兴业进出口有限公司统一社会信用代码:913305978942452331;
运费总价:3 150 美元。
工作任务:
(1) 缮制出口货物报关单;
(2) 准备报关资料。

五、岗位拓展

讨论话题:出口产品采用木箱包装,如何进行出口报关?

湖州兴业进出口有限公司在 2019 年 9 月向乌克兰出口一批灭火器产品(灭火器产品的 HS 编码为 8424100000),灭火器不属于出口法检产品,但是这批灭火器产品采用了木箱包装,这个包装木箱需要申报出口前监管。请问单证员在准备报关时应该如何操作?

讨论引导:
1. 木箱的出口前监管申报资料需要准备哪些?
2. 出口前监管与报关可以同时进行吗?

项目六
办理出口货物投保

一、学习目标

能力目标： 能缮制出口货物投保单，办理投保手续。

知识目标： 明确出口货物投保单的缮制要点，掌握出口保险单证的种类及内容，了解出口信用保险。

二、工作任务

（一）任务描述

2019年4月1日，单证员张洁在收到湖州中远国际货运有限公司的做箱通知后，确定了4月6日的船期，然后按照信用证中的保险条款及商业发票、做箱通知等单据，缮制出口货物投保单并向保险公司办理出口货物投保手续。

（二）任务分析

总体任务	根据信用证要求办理出口货物投保
任务分解	任务一：整理投保资料
	任务二：缮制出口货物投保单
	任务三：办理投保手续

（三）操作示范

第一步：整理投保资料。

信用证中的保险条款为：

+ MARINE INSURANCE POLICY FOR 110PCT OF INVOICE VALUE, BLANK ENDORSED, COVERING ALL RISKS AND WAR RISK, CLAIMS PAYABLE AT DESTINATION.

信用证中的保险条款要求投保加成一成，空白背书，投保一切险和战争险，索赔地点在目的地。张洁根据商业发票（见样单2-4）和做箱通知（见样单3-3）等相关单据，准备缮制出口货物投保单。

第二步：缮制出口货物投保单。

由于销售合同和信用证中没有指定保险公司，张洁决定按照惯例向中国人民财产保险股份有限公司投保。该公司的出口货物投保单见样单6-1。

样单6-1　出口货物投保单

PICC 中国人民财产保险股份有限公司
PICC Property and Casualty Company limited

货物运输保险投保单
APPLICATION FORM FOR CARGO TRANSPORTATION INSURANCE

被保险人
INSURED：
发票号(INVOICE NO.)
合同号(CONTRACT NO.)
信用证号(L/C NO.)
发票金额(INVOICE AMORNT)　　　　　　　　　投保加成(PLUS)
兹有下列物品向中国人民财产保险股份有限公司湖州市分公司投保。(INSURANCE IS REQUIRED ON THE FOLLOWING COMMODITTES：)

标记 MARKS & NO.	包装及数量 QUANTTTY	保险货物项目 DESCRIPTION OF GOODS	保险金额 AMOUNT INSURED

启运日期：　　　　　　　　　　　　　　装载运输工具：
DATE OF COMMENCEMENT：_____　PER CONVEYANCE：_____
自　　　　　　经　　　　　　　　　　至
FROM _____ VIA _____ TO _____
提单号：　　　　　　　　　　　　　　　赔款偿付地点：
B/L NO.：_____　　　　　　　　　CLAIM PAYABLE AT _____
投保险别：(PLEASE INDICATE THE CONDITIONS &/OR SPECIAL COVERAGES：)

请如实告知下列情况：(如"是"在[　]中打"√"，"不是"打"×")IF ANY,PLEASE MARK "√" OR "×"：
1. 货物种类：袋装[　] 散装[　] 冷藏[　] 液体[　] 活动物[　] 机器/汽车[　]
   危险品等级[　]
   GOODS：BAG/JUMBO　BULK　REEFER　LIQUID　LIVE ANIMAL　MACHINE/AUTO
   DANGEROUS CLASS
2. 集装箱种类：普通[　] 开顶[　] 框架[　] 平板[　] 冷藏[　]
   CONTAINER　ORDINARY　OPEN　FRAME　FLAT　REFRIGERATOR
3. 转运工具：海轮[　] 飞机[　] 驳船[　] 火车[　] 汽车[　]
   BY TRANSIT：SHIP　PLANE　BARGE　TRAIN　TRUCK
4. 船舶资料：船籍[　] 船龄[　]
   PARTICULAR OF SHIP：　RIGISTRY　　AGE
备注：被保险人确认对本保险合同条款和内容已经完全了解。　　　投保人(签名盖章)
　　　THE ASSURED CONFIRMS HEREWITH THE TERMS　　APPLICANT'S SIGNATURE
　　　AND CONDITIONS OFTHESE INSURANCE CONTRACTS
　　　FULLY UNDERSTOOD.
　　　　　　　　　　　　　　　　　　　　　　　　　　　　　电话(TEL)：
　　　　　　　　　　　　　　　　　　　　　　　　　　　　　地址(ADD)：

投保日期(DATE)：

出口货物投保单的缮制要点如下,此处只选取了部分与保险单密切相关的栏目进行讲解。

(1) 被保险人(Insured)。

此项要按照保险利益的实际有关人填写,一般应是出口商的名称。

(2) 标记(Marks & No.)。

此项应该和提单上所载的标记符号相一致,特别是要同刷在货物外包装上的实际标记符号一样,以免发生赔案时,引起检验、核赔、确定责任的混乱。如果标记繁杂,可以写成"与××号发票相同"(as per invoice No. ×××)。

(3) 包装及数量(Quantity)。

此项要将包装的性质,如箱、包、件、捆,以及数量都写清楚。

(4) 保险货物项目(Description of Goods)。

此项一般应按商业发票上的具体货物名称填写,如果货物项目较多,可以用统称,但不得与商业发票或其他单据上的所列货物名称相矛盾。

(5) 保险金额(Amount Insured)。

此项通常按照发票 CIF 价加成 10%~20% 计算,如果发票价为 FOB 带保险或 CFR,应将运费、保费相应加上去,再另行加成。需要指出的是,保险合同是补偿性合同,被保险人不能从保险赔偿中获得超过实际损失的赔付,因此,溢额投保(如过高的加成、明显偏离市场价格的投保金额等)是不能得到全部赔付的。保险金额不能出现小数,出现小数时无论多少一律进位。

(6) 装载运输工具(Per Conveyance)。

如果是海运,此项需写明船名、航次。

(7) 航程或路线(From... To...)。

此项应写明从何地运至何地,如果有转运,还要注明中转港的名称。

(8) 赔款偿付地点(Claim Payable at)。

除特别声明外,一般在保险目的地支付赔款。

(9) 投保险别(Conditions)。

此项按信用证要求填写,必须注明具体险别,如有特别要求,也在此项下一并填写。

(10) 投保日期(Date)。

此项所填日期应在开航前,不能迟于提单上的出航日期。

第三步:办理投保手续。

2019 年 4 月 3 日,张洁拿着缮制好的出口货物投保单(见样单 6-2)到中国人民财产保险股份有限公司湖州分公司办理投保手续。

样单 6-2　出口货物投保单

PICC　中国人民财产保险股份有限公司
PICC Property and Casualty Company limited
货物运输保险投保单
APPLICATION FORM FOR CARGO TRANSPORTATION INSURANCE

被保险人
INSURED: HUZHOU ZHENGCHANG TRADING CO., LTD.
发票号(INVOICE NO.) ZC19311
合同号(CONTRACT NO.) ZC190211

信用证号(L/C NO.) M51145160747856

发票金额(INVOICE AMOUNT) USD37 604.88　　　　　投保加成(PLUS) 10 %

兹有下列物品向中国人民财产保险股份有限公司湖州市分公司投保。(INSURANCE IS REQUIRED ON THE FOLLOWING COMMODITTES：)

标记 MARKS & NO.	包装及数量 QUANTTTY	保险货物项目 DESCRIPTION OF GOODS	保险金额 AMOUNT INSURED
MAIJER ZC190211 BUSAN C/NO. 1-1801	1 801CTNS	RATTAN CURTAIN	USD41 366.00

启运日期：　　　　　　　　　　　　　　　装载运输工具：
DATE OF COMMENCEMENT：APR.6,2019　　PER CONVEYANCE：GOLDEN COMPANION　907N
自　　　　　　　　经　　　　　　　　　　至
FROM SHANGHAI　　　VIA　　　　　　　　TO BUSAN
提单号：　　　　　　　　　　　　　　　　赔款偿付地点：
B/L NO.：COSG55896212　　　　　　　　　CLAIM PAYABLE AT BUSAN
投保险别：(PLEASE INDICATE THE CONDITIONS &./OR SPECIAL COVERAGES：)
COVERING ALL RISKS AND WAR RISK

请如实告知下列情况：(如"是"在[　]中打"√","不是"打"×") IF ANY,PLEASE MARK "√" OR "×"：

1. 货物种类：袋装[　] 散装[　] 冷藏[　] 液体[　] 活动物[　] 机器/汽车[　]
   危险品等级[　]
   GOODS：BAG/JUMBO　BULK　REEFER　LIQUID　LIVE ANIMAL　MACHINE/AUTO
   DANGEROUS CLASS
2. 集装箱种类：普通[√] 开顶[　] 框架[　] 平板[　] 冷藏[　]
   CONTAINER　ORDINARY　OPEN　FRAME　FLAT　REFRIGERATOR
3. 转运工具：海轮[　] 飞机[　] 驳船[　] 火车[　] 汽车[　]
   BY TRANSIT：SHIP　PLANE　BARGE　TRAIN　TRUCK
4. 船舶资料：船籍[　] 船龄[　]
   PARTICULAR OF SHIP：RIGISTRY　AGE

备注：被保险人确认对本保险合同条款和内容已经完全了解。　　　投保人(签名盖章)
　　　THE ASSURED CONFIRMS HEREWITH THE TERMS　　　APPLICANT'S SIGNATURE
　　　AND CONDITIONS OFTHESE INSURANCE CONTRACTS
　　　FULLY UNDERSTOOD.

　　　　　　　　　　　　　　　　　　　　　　　　　　电话(TEL)：
　　　　　　　　　　　　　　　　　　　　　　　　　　地址(ADD)：

投保日期(DATE)：　APR.1,2019

教学视频

(四)任务解决

　　中国人民财产保险股份有限公司湖州分公司在审核相关资料后,确认承保,签发货物运输保险单(见样单6-3)。

样单 6-3　货物运输保险单

PICC 中国人民保险

总公司设于北京　　一九四九年创立　　保单号次：
Head Office：Beijing　Established in 1949　POLICY NO.：PYIE201931120504002003

货物运输保险　保险单　CARGO TRANSPORTATION INSURANCE POLICY

发票号（INVOICE NO.）ZC19311
合同号（CONTRACT NO.）ZC190211
信用证号（L/C NO.）M51145160747856
被保险人：
Insured：HUZHOU ZHENGCHANG TRADING CO.，LTD.

中国人民财产保险股份有限公司（以下简称"本公司"）根据被保险人的要求，以被保险人向本公司缴付约定的保险费为对价，按照本保险单列明条款承保下述货物运输保险，特订立本保险单。
THIS POLICY OF INSURANCE WITNESSES THAT PICC PROPERTY AND CASUALTY COMPANY LIMITED(HEREINAFIFR CALLED "THE COMPANY"). AT THE REQUEST OF THE INSRED AND IN CONSIDERATION OF THE AGREED PRMIUM PAID TO THE COMPANY BY THE INSURED, UNDERTAKES TO INSURE THE UNDERMETONED GOODS IN TRANSPORTATION SUBJECT TO THE CONDITIONS OF THIS POLICY AS PER THE CLAUSES PRINTED OVERLEAF.

标记 MARKS & NO.	包装及数量 PACKAGE & QUANTITY	保险货物项目 GOODS	保险金额 AMOUNT INSURED
MAIJER ZC190211 BUSAN C/NO. 1-1801	1 801CTNS	RATTAN CURTAIN	USD41 366.00

总保险金额
TOTAL AMOUNT INSURED：US DOLLARS FORTY ONE THOUSAND THREE HUNDRED AND SIXTY SIX ONLY.

保费：　　　　　　　启运日期：　　　　　　　运载运输工具：
PREMIUM：　　　　　DATE OF COMMENCEMENT：　PER CONVEYANCE：
AS ARRANGED　　　 APR.6,2019　　　　　　　GOLDEN COMPANION 907N
自　　　　　　　　　经　　　　　　　　　　　至
FROM SHANGHAI, CHINA　VIA　　　　　　　　TO BUSAN, KOREA REP.

承保险别
CONDITIONS：
COVERING ALL RISKS AND WAR RISK AS PER OCEAN MARINE CARGO CLAUSES (1/1/1981) OF THE PEOPLE'S INSURANCE COMPANY OF CHINA.

所保货物如果发生保险单项下可能引起索赔的损失或损坏，应立即通知本公司下述代理人查勘。如有索赔，应向本公司提交保单正本(本保单共<u>贰</u>份正本)及有关文件。如一份正本已用于索赔，其余正本自动失效。
IN THE EVENT OF LOSS OR DAMAGE WHICH MAY RESULT IN A CLAM UNDER THIS POLICY, IMMEDIATE NOTICE MUST BE GIVEN TO THE COMPANY'S AGENT AS MENTIONED HEREUNDER. IN THE EVENT OF CLAIMS, IF ANY, ONE OF THE ORIGINAL POLICY WHICH HAS BEEN ISSUED IN <u>2</u> ORIGINAL(S) TOGETHER WITH THE RELEVANT DOCUMENTS SHALL BE SURRENDERED TO THE COMPANY. IF ONE OF THE ORIGINAL POLICY HAS BEEN ACCOMPLISHED, THE OTHERS SHALL BE VOID.

CHYIPSUNG SHIPPING CORPORATION
BUSAN 11TH FLOOR，YUCHANG BLDG
NO. 25M4-YA,NO. 75,BUSAN,KOREA REP.
POST CODE：600847
TEL：82-51-4786551/5
FAX：82-51-47865516
Authorized Signature

中国人民财产保险股份有限公司湖州市分公司
PICC PROPERTY AND CASUALTY COMPANY LIMITED HUZHOU BRANCH

赔款偿付地点
CLAIM PAYABLE AT KOREA REP. IN USD
出单日期
ISSUING DATE APR 5,2019

三、知识链接

（一）出口货物运输险投保程序

在国际货物买卖过程中，由哪一方负责办理投保国际贸易运输保险，应根据买卖双方商订的价格条件来确定。凡按 CIF 条件成交的出口货物，由出口商向当地保险公司逐笔办理投保手续。凡按 FOB 或 CFR 条件成交的出口货物，保险一般应由进口商办理，也可以由出口商代为办理，但保险费应单独列支。

根据销售合同或信用证规定，在备妥货物并已确定装运日期和运输工具后，相关工作人员应按约定的保险险别和保险金额，向保险公司投保。投保时应填制投保单并支付保险费，保险公司出具保险单或保险凭证。投保的日期应不迟于货物装船的日期。对于投保金额，若销售合同没有明确规定，一般为 CIF 价格加成 10%。若进口商要求提高加成比率，一般情况下可以接受，但增加的保险费应由进口商担负。

（二）投保注意事项

相关工作人员在投保时一般应注意以下事项。
（1）投保申报情况必须属实。
（2）投保险别、币制与其他条件必须和信用证上所列保险条款的要求相一致。
（3）投保险别和条件要和销售合同上所列保险条件相符合。
（4）投保后如果发现投保项目有错漏，例如，保险目的地变动、船名错误以及保险金额增减等，要及时向保险公司申请批改。
（5）FOB,CFR 下可以由出口商按照信用证或销售合同的规定代办保险，但保险费必须由进口商额外支付。

（三）保险单据

1. 保险单据的定义

国际贸易货物的运输保险单是指承保人向被保险人签发的，对保险标的物承担保险条款中规定的意外事故的损失和负责赔偿的契约凭证。在国际贸易中，保险单与转让海运提单一样,也可由被保险人背书转让。在 CIF 价格术语下,保险单是卖方必须提供的主要单据之一。

2. 保险单据的种类

在国际贸易业务中,常用的保险单据主要包括以下几种。

(1) 保险单(Insurance Policy)。

保险单俗称大保单。它是保险人和被保险人之间成立保险合同关系的正式凭证。因险别的内容和形式有所不同,海上保险最常用的形式有船舶保险单、货物保险单、运费保险单、船舶所有人责任保险单等。其内容除载明被保险人、保险标的(如果是货物,则应填明数量及标志)、运输工具、险别、起讫地点、保险期限、保险价值和保险金额等项目外,还附有关于保险人责任范围以及保险人和被保险人的权利和义务等方面的详细条款。如果当事人双方对保险单上所规定的权利和义务需要增补或删减,可在保险单上加贴条款或加注字句。保险单是被保险人向保险人索赔或对保险人上诉的正式文件,也是保险人理赔的主要依据。保险单可转让,通常是被保险人向银行进行押汇的单证之一。

(2) 保险凭证(Insurance Certificate)。

保险凭证俗称小保单,是保险单的一种简化形式。它是保险人签发给被保险人,证明货物已经投保和保险合同已经生效的文件。保险凭证无保险条款,表明按照本保险人的正式保险单上所载的条款办理。保险凭证具有与保险单同等的效力,但在信用证规定提交保险单时,一般不能用保险凭证。

(3) 预约保单(Open Policy 或 Open Cover)。

预约保单又称开口保单、敞口保单,是保险公司承保被保险人在一定时期内发运的,以 CIF 价格条件成交的出口货物或以 FOB、CFR 价格条件进口货物的保险单。预约保单是载明保险货物的范围、承保险别、保险费率、每批运输货物的最高保险金额以及保险费计算办法,但不约定保险总金额的保险合同。预约保单是基于保险人与被保险人之间长期合作关系而签订的预约保险或保险约定,可以避免繁杂的保险手续,可以防止漏保。预约保单具有保费定期结算、可以优惠,以及可以减少被保险人的资金占用的优点。

凡属预约保单范围内的出口货物,一经启运,被保险人应立即以启运通知书或其他书面形式将该批货物的名称、数量、保险金额、运输工具的种类和名称、航程的起讫地点、开航日期等情况通知保险人,保险人据此签发正式的保险单证。预约保单主要适用于经常有大量进出口货物的情况。

(4) 批单(Endorsement)。

当保险单、保险凭证、预约保单签发生效以后,如果需要变更保险合同的内容,被保险人应向保险公司提出批改申请,由保险公司出具批单,从而对原保险单据的内容进行变更或补充。

一般情况下,批单须粘贴在原保险单据上,并加盖骑缝章,作为保险单的一部分。批单是保险人与被保险人变更保险合同的证明文件。保险单据一经批改,保险人就应按批改后的内容承担责任。

3. 保险单据的责任起讫

责任起讫亦称保险期间或保险期限,是指保险人承担责任的起讫时限。由于海运货物保险是特定航程中货物的保险,因此海运货物的保险一般没有固定具体的起讫日期。我国货物基本险的保险期限一般采取"仓至仓"的原则。战争险的保险责任期限以水面危险为限,即自货物在启运港装上海轮或驳船时开始,直到卸离海轮或驳船为止。如果不卸离海轮或驳船,则从海轮或驳船到达目的港的当天午夜起算满 15 天,保险责任自行终止。

"仓至仓"简称 W/W,它的含义是:保险责任自被保险货物运离保险单所载启运地仓库或储存处所时开始,在正常运输过程中(包括海上、湖上、内河和驳船运输)继续有效,直至货物运交保险单所载目的地收货人的最后仓库为止。如果被保险货物在最后卸货港全部卸离海轮或驳船后 60 天内未完成最后交货,则保险责任在 60 天届满时终止。

4. 保险单的缮制

(1) 保险人(Insurer)。

保险人即保险公司,通常保险公司的全称及公司标记会用醒目的字体预先印制在保险单的最上端,该项目可以帮助被保险人明确保险责任的承担者。

(2) 保单号次(Policy No.)。

保险单的右上方一般预先印有一个与上、下套保险单前后相连的流水编号,但这还不是真正的保险单编号,保险单编号一般在缮制保险单时才编定。不同保险公司编制保险单编号的规定不尽相同,但一般保险单编号都要反映保险公司下属分公司的编号、出单年份以及同险种保险业务连续号。

(3) 被保险人(Insured)。

被保险人是保险单的抬头。由于保险单可以转让,被保险人只要在保险单背面签章背书,保险单的权益就可以进行转让。所以,除非信用证上有明确规定,否则投保人便被作为被保险人。

根据信用证的有关规定,常见的被保险人的填制方法有以下几种。

① 一般情况下,投保人与被保险人系同一人。信用证若无明确规定,由卖方投保时,被保险人一栏应填写信用证上受益人的名称,并由该受益人在保单后背面做背书。

② 信用证规定须转让给开证行或第三方时,则被保险人一栏内在信用证受益人名称之后应再打上"Held to the Order of ×××",并由该受益人在保单背面做背书。

③ 信用证指定以"个人名义"或"来人"(To Order)为抬头人时,则在被保险人一栏内直接打上"×××"或"To Order",信用证上的受益人不要背书。

④ 信用证指定"Endorse To the Order of ×××"时,则在被保险人一栏内仍打上信用证的受益人名称,同时在保险单背面信用证上的受益人背书的上方打上"Held/Pay to the Order of ×××"。

(4) 标记(Marks & No.)。

按信用证规定,保险单上的标记应与发票、提单上的相应内容一致。若来证无特殊规定,一般可简单填成"As Per Inv. No. ×××"。

(5) 包装及数量(Quantity)。

本栏应填写大包装件数,并应与提单上同一栏目内容相同。填写本栏时还应注意以下几个事项。

有包装的填写最大包装件数;有包装但以重量计价的,应把包装重量与计价重量都注上;裸装货物要注明本身件数;煤炭、石油等散装货物应注明"In Bulk"再填净重;以单位包装件数计价的,可只填总件数。

(6) 保险货物项目(Description of Goods)。

保险单内必须显示对货物的描述。若货物的名称单一,可按发票上的名称填写;若货物的项目很多,该描述可以用统称,但不得与信用证和其他单据上对货物的描述相矛盾。

(7) 保险金额(Amount Insured)。

一般情况下,保险金额需要以信用证规定的货币种类及金额表示。若信用证未对保险金额做出规定,则一般按照发票金额加成 10% 计算;要求加成比例超过 10% 的,保险公司会根据实际情况决定是否接受。保险金额不能出现小数,出现小数时无论多少一律向上进位。

发票金额中往往含有佣金或折扣,在计算保险金额时需要区别对待。通常,除非信用证中另有规定,否则佣金无须扣除,直接以发票金额为基数加成计算保险金额即可;而发票金额中如果包含折扣,那么需要先从发票金额中扣除折扣,然后加成计算保险金额。

(8) 总保险金额(Total Amount Insured)。

总保险金额的币种须与信用证或销售合同的规定相一致,而且应使用币种的全称。另外需要注意的是,大小写金额必须相符,并且由于保险金额精确到个位,因此大写金额后应加上"ONLY"字样,以防涂改。

(9) 保费(Premium)。

因为保险费费率一般不公开,所以在保费栏内通常打"As Arranged"(按照约定)字样。

若信用证要求注明"保费已付"(Premium Paid),可以将原先印制的"As Arranged"删除,然后改打为"Paid"或"Prepaid"。

(10) 运载工具(Per Conveyance)。

运载工具要与运输单据中的相应内容一致,并应按照实际情况填写。海运方式下填写船名和航次,当整个运输由两段或两段以上的运程完成时,应分别填写船名,中间用"/"隔开。铁路运输方式下加填运输方式为"by Railway"或"by Train",最好再填上车号,如 By Train: WAGON NO. ×××。航空运输方式下填"by Air",邮包运输为"By Parcel Post"。除非信用证另有规定,否则如果保险单中只有船名而没有注明航次的,银行应予接受。

(11) 启运日期(Date of Commencement)。

海运可以填写"as per B/L";空运可以填写"as per AWB"。

(12) 起讫地点(From... to...)。

在选用海运直达船运输的情况下,"From..."即为提单中的"Port of loading","to..."即为提单中的"Port of Discharge"。若信用证上的目的地(一般为内陆港)非提单中的卸货港,则保险单上的起讫地点应按信用证规定的原样填写。货物如果转船,也应把转船地点填上。例如,从上海经香港转运纽约时应填写为:From Shanghai to New York W/T at Hongkong。

(13) 承保险别(Conditions)。

本栏系保险单的核心内容,填写时注意保险险别及文句应与信用证严格一致,应根据信用证或销售合同中的保险条款要求填制,即使信用证中有重复语句,为了避免混乱和误解,最好按信用证规定的顺序填写。如果信用证没有规定具体险别,则可投保一切险(ALL RISKS)、水渍险(WA 或 WPA)、平安险(FPA)三种基本险中的任何一种。如果信用证中规定使用伦敦协会条款,包括修订前和修订后的,可以按信用证规定承保,保单应按要求填制。投保的险别除注明险别名称外,还应注明险别适用的文本及日期。

(14) 保险人在货运目的地的检验代理人(Name Survey Agent)。

保险人选择的检验代理人应位于货运目的地,若当地没有符合条件的检验代理人,则应尽可能就近选择。本栏除了填写检验代理人的名称外,还应填写详尽的地址及联系方式,以便被保险人在货物出险后与其联系。

(15) 赔款偿付地点(Claim Payable at)。

如果信用证中没有特殊规定,一般应在本栏填写信用证规定的目的港或打上"Destination"。

当信用证要求以汇票货币为赔付货币时,则在赔付地点之后加注"in the Currency of the Draft";若信用证明确规定以某种货币为赔付货币时,则在赔付地点后直接注明。

(16) 出单日期(Issue Date)。

由于保险公司提供"仓至仓"服务,因此保险手续要求货物离开出口仓库前办理,保险单的签发日期应为货物离开仓库的日期或至少填写早于提单签发的日期、发运日或接受监管日。

(17) 出单人(Issued by)。

保险单必须在表面上由保险公司或保险人或他们两者的代理人开立和签署。除非信用证另有规定,否则银行可以接受保险经纪人以保险公司代理人身份开立和签署保险证明。

(四) 出口信用保险

教学视频

1. 出口信用保险的定义

出口信用保险(Export Credit Insurance)也叫出口信贷保险,是各国政府为提高本国产品的国际竞争力,推动本国的出口贸易,保障出口商的收汇安全和银行的信贷安全,促进经济发展,以国家财政为后盾,为企业在出口贸易、对外投资和对外工程承包等经济活动中提供风险保障的一项政策性支持措施,属于非营利性的保险业务。出口信用保险是政府对市场经济的一种间接调控手段和补充,是世界贸易组织(WTO)补贴和反补贴协议原则上允许的支持出口的政策手段。

2. 出口信用保险承保的风险

出口信用保险承保的风险主要是人为原因造成的商业信用风险和政治风险。

(1) 商业信用风险。

商业信用风险也称买家风险,主要包括买方因破产而无力支付债务、买方拖欠货款、买方因自身原因而拒绝收货及付款等风险。

(2) 政治风险。

政治风险也称国家风险,主要包括因买方所在国禁止或限制汇兑、实施进口管制、撤销进口许可证、发生战争等卖方、买方均无法控制的情况,导致买方无法支付货款等风险。

以上这些风险,是无法预计、难以计算发生概率的,因此,也是商业保险无法承受的。

3. 中国出口信用保险的投保流程

我国的出口信用保险主要由中国出口信用保险公司(以下简称"中国信保")承保。中国信保是由国家出资建立的、具有独立法人地位的国有政策性保险公司。其投保流程一般可以划分为以下四个阶段。

(1) 第一阶段,预约保险。

中国信保和出口商事先约定对未来发生的出口业务投保和承保的条件。

(2) 第二阶段,进口商投保。

有了具体的进口商之后,出口商要先申请进口商信用限额;中国信保根据进口商信用实力批复限额,以确定可能承担的对该进口商的最高风险。

(3) 第三阶段,出口投保。

出口商出口后,向中国信保及时申报出口,中国信保将计收相应保险费,并承担该申报项下的收汇风险责任。

(4) 第四阶段,损失补偿。

如果发生损失,出口商及时向中国信保提出索赔申请,并提供相关材料。中国信保核定企业损失后,在规定时间内向企业支付赔款。

4. 出口信用保险的主要业务

出口信用保险有短期出口信用保险和中长期出口信用保险两种主要业务。

(1) 短期出口信用保险。

短期出口信用保险简称"短期险"。短期险一般承保放账期在180天以内的收汇风险,根据实际情况,短期险还可扩展承保放账期在180天以上、360天以内的出口以及银行或其他金融机构开具的信用证项下的出口风险。

短期险主要适用于以下两种情况。

① 信用期限在1年以内的出口业务。

② 出口商从事以信用证(L/C)、付款交单(D/P)、承兑交单(D/A)、赊销(OA)等结算方式的业务。

短期险损失赔偿比例如下。

① 由政治风险造成损失的最高赔偿比例为90%。

② 由进口商破产、无力偿付债务、拖欠等其他商业风险造成损失的最高赔偿比例为90%。

③ 由进口商拒收货物所造成损失的最高赔偿比例为80%。

(2) 中长期出口信用保险。

中长期出口信用保险简称"中长期险",可分为出口买方信贷保险、出口卖方信贷保险、再融资保险和海外融资租赁保险四大类。中长期险承保放账期在1年以上,一般不超过10年的收汇风险,主要用于高科技、高附加值的大型机电产品和成套设备等资本性货物的出口以及海外投资,如以BOT、BOO或合资等形式在境外兴办企业等。中长期险旨在鼓励出口商积极参与国际竞争,支持银行等金融机构为出口贸易提供信贷融资。

中长期险通过承担保单列明的商业风险和政治风险,使被保险人得以有效规避以下风险。

① 出口商收回延期付款的风险;

② 融资机构收回贷款本金和利息的风险。

四、能力训练

(一) 安吉林木饰品有限公司操作案例

接"项目五 办理出口货物报关"中"能力训练"部分安吉林木饰品有限公司操作案例。

2019年5月12日,安吉林木饰品有限公司的单证员收到上海大洲货代公司的进仓通知(见样单5-5),然后根据信用证中的保险单条款要求及商业发票(见样单3-6)缮制投保单,向保险公司办理投保手续。

信用证中的保险单条款为：

+ INSURANCE POLICY OR CERTIFICATE ISSUED FOR 110 PCT OF INVOICE VALUE, MADE OUT TO THE ORDER OF CAJA DE AHORROS YM. P. DE NAVARRA COVERING 'FPA', 'FROM WAREHOUSE TO WAREHOUSE' AND STATING 'CLAIMS, IF ANY, PAYABLE IN SPAIN', IN 1 ORIGINAL AND 1 COPY.

工作任务：
(1) 缮制出口货物投保单；
(2) 办理投保手续。

(二) 浙江米林进出口有限公司操作案例

2019年8月12日,浙江米林进出口有限公司的单证员小张收到宁波中外运代理公司的做箱通知,小张根据销售合同(见样单6-4)、商业发票(见样单6-5)、装箱单(见样单6-6)以及做箱通知(见样单6-7)中的信息缮制出口货物投保单,并到保险公司办理投保手续。

样单6-4 销售合同

浙江米林进出口有限公司
ZHEJIANG MILIN IMP AND EXP CO., LTD.
ROOM 20FC, AIHUA GARDEN, 288 BINHE ROAD, NINGBO, ZHEJIANG, CHINA

销售确认书
SALES CONFIRMATION

号码：
No. CMH13-022
日期：
Date: JUL. 10, 2019
签约地点：
Signed at: NINGBO

买方：
Buyers: ATICO INTERNATIONAL LIMITED
地址：
Address 48 NYAYA MARG, CHANAKYAPURI, NEW DELHI, INDIA

兹买卖双方同意成交下列商品,订立条款如下：
The undersigned Sellers and Buyers have agreed to close the following transactions according to the terms and conditions stipulated below：

商品名称及规格 Name of Commodity and Specification	数量 Quantity	单价 Unit Price	金额 Amount
UNDYED AND UNPRINTED SILK FABRIC	95 907.2M	CIF USD2.32/M	USD222 504.70

1. 数量与金额允许增或减5%

   More or Less：5% MORE OR LESS IN AMOUNT AND QUANTITY IS ALLOWED.

2. 包装：

   Packing：IN CARTONS

3. 装运期：

   Time of Shipment：NOT LATER THAN AUG. 30, 2019

4. 装运口岸和目的港：

   Port of Loading and Destination：FROM NINGBO,CHINA TO NEW DELHI,INDIA

5. 付款条件：

   Terms of Payment：BY T/T

6. 保险：由卖方按发票金额110%投保_____险

   Insurance：TO BE EFFECTED BY SELLERS FOR 110% OF FULL INVOICE VALUE COVERING FPA.

7. 备注：

   Remarks：

买方	卖方：浙江米林进出口有限公司
THE BUYER：	THE SELLER：
ATICO INTERNATIONAL LIMITED	ZHEJIANG MILIN IMP AND EXP CO., LTD.
Jim	李一航

样单 6-5　商业发票

浙江米林进出口有限公司

ZHEJIANG MILIN IMP AND EXP CO., LTD.

ROOM 20FC,AIHUA GARDEN,288 BINHE ROAD,NINGBO,ZHEJIANG,CHINA

COMMERCIAL INVOICE

TO：ATICO INTERNATIONAL LIMITED　　　　　　INVOICE NO.：MH13-050

48 NYAYA MARG,CHANAKYAPURI,NEW DELHI,INDIA　INVOICE DATE：AUG. 1,2019

　　　　　　　　　　　　　　　　　　　　　　　S/C NO.：CMH10-022

　　　　　　　　　　　　　　　　　　　　　　　S/C DATE：JUL. 10,2019

FROM：NINGBO,CHINA　　　　　　　　　　　　TO：NEW DELHI,INDIA

LETTER OF CREDIT NO.：T/T　　　　　　　　　ISSUED BY：

MARKS AND NUMBERS	NUMBER AND KIND OF PACKAGE DESCRIPTION OF GOODS	QUANTITY	UNIT PRICE	AMOUNT
	UNDYED AND UNPRINTED SILK FABRIC	95 907.2M	CIF USD2.32/M	USD222 504.70

SAY TOTAL：SAY U. S. DOLLARS TWO HUNDRED TWENTY-TWO THOUSAND FIVE HUNDRED AND FOUR POINT SEVENTY.

浙江米林进出口有限公司

ZHEJIANG MILIN IMP AND EXP CO., LTD.

李一航

样单 6-6 装箱单

浙江米林进出口有限公司
ZHEJIANG MILIN IMP AND EXP CO., LTD.
ROOM 20FC, AIHUA GARDEN, 288 BINHE ROAD, NINGBO, ZHEJIANG, CHINA

PACKING LIST

TO: ATICO INTERNATIONAL LIMITED   INVOICE NO.: MH13-050
    48 NYAYA MARG, CHANAKYAPURI,   INVOICE DATE: AUG.1,2019
    NEW DELHI, INDIA   S/C NO.: CMH10-022
FROM: NINGBO, CHINA   TO: NEW DELHI, INDIA
LETTER OF CREDIT NO.: T/T

MARKS AND NUMBERS	DESCRIPTION OF GOODS	QUANTITY	PACKAGE	G.W	N.W	MEAS.
NEW DELHI	UNDYED AND UNPRINTED SILK FABRIC	95 907.2M	130CTNS	6370KGS	5563KGS	25.77CBM
	TTL	95 907.2M	130CTNS	6370KGS	5563KGS	25.77CBM

SAY TOTAL: ONE HUNDRED AND THIRTY CARTONS ONLY.

                                    浙江米林进出口有限公司
                              ZHEJIANG MILIN IMP AND EXP CO., LTD.
                                              李一航

样单 6-7 做箱通知

做箱通知

TO：宁波米林/张小姐

货名：真丝绸
唛头：NEW DELHI
船名/航次：RAJIV GANDHI V.0116W
B/L NO.：CPC1907B15015
目的港：NEW DELHI, INDIA
做箱地址：宁波滨河路288号
箱型：20GP*1

装箱时间：2019年8月13日上午9点
预计开船日：2019年8月15日

注：预配数据为130CTNS,6370KGS,25.77CBM。
请确认核对数据，如无误请签OK传回我司，谢谢配合！

                                            FROM：宁波中外运/小陈
                                                  2019年8月12日

工作任务：
(1) 缮制出口货物投保单；
(2) 办理投保手续。

五、岗位拓展

讨论话题：保险单倒签问题。

浙江米林进出口有限公司与澳大利亚一家公司以 CIF 成交一批童装，付款方式是信用证，船期是 2019 年 9 月 4 日，直达船。9 月 6 日船已开后，浙江米林进出口有限公司的单证员才想起来没有办保险。

讨论引导：
(1) 如果不办保险，会存在哪些风险？
(2) 如果 9 月 6 日向保险公司投保，是否可行？需要提供哪些文件？

项目七
缮制其他结汇单证

一、学习目标

能力目标: 能根据信用证和销售合同制作装运通知、受益人证明等其他结汇单证,能制作汇票。

知识目标: 明确装运通知、受益人证明和汇票等其他结汇单证的缮制要点。

二、工作任务

(一) 任务描述

2019年4月8日,单证员张洁从湖州中远国际货运有限公司处拿到海运提单(B/L NO.:COSG55896212),张洁对照信用证中的结汇单据条款,并参考海运提单(见样单7-1)里的信息,缮制其他结汇单证,并处理信用证中要求的其他相关事项。

教学视频

样单7-1 海运提单

Shipper HUZHOU ZHENGCHANG TRADING CO., LTD. 42 HONGQI ROAD, HUZHOU, CHINA	BILL OF LADING B/L No.:COSG55896212
Consignee TO SHIPPER'S ORDER	**COSCO** 中国远洋运输公司
Notify Party MAIJER FISTRTION INC. 3214,WALKER, NAKAGYO-KU,KYUNG-BUK, KOREA REP.	CHINA OCEAN SHIPPING COMPANY ORIGINAL

* Pre Carriage by	* Place of Receipt		
Ocean Vessel Voy. No. GOLDEN COMPANION 907N	Port of Loading SHANGHAI, CHINA		
Port of Discharge BUSAN PORT, KOREA REP.	* Final Destination BUSAN PORT, KOREA REP.	Freight Payable at	Number Original Bs/L THREE

续表

Marks and Numbers	Number and Kind of Packages; Description of Goods	Gross Weight	Measurement
MAIJER ZC190211 BUSAN C/NO. 1-1801 TGHU2187451/2125007	SHIPPER'S LOAD, COUNT & SEAL RATTAN CURTAIN 1 801CARTONS 1×40'FCL CY-CY ON BOARD APR. 6,2019	22 512.5KGS	56.28CBM

TOTAL PACKAGES (IN WORDS)　SAY ONE THOUSAND EIGHT HUNDRED AND ONE CARTONS ONLY	
Freight and Charges FREIGHT PREPAID	Number of Original B/L THREE Place and Date of Issue SHANGHAI APR. 6,2019 Signed for the Carrier COSCO CONTAINER LINES 杨利 AS CARRIER

* Applicable only when Document Used as a Through Bill of Loading

海运提单的缮制要点如下。

(1) 托运人(Shipper)。

托运人一般为信用证中的受益人。如果开证人为了贸易上的需要,要求做第三者提单(Third Party B/L),也可照办。

(2) 收货人(Consignee)。

本栏为提单的抬头。如果是记名提单,则可填上具体的收货公司或收货人名称;如果是指示提单,则填"指示"(Order)或"凭指示"(To Order);如果需在提单上列明指示人,则可根据不同要求,做成"凭托运人指示"(To Order of Shipper)、"凭收货人指示"(To Order of Consignee)或"凭银行指示"(To Order of ××× Bank)。

(3) 被通知人(Notify Party)。

被通知人是船公司在货物到达目的港时发送到货通知的收件人,有时即为进口商。信用证项下的提单,如信用证对提单被通知人有具体规定,则必须严格按信用证中的要求填写。如果是记名提单或收货人指示提单,且收货人又有详细地址的,则本栏可以不填。如果是空白指示提单或托运人指示提单,则本栏必须填写被通知人名称及详细地址,否则船方就无法与收货人联系,收货人也不能及时报关提货,甚至会因超过海关规定的提货时间而导致货物被没收。

(4) 提单号码(B/L No.)。

提单号码一般列在提单右上角,以便于工作联系和查核。托运人向收货人发送装船通知(Shipment Advice)时,也要列明船名和提单号码。

(5) 船名、航次(Name of Vessel,Voyage No.)。

本栏应完整填写装载货物的船名及航次。

(6) 装货港(Port of Loading)。

本栏应完整填写实际装船港口的具体名称。

(7) 卸货港(Port of Discharge)。

本栏应填列货物实际卸下的港口名称。如属转船,则第一程提单上的卸货港填转船港,收货人填二程船公司;第二程提单装货港填转船港,卸货港填最后目的港。如果由第一程船公司出联运提单(Through B/L),则卸货港即可填最后目的港,提单上列明第一程和第二程船名,经某港转运的,要填写"VIA ×××"字样。

(8) 唛头(Marks and Numbers)。

信用证有规定的,必须按信用证上的规定填列唛头,否则可按发票上的唛头填列。

(9) 件数和包装种类(Number and Kind of Packages)。

件数和包装种类要按箱子实际包装情况填列。一张提单有几种不同包装的应分别列明,在总数及大写部分则可以使用 Packages。托盘及集装箱也可作为包装填列,散装应注明"In Bulk"。

(10) 货物描述(Description of Goods)。

货物描述可以写货物的统称,但货物名称必须与信用证上规定的一致。

(11) 毛重、尺码(Gross Weight,Measurement)。

除信用证另有规定外,毛重一般以千克为单位列出,体积以立方米为单位列出。

(12) 运费和费用(Freight and Charges)。

运费和费用一般为预付(Freight Prepaid)或到付(Freight Collect)。如果以 CIF 或 CFR 方式出口,一般均填上"运费预付"字样,千万不可漏列,否则收货人会因运费问题提不到货,虽可查清情况,但拖延提货时间,也将造成损失。如果系 FOB 方式出口,则可填写"运费到付"字样,除非收货人委托发货人垫付运费。

(13) 提单的份数(Number of Original B/L)。

提单份数一般按信用证要求出具,如果为"Full Set of",一般理解成三份正本若干份副本。等其中一份正本完成提货任务后,其余各份失效。

(14) 提单的签发地点和日期 (Place and Date of Issue)。

提单必须由承运人、船长或他们的代理签发,并应明确表明签发人的身份。一般表示方法有:"Carrier""Captain",或"As Agent for the Carrier:×××"等。提单还是结汇的必需单据,特别是在跟单信用证结汇时,银行要求所提供的单证必须一致,因此提单上所签的日期必须与信用证或销售合同上所要求的最后装船期一致或先于装船期。如果出口商估计货物无法在信用证装船期前装上船,应尽早通知进口商,要求修改信用证,而不应利用"倒签提单""预借提单"等欺诈行为取得货款。

(二) 任务分析

总体任务	根据信用证(L/C NO.:M51145160747856)的结汇单据条款来制作其他结汇单证
任务分解	任务一:分析信用证结汇单据条款
	任务二:缮制装运通知并完成相关操作
	任务三:缮制受益人证明并完成相关操作
	任务四:缮制汇票

（三）操作示范

第一步：分析信用证结汇单据条款。

信用证中的结汇单据条款如下。

DOCUMENTS REQUIRED　　　46A：

+ SIGNED COMMERCIAL INVOICE IN 3 FOLDS CERTIFIED THE GOODS ARE OF CHINESE ORIGIN.

+ PACKING LIST IN 3 FOLDS

+ FULL SET OF ORIGINAL CLEAN ON BOARD MARINE BILL OF LADING MADE OUT TO SHIPPER'S ORDER AND BLANK ENDORSED, MARKED FREIGHT PREPAID AND NOTIFY APPLICANT QUOTING FULL NAME AND ADDRESS.

+ MARINE INSURANCE POLICY FOR 110PCT OF INVOICE VALUE, BLANK ENDORSED, COVERING ALL RISKS AND WAR RISK, CLAIMS PAYABLE AT DESTINATION.

+ ORIGINAL CERTIFICATE OF ORIGIN ASIA-PACIFIC TRADE AGREEMENT PLUS ONE COPY ISSUED BY CIQ.

+ SHIPMENT ADVICE WITH FULL DETAILS INCLUDING SHIPPING MARKS, CARTON NUMBERS, VESSEL'S NAME, BILL OF LADING NUMBER, VALUE AND QUANTITY OF GOODS MUST BE SENT WITHIN 3 DAYS OF THE DATE OF SHIPMENT TO US.

+ BENEFICIARY SIGNED STATEMENT CERTIFYING THAT COPIES OF INVOICE, BILL OF LADING AND PACKING LIST HAVE BEEN FAXED TO APPLICANT ON FAX NO. 0082-54-8545×× × WITHIN 3 DAYS OF BILL OF LADING DATE.

信用证的结汇单据条款中要求提交的单据有：商业发票一式三份、装箱单一式三份、全套提单、保险单、《亚太贸易协定》原产地证书一正一副、装运通知、受益人证明。

在所要求的结汇单据中，只有装运通知和受益人证明还没有缮制，其他相关单据都已完成，接下来就要按条款要求缮制这两份单据。

第二步：缮制装运通知并完成相关操作。

信用证中的装运通知条款如下。

+ SHIPMENT ADVICE WITH FULL DETAILS INCLUDING SHIPPING MARKS, CARTON NUMBERS, VESSEL'S NAME, BILL OF LADING NUMBER, VALUE AND QUANTITY OF GOODS MUST BE SENT WITHIN 3 DAYS OF THE DATE OF SHIPMENT TO US.

张洁认真分析了信用证中的装运通知条款。

信用证要求装运通知中要包括唛头、包装数量、船名、提单号码、货物价值、货物数量等信息，并要在提单签发后3天内将装运通知发送给买方。

张洁根据信用证中装运通知条款的要求以及从提单中确认的信息，缮制好装运通知（见样单7-2）作为结汇单证并立刻发送一份给买方。

样单 7-2 装运通知

湖州正昌贸易有限公司
HUZHOU ZHENGCHANG TRADING CO., LTD.
42 HONGQI ROAD, HUZHOU, CHINA
TEL：＋86-0572-2365×××　　FAX：＋86-0572-2365×××

SHIPPING ADVICE

MESSERS：MAIJER FISTRTION INC.　　　　　　DATE：APR. 8, 2019
　　　　　3214, WALKER, NAKAGYO-KU, KYUNG-BUK,　L/C NO.：M51145160747856
　　　　　KOREA REP.　　　　　　　　　　　　INVOICE NO.：ZC19311

COMMODITY：RATTAN CURTAIN
QUANTITY：14 408PCS
PACKAGES：1 801CARTONS
GROSS WIGHT：22 512.5KGS
NET WEIGHT：18 910.5KGS
TOTAL AMOUNT：USD37 604.88
SHIPPING MARKS：MAIJER
　　　　　　　　ZC190211
　　　　　　　　BUSAN
　　　　　　　　C/NO. 1-1801
OCEAN VESSEL/VOY. NO.：GOLDEN COMPANION 907N
CONTAINER NO.：TGHU2187451
DATE OF SHIPMENT：APR. 6. 2019
PORT OF LOADING：SHANGHAI, CHINA
PORT OF DESTINATION：BUSAN, KOREA REP.

　　　　　　　　　　　　　　　　　　　　湖州正昌贸易有限公司(章)
　　　　　　　　　　　　　　　　　　　HUZHOU ZHENGCHANG TRADING CO. LTD.,
　　　　　　　　　　　　　　　　　　　　　　　　陈强

　　装运通知没有固定的格式,但其内容要符合信用证的要求,并要与其他单据的相关内容保持一致。装运通知的缮制要点如下。

　　(1) 出单方(Issuer)：出单方的名称和地址,一般是出口商的名称和地址。

　　(2) 单据名称(Name of Document)：一般为"Shipping Advice"或"Advice of shipment",如信用证有具体规定,则应按信用证的要求来缮打该单据的名称。

　　(3) 抬头(To)：按信用证规定填写,通常为进口商、进口商指定的保险公司等。如果信用证没有规定抬头人,则可填进口商。

　　(4) 单据日期(Date)：填写缮制装运通知的日期,日期不能超过信用证约定的出单时间范围。

　　(5) 发票号码(Invoice No.)：填写商业发票的号码,注意要与其他单据相符。

　　(6) 信用证号码(L/C No.)：填写信用证的号码。

　　(7) 商品名称(Commodity)：可按提单中的商品描述来写,不用详细说明。

(8) 成交数量(Quantity)：填写此批货物的成交数量。

(9) 包装数量(Packages)：填写此批货物的包装数量，要与其他单据保持一致。

(10) 毛重(Gross Weight)：填写此批货物的毛重，一般只需填写总毛重即可。

(11) 总金额(Total Amount)：填写此批货物的总金额，主要是进口商买保险时用。

(12) 运输工具(Ocean Vessel/Voy. No.)：填写装载货物的运输船舶的船名和航次。

(13) 装运港(Port of Loading)：填写装运口岸的名称。

(14) 目的港(Port of Destination)：填写目的港的名称。

(15) 签署(Signature)：一般可以不签署，如信用证要求"Certified Copy of Shipping Advice"，通常加盖受益人条形章。

第三步：缮制受益人证明并完成相关操作。

信用证中的受益人证明条款如下。

+ BENEFICIARY SIGNED STATEMENT CERTIFYING THAT COPIES OF INVOICE, BILL OF LADING AND PACKING LIST HAVE BEEN FAXED TO APPLICANT ON FAX NO. 0082-54-8545××× WITHIN 3 DAYS OF BILL OF LADING DATE.

张洁认真分析了受益人证明条款。

信用证在受益人证明中要求证明出口商在提单签发后3天内把发票、提单和装箱单的复印件传真给进口商。

张洁根据信用证中受益人证明条款的要求，把发票、提单和装箱单的复印件传真给买方，同时缮制受益人证明(见样单7-3)作为结汇单证。

样单7-3 受益人证明

湖州正昌贸易有限公司
HUZHOU ZHENGCHANG TRADING CO., LTD.
42 HONGQI ROAD, HUZHOU, CHINA
TEL：+86-0572-2365×××   FAX：+86-0572-2365×××

BENEFICIARY'S STATEMENT

TO：WHOM IT MAY CONCERN   DATE：APR. 8, 2019
                                 INV. NO.：ZC19311
                                 L/C NO.：M51145160747856

WE HEREBY CERTIFY THAT COPIES OF INVOICE, BILL OF LADING AND PACKING LIST HAVE BEEN FAXED TO APPLICANT ON FAX NO. +82-54-8545××× WITHIN 3 DAYS OF BILL OF LADING DATE.

湖州正昌贸易有限公司(章)
HUZHOU ZHENGCHANG TRADING CO. LTD.,
陈强

受益人证明的缮制要点如下。

(1) 出单人(Issuer)：填写受益人(出口商)的名称和地址。

(2) 单据名称(Name of Document)：根据信用证中的规定进行缮制，一般为"Beneficiary's Certificate"或"Beneficiary's Statement"或"Beneficiary's Declaration"。

(3) 单据日期(Date)：按照信用证规定的日期填制，一般为提单签发后的日期。

(4) 抬头人(To)：一般都缮打笼统的抬头人，即"To Whom it May Concern"(致有关当事人)。

(5) 商业发票号码、信用证号码[(INV. No.)/(L/C No.)]：填写商业发票号码、信用证号码。

(6) 证明内容(Certify)：根据信用证要求直接照搬照抄，但有时也应做必要的修改。例如，信用证规定为 Beneficiary's Certificate certifying that each export package to be marked with "MADE IN CHINA"，则受益人证明应作成：We hereby certify that each export package has been marked with "MADE IN CHINA"。

(7) 签署：缮打受益人(出口商)名称，由法人代表或经办人签字盖章。

第四步：缮制汇票。

信用证中的汇票条款为：

AVAILABLE WITH/BY　　＊41A：ANY BANK
　　　　　　　　　　　　　　　　　BY NEGOTIATION
DRAFT AT...　　　　　　42C：AT SIGHT FOR 100 PERCENT OF INVOICE VALUE
DRAWEE　　　　　　　＊42A：＊DAEGU BANK，LTD.，THE DAEGU

张洁完成相关结汇单证的缮制后，根据汇票条款缮制汇票(见样单 7-4)。

样单 7-4　汇票

凭　　　　　　　　　　　　　　　　信用证
Drawn under (1)　　　　　　　　　L/C NO. (2)
日期
Dated (3)　　　　　　　支取 Payable with Interest @(4)　　％按息付款
号码　　　　　　　　　汇票金额　　　　　　　　湖州
NO. (5)　　　　　　　　Exchange for (6)　　　　　Huzhou, (7)
见票_____日后(本汇票之副本未付)付交
　　　AT (8)　　　　Sight of this FIRST of Exchange (Second of Exchange Being Unpaid)
Pay to the order of (9) _____ the Sum of
(10)
此致
TO：(11)
　　　(12)

教学视频

汇票的缮制要点如下。

(1) 出票根据(Draw under)。

出票根据处应填写开证行名称和地址。在托收项下，出票根据处则应填写销售合同号(发票号)、商品件数、商品名称等。

(2) 信用证号码(L/C No.)。

本栏填写信用证的号码。在托收项下，本栏空白。

(3) 日期(Dated)。

此处的日期即为开证日期,应填写信用证开立的日期。

(4) 年息(Payable with Interest @ ％ Per Annum)。

年息由结汇银行填写,用以清算企业与银行间的利息费用,企业可空着不填。

(5) 号码(No.)。

号码栏填写本交易单据中发票的号码。

(6) 汇票小写金额(Exchange for)。

汇票上有两处相同案底的栏目,较短的一处填写小写金额,较长的一处填写大写金额。金额数要求保留小数点后两位,货币名称应与信用证规定和发票上的货币名称一样,汇票金额的多少应根据信用证中具体规定而填写。

(7) 汇票的出票日期(Date)。

信用证项下,一般以议付日期作为汇票的出票日期,指受益人把汇票交给议付行的日期,由银行填写。

(8) 付款期限(At... Sight)。

汇票的付款期限分为即期和远期两种。

若是即期汇票,一般在"At"和"Sight"之间的横线上填上一排"***"或"——"等,注意此处不得留空。

若是远期汇票,则按信用证或销售合同的规定打上相应的内容。如果信用证或销售合同规定"At 30 Days after Sight",表示见票后 30 天付款,应在本栏缮制"At 30 Days after Sight"。

(9) 受款人(Payee)。

受款人也称为收款人,为汇票抬头,应根据信用证内容填写。在信用证支付的条件下,汇票中收款人这一栏填写的应是银行的名称和地址,一般是议付行的名称和地址。托收方式下一般以托收行指示性抬头为汇票收款人。

(10) 汇票大写金额(the Sum of)。

汇票大写金额要求顶格填写,不留任何空隙,以防有人故意在汇票金额上做手脚。大写金额由两部分构成:一是货币名称,二是货币金额。例如,USD21 312.56 大写:Say U. S. Dollars Twenty-One Thousand Three Hundred and Twelve and Point Fifty-Six.

(11) 受票人(Drawee)。

受票人指汇票的付款人(Payer),本栏按照信用证的要求来填写,如果信用证未做任何规定,付款人即为开证行。托收项下以进口商为付款人,应填写进口商的名称和详细地址。

(12) 出票人(Drawer)。

出票人即出具汇票的人,一般为出口商。习惯上工作人员会在汇票的右下角空白处盖上出票人全称印章和其负责人手签印章。

(四) 任务解决

张洁缮制好汇票(见样单 7-5),做好交单准备。

样单 7-5　汇票

```
凭                                              信用证
Draw under DAEGU BANK, LTD., THE DAEGU          L/C No. M51145160747856
日期
Dated MAR.5, 2019      支取 Payable with Interest @_____ ‰按息付款
号码                    汇票金额                    湖州
NO. ZC19311            Exchange for USD37 604.88   Huzhou _____
见票_____日后(本汇票之副本未付)付交
      At   ***   Sight of this FIRST of Exchange (Second of Exchange Being Unpaid)
Pay to the order of BANK OF CHINA, HUZHOU BRANCH the Sum of
SAY U. S. DOLLARS THIRTY-SEVEN THOUSAND SIX HUNDRED AND FOUR AND POINT
EIGHTY-EIGHT.
此致
To：DAEGU BANK, LTD., THE DAEGU
                                        HUZHOU ZHENGCHANG TRADING CO., LTD.
                                                       陈强
```

三、知识链接

（一）海运提单

1. 含义

海运提单（Marine Bill of Lading），简称"提单"（B/L），是由船长、承运人或其代理人签发的，证明收到其承运的货物或已装船，将约定的货物运至特定的目的地，并交付于收货人或提单持有人的物权凭证，也是承运人和托运人之间运输合同的证明。

2. 作用

（1）提单是承运人或其代理人签发的货物收据，证实已按提单所列内容收到货物。

（2）提单是代表货物所有权的凭证，收货人或提单的合法持有人有权凭提单向承运人提取货物。由于提单是一种物权凭证，因此提单可以进行转让或抵押。

（3）提单是承运人与托运人之间运输协议的证明，是承运人与托运人处理双方在运输中的权利和义务问题的主要依据。

（4）提单是收取运费的证明，在运输过程中起到办理货物的装卸、发运和交付等方面的作用。

（5）提单是向船公司或保险公司索赔的重要依据。

3. 种类

根据不同的标准，我们可将提单分为不同的类型。

（1）根据货物是否装船进行分类。

根据货物是否装船，我们可以把提单分为已装船提单和收货待运提单。

教学视频

① 已装船提单[(On Board B/L)/(Shipped B/L)],是指货物装船后由承运人或其授权代理人根据大副收据签发给托运人的提单。如果承运人签发了已装船提单,就是确认他已将货物装在船上。这种提单除载明一般事项外,通常还必须注明装载货物的船名称和装船日期。

② 收货待运提单(Received for Shipment B/L),又称备运提单,是指船公司已收到指定货物,等待装运货物期间签发的提单。所以,这种提单未载明所装船的船名和装船时间。在跟单信用证支付方式下,银行一般都不肯接受这种提单。待运货物一旦装运后,经承运人或其代理人在收货待运提单上批注货物已装上某船只及装船日期并签署后,收货待运提单就变成了已装船提单。

(2) 根据提单有无不良批注进行分类。

根据有无不良批注,我们可以将提单分为清洁提单和不清洁提单。

① 清洁提单(Clean B/L),是指货物在装运时表面状况良好,未批注有关货物受损或包装不良情况的提单。UCP600第二十七条规定,"银行只接受清洁运输单据。清洁运输单据指未载有明确宣称货物或包装有缺陷的条款或批注的运输单据。"可见,在以跟单信用证为付款方式的贸易中,通常卖方只有向银行提交清洁提单才能取得货款。清洁提单是收货人转让提单时必须具备的单据,同时也是履行货物销售合同规定的交货义务的必要单据。

② 不清洁提单(Unclean B/L),货物装船时,若承运人发现货物有包装不牢、破残、渗漏、玷污、标志不清等现象,大副将在收货单上对此加以批注,并将此批注转移到提单上,这种提单称为不清洁提单。一般情况下,银行不接受不清洁提单。

(3) 根据提单的抬头不同进行分类。

根据提单的抬头不同,我们可以将提单分为记名提单、指示提单和不记名提单。

① 记名提单(Straight B/L)又称收货人抬头提单,是指提单上的收货人栏中已具体填写收货人名称的提单。使用记名提单时,提单所记载的货物只能由提单上特定的收货人提取,或者说承运人在卸货港只能把货物交给提单上所指定的收货人。如果承运人将货物交给提单指定的收货人以外的人,即使该人占有提单,承运人也应承担货物损失的责任。记名提单失去了代表货物可转让流通的便利,但同时也可以避免在转让过程中可能带来的风险。

② 指示提单(Order B/L),是指收货人栏内填写了"凭指示"(To Order)或"凭×××指示"(To Order of ×××)的提单,前者为不记名指示提单,又称为空白抬头,后者为记名指示提单。如果在收货人栏内只填记"To Order"字样,这种提单在托运人未指定收货人或受让人之前,货物所有权仍属于卖方。在信用证支付方式下,托运人就是以议付银行或收货人为受让人,通过转让提单而取得议付货款的。指示提单是一种可转让提单。提单的持有人可以通过背书的方式把它转让给第三者,而无须经过承运人认可。如果收货人栏内填记"To Order of ×××",指名的"×××"既可以是银行的名称,也可以是托运人,这种提单在转让时需要由指名的"×××"先进行背书。

指示提单流通性强,所以在国际贸易中较为常用。

③ 不记名提单(Bearer B/L),是指收货人栏内只写明"交持有人"(To Bearer),而不填

写具体收货人名称的提单。不记名提单不需要背书即可流通转让,只要把提单交给受让人即可。承运人应将货物交给提单持有人,谁持有提单,谁就可以提货,承运人交付货物只凭单,不凭人。不记名提单若丢失或被窃,风险极大,若转入善意的第三者手中时,极易引起纠纷,故在国际贸易中使用很少。

(4) 根据提单内容的繁简进行分类。

根据内容的繁简,我们可以将提单分为全式提单和略式提单。

① 全式提单(Long Form B/L),是指除正面印就的提单格式所记载的事项外,在提单的背面详细注明承运人和托运人之间各自的权利、义务的提单。由于条款繁多,因此全式提单又称繁式提单。在海运的实际业务中大量使用的都是这种全式提单。

② 略式提单(Short Form B/L,Simple B/L),是指只在正面列出了必须记载的内容,而背面没有任何内容的提单。略式提单一般在正面印有"简式"(Short Form)字样,以示区别。略式提单中通常列有如下条款:"本提单货物的收受、保管、运输和运费等事项,均按本提单全式提单的正面、背面的铅印、手写、印章和打字等书面条款和例外条款办理,该全式提单存于公司及其分支机构或代理处,可供托运人随时查阅。"

(5) 根据船舶的不同运营方式进行分类。

按船舶的不同运营方式,我们可以将提单分为班轮提单和租船提单。

① 班轮提单(Liner B/L),是指班轮承载货物后,由班轮公司签发给托运人的提单。

② 租船提单(Charter Party B/L),是指承运人根据租船合同而签发的提单。租船提单多用于大宗物品的运输。当货方向船方租船时,须订立租船合同。租船提单上常注明:"一切条件、条款和免责事项按照××××年××月××日的租船合同。"

(6) 其他类型的提单。

① 甲板提单(On Deck B/L)又称舱面提单,是指承运人对装上舱面甲板的货物所签发的提单。一般货物均应装在舱里,装在舱面容易受损。但有些货物(如危险品、活禽或体积过大的货物等)只能装在甲板上。承运人签发此类提单时要注明"货装甲板"。按照UCP600的规定,除非信用证另有规定,银行不接受甲板提单。

② 预借提单(Advanced B/L),是指由于信用证规定的装运期和交单结汇期已到,货主因故未能及时备妥货物或尚未装船完毕的,应托运人要求由承运人或其代理人提前签发的已装船提单。这种提单往往是当托运人未能及时备妥货物或船期延误,船舶不能按时到港接受货载,估计货物装船完毕的时间可能超过信用证规定的结汇期时,托运人采用从承运人那里借出提单用以结汇的,当然必须出具保函。签发这种提单承运人要承担更大的风险,可能构成承、托双方合谋对收货人进行欺诈的情况。

③ 过期提单(Stale B/L),过期提单有两种情形:一种是由于航线较短或银行单据流转速度太慢,以至于提单晚于货物到达目的港,收货人提货受阻形成过期提单;另一种则是由于出口商在取得提单后未能及时到银行议付形成过期提单。UCP600第十四条规定:如信用证无特殊规定,银行将拒受在运输单据签发日期后超过21天才提交的单据。在任何情况下,交单不得晚于信用证到期日。

④ 倒签提单(Anti-dated B/L),由于货物实际装船完毕日期迟于信用证规定的装运日期,若仍按实际装船日期签发提单,肯定影响结汇,为了使签发提单日期与信用证规定的装

运日期相吻合,以便结汇,承运人应托运人的要求,在提单上仍按信用证规定的装运日期签发,这种提单称为倒签提单。

⑤ 运输代理行提单(House B/L),是指由运输代理行签发的提单。在航运实践中,为了节省费用、简化手续,有时运输代理行将不同托运人发运的零星货物集中在一套提单上托运,而由承运人签发给运输代理行一组提单,由于提单只有一套,各个托运人不能分别取得提单,只好由运输代理行向各托运人签发运输代理行的提单。由于集装箱运输的发展,运输代理行组织的拼箱货使用这种提单有利于提高效率,所以这种提单的使用正在扩展。一般情况下,运输代理行提单不具有提单的法律地位,它只是运输代理行收到托运货物的收据,而不是一种可以转让的物权凭证,故不能凭此向承运人提货。

(二)装运通知

装运通知(Shipping Advice)又称 Declaration of Shipment 或 Notice of Shipment,是出口商在订妥舱位或货物装船后,以传真、电子邮件或快递等方式将货物详细装运情况及时通知进口商等相关当事人的单据。出口商做此项通知时,有时还附上或另行寄上货运单据副本,以便进口商明了装货内容。

装运通知的作用主要有两个方面。第一,在 CIF 条件下,让收货人等有关当事人及时了解货物装运情况,以便做好筹措资金、付款和接货等其他准备工作。第二,在 FOB 或 CFR 条件下,装运通知是进口商办理进口货物保险的凭证。按照国际惯例,在以 FOB、CFR 条件成交的情况下,由进口商办理保险。出口商在货物装船后应立即通知进口商或其指定的保险公司,以便进口商及时办理投保或使预约保险单生效。若因装船通知迟发或漏发而造成进口商漏办保险或未能及时办理保险,由此造成的损失将由出口商承担。在实际操作中,有些公司也会简化装运通知本身,把提单草稿发给进口商,提醒对方办理保险事宜。

(三)受益人证明

受益人证明(Beneficiary's Certificate)是一种由受益人自己出具的证明,以便证明自己履行了信用证规定的义务或证明自己按信用证的要求办事,例如,证明交货的品质,证明运输包装的处理,证明按要求寄单等。受益人证明一般没有固定格式,内容按实际情况来缮制即可。

(四)船籍证明与航程证明

船籍证明(Ship's Nationality Certificate)常与航程证明(Itinerary Certificate)合并在一起。船籍证明是用以说明载货船舶国籍的证明。有时进口商出于政治原因,对装货船舶的国籍予以限制,要求出口商仅装某些国家或不装某些国家的船舶,并要求出口商提供相应证明。航程证明是用以说明载货船舶在航程中停靠港口的证明。有时进口商出于政治原因或为了避免航行途中货船被扣的风险,对装货船舶的航行路线、停靠港口予以限制,要求船只不经过某些地区或不在某些港口停靠,并要求出口商提供相应证明。

(五) 汇票

1. 定义

汇票(Bill of Exchange/Draft)是出票人签发的,委托付款人在见票时或者在指定日期无条件支付确定的金额给某人或其指定的人或持票人的票据。

2. 当事人

从以上定义可知,汇票是一种无条件支付的委托,有三个当事人:出票人、受票人和受款人。

(1) 出票人(Drawer)。

出票人是指开立票据并将其交付给他人的法人、其他组织或者个人。出票人对收款人及正当持票人承担票据在提示付款或承兑时必须付款或者承兑的保证责任。出票人一般是出口商,是真正的债权人。

(2) 受票人(Drawee/Payer)。

受票人就是付款人,即接受支付命令的人。在进出口业务中,受票人通常为进口商或银行。在托收支付方式下,付款人一般为进口商或债务人;在信用证支付方式下,付款人一般为开证行或其指定的银行。

(3) 受款人(Payee)。

受款人也称为收款人,是汇票的抬头人,是指受领汇票所规定的金额的人。在进出口业务中,受款人一栏一般填写出票人提交单据的银行。

3. 汇票的票据行为

汇票使用过程中的各种行为,都由《中华人民共和国票据法》(以下简称《票据法》)加以规范,主要有出票、提示、承兑和付款。如需转让,通常应经过背书行为。如汇票遭拒付,还须做成拒绝证书和行使追索权。

(1) 出票(Draw/Issue)。

出票是指出票人签发汇票并交付给收款人的行为。出票包括两个动作:一是写成汇票,即在汇票上写明有关内容并签名;二是交付,即将汇票交付给收款人。只有经过交付,才真正建立了债权关系,完成了出票手续。出票后,出票人即承担保证汇票得到承兑和付款的责任。如果汇票遭到拒付,出票人应接受持票人的追索,清偿汇票金额、利息和有关费用。

(2) 提示(Presentation)。

提示是指持票人将汇票提交付款人要求承兑或付款的行为,是持票人要求取得票据权利的必要程序。付款人看到汇票叫作见票(Sight)。如果是即期汇票,付款人见票后应立即付款;如果是远期汇票,付款人见票后先承兑,到期再付款。

(3) 承兑(Acceptance)。

承兑是指付款人在持票人向其提示远期汇票时,在汇票上签名,承诺于汇票到期时付款的行为。具体做法是付款人在汇票正面写明"承兑(Accepted)"字样,注明承兑日期,签章后交还持票人。付款人一旦对汇票做承兑,即成为承兑人,以主债务人的地位承担汇票到期时付款的法律责任。

(4) 付款(Payment)。

付款是指付款人在汇票到期日,向提示汇票的合法持票人足额付款。持票人收款后将汇票注销并交给付款人作为收款证明,汇票所代表的债务债权关系即告终止。

(5) 背书(Endorsement)。

《中华人民共和国票据法》规定,除出票人在汇票上记载"不得转让"外,汇票的收款人可以以记名背书的方式转让汇票权利,即在汇票背面签上自己的名字,并记载被背书人的名称,然后把汇票交给被背书人(即受让人),受让人成为持票人,是票据的债权人。受让人有权以背书方式再行转让汇票的权利。在汇票经过不止一次转让时,背书必须连续,即被背书人和背书人名字应前后一致。对受让人来说,所有以前的背书人和出票人都是他的"前手",对背书人来说,所有他转让以后的受让人都是他的"后手","前手"对"后手"承担汇票得到承兑和付款的责任。在金融市场上,最常见的背书转让为汇票的贴现,即远期汇票经承兑后,尚未到期,持票人背书后,由银行或贴现公司作为受让人,从票面金额中扣减按贴现率结算的贴息后,将余款付给持票人。

(6) 拒付和追索(Dishonor & Recourse)。

持票人向付款人提示,付款人拒绝付款或拒绝承兑,均称拒付。另外,付款人逃匿、死亡或宣告破产,以致持票人无法实现提示,也称拒付。出现拒付时,持票人有追索权,即有权向其"前手"(背书人、出票人)要求偿付汇票金额、利息和其他费用。持票人在追索前必须按规定做成拒绝证书和发出拒付通知。拒绝证书由付款地公证机构出具,也可由付款人自行出具退票理由书或有关的司法文书,用以证明持票人已进行提示而未获结果。拒付通知用以通知"前手"关于拒付的事实,使其准备偿付并进行再追索。

4. 汇票的种类

根据不同的标准,我们可将汇票分为不同的种类。

(1) 根据出票人不同进行分类。

根据出票人不同,我们可将汇票分为银行汇票和商业汇票。

① 银行汇票(Banker's Bill),是指出票人是银行,受票人也是银行的汇票。银行汇票由银行签发后,交汇款人,由汇款人寄交国外收款人。收款人凭银行汇票从付款行取款,这种汇款方式叫作顺汇法。

② 商业汇票(Trade Bill),是指出票人是商号或个人,付款人可以是商号、个人,也可以是银行的汇票。在国际贸易结算中,出口商用逆汇法,向国外进口商收取货款并签发的汇票,即属商业汇票。

(2) 根据有无随附商业单据进行分类。

根据有无随附商业单据,我们可将汇票分为光票和跟单汇票。

① 光票(Clean Bill),是指不附带商业单据的汇票。银行汇票多是光票。在国际贸易中,对少量货款或佣金、保险费、运费等其他费用,可采用光票向对方收款或付款。

② 跟单汇票(Documentary Bill),是指附带有商业单据的汇票。商业汇票一般为跟单汇票。在国际贸易中,跟单汇票使用较为广泛。

(3) 根据付款时间进行分类。

根据付款时间不同,我们可将汇票分为即期汇票和远期汇票。

① 即期汇票(Sight Bill),是指在提示或见票时立即付款的汇票。

② 远期汇票(Time Bill),是指在一定期限或特定日期付款的汇票。远期汇票的付款时间有以下几种规定办法:见票后若干天付款(At ××× days after sight)、出票后若干天付款(At ××× days after date)、提单签发日后若干天付款(At ××× days after date of B/L)、指定日期付款(Fixed date)。

(4) 根据承兑人不同进行分类。

根据承兑人不同,我们可将汇票分为商业承兑汇票和银行承兑汇票。

① 商业承兑汇票(Trader's Acceptance Bill),是指企业或个人承兑的远期汇票。托收中使用的远期汇票即属于商业承兑汇票。商业承兑汇票是建立在商业信用基础上的。

② 银行承兑汇票(Banker's Acceptance Bill),是指银行承兑的远期汇票。信用证中使用的远期汇票即属于银行承兑汇票。银行承兑汇票是建立在银行信用基础上的,所以银行承兑汇票比商业承兑汇票更易于被人们接受。

一张汇票往往可以同时具备几种性质。例如,一张商业汇票同时又可以是即期的跟单汇票;一张远期的商业跟单汇票,同时又可以是银行承兑汇票。

四、能力训练

(一) 安吉林木饰品有限公司操作案例

接"项目六 办理出口货物投保"中"能力训练"部分安吉林木饰品有限公司操作案例。2019年5月21日,安吉林木饰品有限公司的单证员收到上海大洲货代公司寄来的海运提单。单证员根据销售合同(见样单1-7)和信用证(见样单2-6),分析信用证中的结汇单据条款,缮制其他结汇单证,准备交单。

其他补充资料:

集装箱号码:COSU457896;

封志号:671234。

工作任务:

(1) 分析信用证中的结汇单据条款;

(2) 缮制受益人证明;

(3) 缮制汇票。

(二) 湖州兴业进出口有限公司操作案例

接"项目五 办理出口货物报关"中"能力训练"部分湖州兴业进出口有限公司操作案例。2019年6月10日,湖州兴业进出口有限公司的单证员收到上海货代公司寄来的海运提单(B/L NO.:COSU6018011491)。单证员根据销售合同(见样单1-9)、信用证(见样单2-7)和海运提单(见样单7-6),分析信用证中的结汇单据条款,缮制其他结汇单证,准备交单。

样单 7-6 海运提单

1. Shipper Insert Name, Address and Phone HUZHOU XINGYE INDUSTRY CO. ,LTD. 18TH FLOOR, MEIXIN BUILDING, HUZHOU, ZHEJIANG, CHINA		B/L No. COSU6018011491
2. Consignee Insert Name, Address and Phone TO SHIPPER'S ORDER		中远集装箱运输有限公司 **COSCO CONTAINER LINES** TLX: 33057 COSCO CN FAX: +86(021)6545-8984 **ORIGINAL** **Port-to-Port or Combined Transport** **BILL OF LADING**
3. Notify Party Insert Name, Address and Phone (It is agreed that no responsibility shall attach to the Carrier or his agents for failure to notify) TUFFCO 3052 SFAX TUNISIE		RECEIVED in external apparent good order and condition except as other-Wise noted. The total number of packages or unites stuffed in the container, The description of the goods and the weights shown in this Bill of Lading are furnished by the Merchants, and which the carrier has no reasonable means of checking and is not a part of this Bill of Lading contract. The carrier has Issued the number of Bills of Lading stated below, all of this tenor and date, One of the original Bills of Lading must be surrendered and endorsed or signed against the delivery of the shipment and whereupon any other original Bills of Lading shall be void. The Merchants agree to be bound by the terms and conditions of this Bill of Lading as if each had personally signed this Bill of Lading. SEE clause 4 on the back of this Bill of Lading (Terms continued on the back here of, please read carefully). * Applicable Only When Document Used as a Combined Transport Bill of Lading.
4. Combined Transport * Pre-carriage by	5. Combined Transport * Place of Receipt	
6. Ocean Vessel Voy. No. ITAL FIDUCIA 019W	7. Port of Loading SHANGHAI PORT	
8. Port of Discharge SFAX PORT, TUNISIA	9. Combined Transport * Place of Delivery	

Marks &. Nos. Container/Seal No.	No. of Containers or Packages	Description of Goods (If Dangerous Goods, See Clause 20)	Gross Weight	Measurement
TU (PRODUCT'S NAME) QTY: C/NO.: COSU1927243 SEAL 8954588	870CTNS 1×40'FCL	FIRE EXTINGUISHER ( ) AS PER PROFORMA INVOICE NO. 2019TU02 DTD 29/03/2019 NUMBER OF L/C: CDI702/8053/2019 FREIGHT PREPAID	19 140KGS ON BOARD JUN 8,2019	31.32CBM
		Description of Contents for Shipper's Use Only (Not part of This B/L Contract)		

10. Total Number of containers and/or packages (in words) SAY EIGHT HUNDRED AND SEVENTY CARTONS ONLY.
    Subject to Clause 7 Limitation

11. Freight &. Charges Declared Value Charge	Revenue Tons	Rate	Per	Prepaid	Collect

续表

Ex. Rate:	Prepaid at	Payable at	Place and date of issue SHANGHAI 8 JUN 2019
	Total Prepaid	No. of Original B(s)/L THREE(3)	Signed for the Carrier, COSCO CONTAINER LINES AS CARRIER
LADEN ON BOARD THE VESSEL DATE　　　　　　BY			

工作任务：

（1）分析信用证中的结汇单据条款；

（2）缮制受益人证明；

（3）缮制装运通知。

五、岗位拓展

讨论话题：结汇单据的缮制问题。

湖州兴业进出口有限公司与阿曼的一家公司成交一批纺织服装，货物于2019年3月底出运。公司的单证员在缮制结汇单据时发现中间有些条款较复杂。请仔细分析以下结汇单据条款，说明缮制要点，并指出其中是否存在风险。

+ ONE ORIGINAL AND SIX COPIES OF INVOICE DULY SIGNED BY THE BENEFICIARY CERTIFYING ORIGIN OF THE GOODS.

+ A COPY OF FAX ADVICE ALONG WITH TRANSMISSION REPORT SENT BY THE BENEFICIARY WITHIN SEVEN WORKING DAYS OF SHIPMENT TO THE APPLICANT ON FAX. 00968 24820×× × AND THE INSURER AXA INSURANCE (GULF) B.S.C. (C), 833, RUWI, P.C. 112 FAX: 00968 24400×× × ADVISING ALL DETAILS OF THE SHIPMENT AND INDICATING OPEN COVER/POLICY NUMBER 65/MO/000873.

+ BENEFICIARY CERTIFICATE SIGNED BY THE AUTHORISED OFFICERS TO THE EFFECT THAT PRODUCT/CARGOES HAD BEEN DELIVERED IN CONFORMITY WITH THE TERMS OF THE L/C, THAT ALL NECESSARY DOCUMENTS HAVE BEEN FORWARDED TO THE CONSIGNEE AND THAT PAYMENT OF THE INVOICE FOR DELIVERY IS PROPERLY DUE TO THEM AND WOULD BE EXCLUSIVELY USED FOR THE SETTLEMENT OF THE INVOICE.

项目八
交单收汇

一、学习目标

能力目标： 能审核相关结汇单证，向银行办理交单手续。

知识目标： 掌握单证审核的要点，了解审单的操作流程。

二、工作任务

（一）任务描述

2019年4月9日，张洁在完成相关结汇单证制作后，就按照销售合同和信用证的要求对全套单证进行一一审核。审核及修改完成后，张洁整理全套单证，填好客户交单联系单向中国银行湖州市分行交单。等款项到账后张洁又到银行办理结汇手续，通过国际贸易单一窗口自行打印报关单并加盖企业公章，和出口货物销售统一发票退税联等一齐交给公司财务，由公司财务人员到国税局办理相关退税手续。

（二）任务分析

总体任务	根据销售合同（S/C NO.：ZC190211）及信用证（L/C NO.：M51145160747856）的要求审核全套结汇单证，办理交单手续
任务分解	任务一：审核全套结汇单证
	任务二：办理交单手续
	任务三：办理收汇退税手续

（三）操作示范

第一步：审核全套结汇单证。

张洁把前段时间就这笔业务所做的结汇单证整理出来，并按照销售合同（见样单8-1）和信用证（见样单8-2）对汇票（见样单8-3）、商业发票（见样单8-4）、装箱单（见样单8-5）、海运提单（见样单8-6）、保险单（见样单8-7）、原产地证书（见样单8-8）、装运通知（见样单8-9）、受益人证明（见样单8-10）进行一一审核。

样单 8-1 销售合同

湖州正昌贸易有限公司

HUZHOU ZHENGCHANG TRADING CO., LTD.

42 HONGQI ROAD, HUZHOU, CHINA

TEL: +86-0572-2365×××　　FAX: +86-0572-2365×××

销售确认书

SALES CONFIRMATION

号码:
No.: ZC190211

日期:
Date: FEB. 11, 2019

签约地点:
Signed at: HUZHOU

买方:
Buyers: MAIJER FISTRTION INC

地址:
Address: 3214, WALKER, NAKAGYO-KU,
　　　　　KYUNG-BUK, KOREA REP.

电传/传真:
Telex/Fax: 0082-54-8545×××

兹买卖双方同意成交下列商品,订立条款如下:
The undersigned Sellers and Buyers have agreed to close the following transactions according to the terms and conditions stipulated below:

(1) 货号 Article No.	(2) 商品名称及规格 Name of Commodity and Specification	(3) 数量 Quantity	(4) 单价 Unit Price	(5) 金额 Amount
L-2331	RATTAN CURTAIN	14 408PCS	CIF BUSAN USD2.61/PC	USD37 604.88

1. 数量与金额允许增或减5%
   More or Less: 5% MORE OR LESS IN AMOUNT AND QUANTITY IS ALLOWED.
2. 包装:
   Packing: IN CARTONS OF 8PCS EACH
3. 装运期:
   Time of Shipment: NOT LATER THAN MAR. 30, 2019
4. 装运口岸和目的港:
   Port of Loading and Destination: FROM SHANGHAI, CHINA TO BUSAN, KOREA REP. TRANS-SHIPMENT IS ALLOWED AND PARTIAL SHIPMENT IS PROHIBITED.
5. 付款条件:
   Terms of Payment: BY IRREVOCABLE LETTER OF CREDIT AT SIGHT
6. 保险: 由卖方按发票金额110%投保_____险
   Insurance: TO BE EFFECTED BY SELLERS FOR 110% OF FULL INVOICE VALUE COVERING ALL RISKS AND WAR RISK
7. 备注:
   Remarks:

买方:　　　　　　　　　　　　　　　　　卖方: 湖州正昌贸易有限公司
THE BUYER:　　　　　　　　　　　　　　 THE SELLER:
MAIJER FISTRTION INC.　　　　　　　　　 HUZHOU ZHENGCHANG TRADING CO., LTD.
　　ADAM　　　　　　　　　　　　　　　　　　　　陈强

样单 8-2 信用证

MT S700	ISSUE OF A DOCUMENTARY CREDIT
APPLICATION HEADER	*DAEGU BANK, LTD., THE
	*DAEGU
SEQUENCE OF TOTAL	*27: 1/1
FORM OF DOC. CREDIT	*40A: IRREVOCABLE
DOC. CREDIT NUMBER	*20: M51145160747856
DATE OF ISSUE	31C: 190305
APPLICABLE RULES	*40E: UCP LATEST VERSION
EXPIRY	*31D: DATE 190501 PLACE IN CHINA
APPLICANT	*50: MAIJER FISTRTION INC.
	3214, WALKER, NAKAGYO-KU, KYUNG-BUK,
	KOREA REP.
BENEFICIARY	*59: HUZHOU ZHENGCHANG TRADING CO., LTD.
	42 HONGQI ROAD,
	HUZHOU, CHINA
AMOUNT	*32B: CURRENCY USD AMOUNT 37 604.88
AVAILABLE WITH/BY	*41A: ANY BANK
	BY NEGOTIATION
DRAFT AT...	42C: AT SIGHT FOR 100 PERCENT OF INVOICE VALUE
DRAWEE	*42A: *DAEGU BANK, LTD., THE DAEGU
PARTIAL SHIPMENT	43P: NOT ALLOWED
TRANSSHIPMENT	43T: NOT ALLOWED
PORT OF LOADING	44E: CHINESE MAIN PORT
PORT OF DISCHARGE	44F: BUSAN PORT, KOREA REP.
LATEST DATE OF SHIP.	44C: 190415
DESCRIPT. OF GOODS	45A:
	14 408PCS RATTAN CURTAIN AS PER SALES CONFIRMATION NO. ZC190211
	USD2.61/PC CIF BUSAN
DOCUMENTS REQUIRED	46A:

+ SIGNED COMMERCIAL INVOICE IN 3 FOLDS CERTIFIED THE GOODS ARE OF CHINESE ORIGIN.
+ PACKING LIST IN 3 FOLDS
+ FULL SET OF ORIGINAL CLEAN ON BOARD MARINE BILL OF LADING MADE OUT TO SHIPPER'S ORDER AND BLANK ENDORSED, MARKED-FREIGHT PREPAID AND NOTIFY APPLICANT QUOTING FULL NAME AND ADDRESS.
+ MARINE INSURANCE POLICY FOR 110PCT OF INVOICE VALUE, BLANK ENDORSED, COVERING ALL RISKS AND WAR RISK, CLAIMS PAYABLE AT DESTINATION.
+ ORIGINAL CERTIFICATE OF ORIGIN ASIA-PACIFIC TRADE AGREEMENT PLUS ONE COPY ISSUED BY CIQ.
+ SHIPMENT ADVICE WITH FULL DETAILS INCLUDING SHIPPING MARKS, CARTON NUMBERS, VESSEL'S NAME, BILL OF LADING NUMBER, VALUE AND QUANTITY OF GOODS MUST BE SENT WITHIN 3 DAYS OF THE DATE OF SHIPMENT TO US.
+ BENEFICIARY SIGNED STATEMENT CERTIFYING THAT COPIES OF INVOICE, BILL OF LADING AND PACKING LIST HAVE BEEN FAXED TO APPLICANT ON FAX NO. 0082-54-8545×× × WITHIN 3 DAYS OF BILL OF LADING DATE.

ADDITIONAL COND.   47A:
    + A FEE OF USD 80 IS TO BE DEDUCTED FROM EACH DRAWING FOR THE
      ACCOUNT OF BENEFICIARY. IF DOCUMENTS ARE PRESENTED WITH DIS-
      CREPANCY(IES)..
    + UNLESS OTHERWISE EXPRESSLY STATE, ALL DOCUMENTS MUST BE IN
      ENGLISH.
    + MORE OR LESS 5% IN AMOUNT AND QUANTITY IS ALLOWED.

DETAILS OF CHARGES   71B: ALL BANKINGCOMMISSIONS AND CHARGES INCLUDING
                             REIMBURSEMENT COMMISSIONS OUTSIDE SOUTH KO-
                             REA REP. ARE FOR BENEFICIARY'S ACCOUNT.

PRESENTATION PERIOD   48: DOCUMENTS MUST BE PRESENTED FOR NEGOTIATION
                             WITHIN 21 DAYS AFTER THE DATE OF SHIPMENT BUT
                             WITHIN THE VALIDITY OF THE CREDIT.

CONFIRMATION   *49: WITHOUT
INSTRUCTION   78:
    + PLEASE REIMBURSE YOURSELVES BY PRESENTING BENEFICIARY'S
      DRAFT TO THE DRAWEE BANK.
    + ALL DOCUMENTS MUST BE MAILED TO DAEGU BANK, LTD.
      BUSINESS PROCESS SUPPORT DEPT 17FL,
      118, SUSEONG-2-GA, SUSEONG-GU,
      DAEGU,706-712 KOREA REP. IN ONE LOT BY COURIER MAIL.

"ADVISE THROUGH"   57A: BKCHCNBJ92G
                                  * BANK OF CHINA
                                  * HUZHOU
                                  * (HUZHOU BRANCH)

样单 8-3　汇票

凭	信用证
Drawn under DAEGU BANK, LTD., THE DAEGU	L/C No. M51145160747856
日期	
Dated MAR. 5, 2019	支取 Payable with interest @ _____% 按息付款
号码	汇票金额	湖州
NO. ZC19311	Exchange for USD37 604.88	Huzhou _____

见票_____日后(本汇票之副本未付)付交
　　AT *** Sight of this FIRST of Exchange (Second of Exchange Being Unpaid)

Pay to the order of BANK OF CHINA, HUZHOU BRANCH the Sum of
SAY U. S. DOLLARS THIRTY-SEVEN THOUSAND SIX HUNDRED AND FOUR AND POINT EIGHTY EIGHT.

此致
To: MAIJER FISTRTION INC.
　　　　　　　　　　　　　　　　　HUZHOU ZHENGCHANG TRADING CO., LTD.
　　　　　　　　　　　　　　　　　　　　　　　　陈强

样单 8-4 商业发票

湖州正昌贸易有限公司
HUZHOU ZHENGCHANG TRADING CO., LTD.
42 HONGQI ROAD, HUZHOU, CHINA
TEL：+86-0572-2365××× FAX：+86-0572-2365×××

COMMERCIAL INVOICE

TO：MAIJER FISTRTION INC. INVOICE NO.：ZC19311
3214,WALKER, INVOICE DATE：MAR. 25,2019
NAKAGYO-KU,KYUNG-BUK, KOREA REP. S/C NO.：ZC190211
FROM：SHANGHAI,CHINA TO：BUSAN PORT, KOREA REP.
LETTER OF CREDIT NO.：M51145160747856 ISSUED By：DAEGU BANK, LTD., THE DAEGU

MARKS AND NUMBERS	DESCRIPTION OF GOODS	QUANTITY	UNIT PRICE	AMOUNT
MAIJER ZC190211 BUSAN C/NO. 1-1801	ART. NO.：L-2331 RATTAN CURTAIN AS PER SALES CONFIRMATION NO. ZC190211	14 408PCS	CIF BUSAN USD2.61/PC	USD37 604.88

SAY TOTAL：SAY U.S. DOLLARS THIRTY-SEVEN THOUSAND SIX HUNDRED AND FOUR AND POINT EIGHTY EIGHT
WE HEREBY CERTIFIED THE GOODS ARE OF CHINESE ORIGIN.

湖州正昌贸易有限公司
HUZHOU ZHENGCHANG TRADING CO., LTD.
陈强

样单 8-5 装箱单

湖州正昌贸易有限公司
HUZHOU ZHENGCHANG TRADING CO., LTD.
42 HONGQI ROAD, HUZHOU, CHINA
TEL：+86-0572-2365××× FAX：+86-0572-2365×××

PACKING LIST

TO：MAIJER FISTRTION INC. INVOICE NO.：ZC19311
3214,WALKER, NAKAGYO-KU, INVOICE DATE：MAR. 25,2019
KYUNG-BUK, KOREA REP. S/C NO.：ZC190211
FROM：SHANGHAI,CHINA TO：BUSAN PORT, KOREA REP.
LETTER OF CREDIT NO.：M51145160747865

MARKS AND NUMBERS	DESCRIPTION OF GOODS	QUANTITY	PACKAGE	G.W	N.W	MEAS.
MAIJER ZC190211 BUSAN C/NO. 1-1801	ART. NO.：L-2331 RATTAN CURTAIN AS PER SALES CONFIRMATION NO. ZC190211	14 408PCS	1 801CTNS	22 512.5KGS	18 910.5KGS	56.28CBM
	TOTAL	14 408PCS	1 801CTNS	22 512.5KGS	18 910.5KGS	56.28CBM

SAY TOTAL：SAY ONE THOUSAND EIGHT HUNDRED AND ONE CARTONS ONLY.

湖州正昌贸易有限公司
HUZHOU ZHENGCHANG TRADING CO., LTD.
陈强

样单 8-6　海运提单

Sipper HUZHOU ZHENGCHANG TRADING CO. ,LTD. 42 HONGQI ROAD, HUZHOU, CHINA			BILL OF LADING B/L No.：COSG55896212	
Consignee TO SHIPPER'S ORDER			**COSCO** 中国远洋运输公司 CHINA OCEAN SHIPPING COMPANY ORIGINAL	
Notify Party MAIJER FISTRTION INC. 3214, WALKER, NAKAGYO-KU, KYUNG-BUK, KOREA REP.					
* Pre Carriage by	* Place of Receipt			
Ocean Vessel Voy. No. GOLDEN COMPANION 907N	Port of Loading SHANGHAI,CHINA			
Port of Discharge BUSAN PORT, KOREA REP.	* Final Destination BUSAN PORT, KOREA REP.	Freight Payable at		Number Original Bs/L THREE
Marks and Numbers MAIJER ZC190211 BUSAN C/NO. 1-1801 TGHU2187451/2125007	Number and Kind of Packages； Description of Goods SHIPPER'S LOAD, COUNT & SEAL RATTAN CURTAIN 1 801CARTONS 1×40′FCL CY-CY	Gross Weight 22 512.5KGS ON BOARD APR.6,2019		Measurement 56.28CBM
TOTAL PACKAGES (IN WORDS)　　SAY ONE THOUSAND EIGHT HUNDRED AND ONE CARTONS ONLY				
Freight and Charges FREIGHT PREPAID	Number of Original B/L THREE			
~	Place and Date of Issue SHANGHAI APR.6,2019			
~	Signed for the Carrier COSCO CONTAINER LINES 　　　　　杨利 　　　AS CARRIER			
* Applicable only when Document Used as a Through Bill of Loading				

样单 8-7　保险单

PICC 中国人民保险

总公司设于北京　　一九四九年创立　　保单号次：
Head Office：Beijing　Established in 1949　POLICY NO.；PYIE201931120504002003

货物运输保险　保险单　CARGO TRANSPORTATION INSURANCE POLICY

发票号（INVOICE NO.）ZC19311
合同号（CONTRACT NO.）ZC190211
信用证号（L/C NO.）M51145160747856
被保险人：
Insured.：HUZHOU ZHENGCHANG TRADING CO.，LTD.

中国人民财产保险股份有限公司（以下简称"本公司"）根据被保险人的要求，以被保险人向本公司缴付约定的保险费为对价，按照本保险单列明条款承保下述货物运输保险，特订立本保险单。
THIS POLICY OF INSURANCE WITNESSES THAT PICC PROPERTY AND CASUALTY COMPANY LIMITED(HEREINAFIFR CALLED "THE COMPANY"). AT THE REQUEST OF THE INSRED AND IN CONSIDERATION OF THE AGREED PRMIUM PAID TO THE COMPANY BY THE INSURED,UNDERTAKES TO INSURE THE UNDERMETONED GOODS IN TRANSPORTATION SUBJECT TO THE CONDITIONS OF THIS POLICY AS PER THE CLAUSES PRINTED OVERLEAF.

标记 MARKS & NO.	包装及数量 PACKAGE & QUANTITY	保险货物项目 GOODS	保险金额 AMOUNT INSURED
MAIJER ZC190211 BUSAN C/NO. 1-1801	1 801CTNS	RATTAN CURTAIN	USD41 366.00

总保险金额
TOTAL AMOUNT INSURED：US DOLLARS FORTY ONE THOUSAND THREE HUNDRED AND SIXTY SIX ONLY.

保费：　　　　　　　　启运日期：　　　　　　　　运载运输工具：
PREMIUM：　　　　　　DATE OF COMMENCEMENT：　PER CONVEYANCE：
AS ARRANGED　　　　　APR. 6,2019　　　　　　　　GOLDEN COMPANION 907N
自　　　　　　　　　　经　　　　　　　　　　　　至
FROM SHANGHAI,CHINA　VIA　　　　　　　　　　　TO BUSAN, KOREA REP.

承保险别
CONDITIONS：
COVERING ALL RISKS AND WAR RISK AS PER OCEAN MARINE CARGO CLAUSES (1/1/1981) OF THE PEOPLE'S INSURANCE COMPANY OF CHINA.

所保货物如果发生保险单项下可能引起索赔的损失或损坏，应立即通知本公司下述代理人查勘。如有索赔，应向本公司提交报单正本（本报单共有贰份正本）及有关文件。如一份正本已用于索赔，其余正本自动失效。

IN THE EVENT OF LOSS OR DAMAGE WHICH MAY RESULT IN A CLAM UNDER THIS POLICY, IMMEDIATE NOTICE MUST BE GIVEN TO THE COMPANY'S AGENT AS MENTIONED HEREUNDER. IN THE EVENT OF CLAIMS, IF ANY, ONE OF THE ORIGINAL POLICY WHICH HAS BEEN ISSUED IN __2__ ORIGINAL(S) TOGETHER WITH THE RELEVANT DOCUMENTS SHALL BE SURRENDERED TO THE COMPANY. IF ONE OF THE ORIGINAL POLICY HAS BEEN ACCOMPLISHED, THE OTHERS SHALL BE VOID.

CHYIPSUNG SHIPPING CORPORATION
BUSAN 11TH FLOOR , YUCHANG BLDG
NO. 25M4-YA, NO. 75, BUSAN, KOREA REP.
POST CODE：600847
TEL：82-51-4786551/5   FAX：82-51-47865516
赔款偿付地点
CLAIM PAYABLE AT KOREA REP. IN USD
出单日期
ISSUING DATE APR 5,2019

中国人民财产保险股份有限公司湖州市分公司
PICC PROPERTY AND CASUALTY COMPANY LIMITED HUZHOU BRANCH

Authorized Signature

样单 8-8　原产地证书

1. Goods Consigned from (Exporter's Business Name, Address, Country) HUZHOU ZHENGCHANG TRADING CO. ,LTD. 42 HONGQI ROAD, HUZHOU, CHINA	Reference No. B193333331450008 **CERTIRICATE OF ORIGIN** Asia-Pacific Trade Agreement (Combined Declaration and Certificate) Issued in THE PEOPLE'S REPUBLIC OF CHINA
2. Goods Consigned to (Consignee's Name, Address, Country) MAIJER FISTRTION INC. 3214, WALKER , NAKAGYO-KU, KYUNG-BUK, KOREA REP.	3. For Official Use
4. Means of Transport and Route FROM SHANGHAI TO BUSAN BY SEA	

5. Tariff Item Number	6. Marks and Number of Packages	7. Number and Kind of Packages; Description of Goods	8. Origin Criterion (See Notes Overleaf)	9. Gross Weight or Other Quantity	10. Number and Date of Invoices
460122	MAIJER ZC190211 BUSAN C/NO. 1-1801	1 801(ONE THOUSAND EIGHT HUNDRED AND ONE) CARTONS OF RATTAN CURTAIN *******************	A	14 408PCS	ZC19311 MAR. 25,2019

11. Declaration by the Exporter The undersigned hereby declares that the above details and statements are correct, that all the goods were produced in 　　　　　CHINA ·· 　　　　　（Country） and that they comply with the origin requirements specified for these goods in the Asia-Pacific Trade Agreement for goods exported to ············KOREA REP.············ 　　　　（Importing Country） 　　　　　　　　　　*张洁* HUZHOU, CHINA, APR. 2, 2019 ·· Place and date, signature and stamp of authorized signatory	12. Certification It is hereby certified that the declaration by the exporter is correct. HUZHOU, CHINA, APR. 2, 2019 ·· Place and date, signature and stamp of certifying authority

样单 8-9　装运通知

湖州正昌贸易有限公司

HUZHOU ZHENGCHANG TRADING CO., LTD.

42 HONGQI ROAD, HUZHOU, CHINA

TEL：＋86-0572-2365×××　　FAX：＋86-0572-2365×××

SHIPPING ADVICE

MESSERS：MAIJER FISTRTION INC　　　　　　　　DATE：APR. 8, 2019
　　　　　3214, WALKER, NAKAGYO-KU, KYUNG-BUK,　L/C NO.：M51145160747856
　　　　　KOREA REP.　　　　　　　　　　　　　　B/L NO.：COSG55896212
COMMODITY：RATTAN CURTAIN
QUANTITY：14 408PCS
PACKAGES：1 801CARTONS
GROSS WIGHT：22 512.5KGS
NET WEIGHT：18 910.5KGS
TOTAL AMOUNT：USD37 604.88
SHIPPING MARKS：MAIJER
　　　　　　　　ZC190211
　　　　　　　　BUSAN
　　　　　　　　C/NO. 1-1801
OCEAN VESSEL/VOY. NO.：GOLDEN COMPANION 907N
CONTAINER NO.：TGHU2187451
DATE OF SHIPMENT：APR. 6, 2019
PORT OF LOADING：SHANGHAI, CHINA
PORT OF DESTINATION：BUSAN, KOREA REP.

　　　　　　　　　　　　　　　　　　　湖州正昌贸易有限公司（章）
　　　　　　　　　　　　　　　　　　　HUZHOU ZHENGCHANG TRADING CO. LTD.,
　　　　　　　　　　　　　　　　　　　　　　　陈强

样单 8-10 受益人证明

> **湖州正昌贸易有限公司**
> **HUZHOU ZHENGCHANG TRADING CO., LTD.**
> 42 HONGQI ROAD, HUZHOU, CHINA
> TEL：+86-0572-2365×××　　FAX：+86-0572-2365×××
>
> # BENEFICIARY'S STATEMENT
>
> TO：WHOM IT MAY CONCERN　　　　DATE：APR. 8, 2019
> 　　　　　　　　　　　　　　　　INV. NO.：ZC19311
> 　　　　　　　　　　　　　　　　L/C NO.：M51145160747856
>
> WE HEREBY CERTIFY THAT COPIES OF INVOICE, BILL OF LADING AND PACKING LIST HAVE BEEN FAXED TO APPLICANT ON FAX NO. +82-54-8545××× WITHIN 3 DAYS OF BILL OF LADING DATE.
>
> 　　　　　　　　　　　　　　　　湖州正昌贸易有限公司(章)
> 　　　　　　　　　　　　　　　　HUZHOU ZHENGCHANG TRADING CO. LTD.,
> 　　　　　　　　　　　　　　　　陈强

经过认真审核，张洁发现上述单据中存在如下问题。

（1）汇票的付款人不是"MAIJER FISTRTION INC"，应改为"DAEGU BANK, LTD., THE DAEGU"。

（2）商业发票中缺少证明文句，根据信用证中商业发票的条款要求应加上"WE HEREBY CERTIFIED THE GOODS ARE OF CHINESE ORIGIN"。

（3）装箱单中信用证号码打错，应改为 M51145160747856。

（4）装运通知中包装数量打错，应改为 1 801CARTONS。

第二步：办理交单手续。

张洁对单据进行了修改，并按要求对提单、保险单进行了空白背书。在填好客户交单联系单（见样单 9-11）后，张洁向中国银行湖州市分行交单。

样单 8-11 交单联系单

客户交单联系单

致：中国银行湖州市分行

兹随附下列信用证项下出口单据一套，请按国际商会第 600 号出版物《跟单信用证统一惯例》办理寄单索汇。

开证行：DAEGU BANK, LTD., THE DAEGU							信用证号：M51145160747856					
通知行：BANK OF CHINA, HUZHOU							通知行编号：					
最迟装期：190415							效期：190501			交单期限：21 天		
汇票付款期限：AT SIGHT							汇票金额：USD37 604.88					
发票编号：ZC19311							发票金额：USD37 604.88					
单据名称	汇票	发票	海关发票	海运提单正本	海运提单副本	航空运单	货物收据	保险单	装箱/重量单	数量/质量/重量证	产地证	GSP FORM A	检验/分析证	受益人证明	船公司证明	装运通知
份数	2	3		3				2	3		1			1		1

续表

委办事项：打("×"者)				
×附信用证及修改书共 __2__ 页。				
□ 单据中有下列不符点：				
□ 请向开证行寄单，我公司承担一切责任。 □ 请电提不符点，待开证行同意后再寄单。 □ 寄单方式：×特快专递　□ 航空挂号 □ 索汇方式：□ 电索　□ 信索（□ 特快专递　□ 航空挂号）				
核销单编号： 公司联系人：　　　　　联系电话：　　　　　公司签章：				
银行审单记录：		银行接单日期：	寄单日期：	
^		汇票/发票金额：	BP No.：	
^		银行费用	通知/保兑：	银行经办：
^		^	议/承/付：	^
^		^	修改费：	^
^		^	邮费：	^
^		^	电传：	银行复核：
退单记录：		小计：		
^		费用由　　　　承担		

第三步：办理收汇退税手续。

4月28日，公司财务通知张洁此批货款已到公司美元账户，财务去中国银行湖州市分行办理了结汇手续，拿回银行提供的结汇水单。

5月6日，张洁就在中国电子口岸网上交单（见图8-1），并办理退税手续。

图8-1　中国电子口岸业务系统

(四)任务解决

张洁在中国电子口岸网上完成交单手续后,就把相关单据转给公司财务,以供其办理退税手续。

三、知识链接

(一)信用证下交单

信用证下交单是指出口商(信用证受益人)在规定时间内向银行提交信用证规定的全套单据,银行审核这些单据,然后根据信用证条款中的具体付汇方式办理结汇。

交单应注意以下三点。

(1)单据的种类和份数应与信用证的规定相符。

(2)单据内容应正确,包括所用文字应与信用证一致。

(3)交单时间必须在信用证规定的交单期和有效期之内。

教学视频

(二)信用证下审单要求

1. 审单标准

在信用证结算方式下,银行审单的标准是:单证一致、单单一致,即所提交的单据与单据之间内容要一致,单据内容与信用证的要求要一致。

UCP600 在第二条中对相符交单给出了明确的定义:提交的单据必须与信用证条款、UCP600 中的相关适用条款以及国际标准银行实务一致。UCP600 中所规定的"一致",并不是过去银行所倡导的"严格相符",而是相对宽松和灵活的一致,例如,UCP600 第十四条 d 款规定:单据中的数据,在与信用证、单据本身以及国际标准银行实务参照解读时,无须与该单据本身中的数据、其他要求的单据或信用证中的数据等同一致,但不得矛盾。第十四条 e 款规定:除商业发票外,其他单据中的货物、服务或履约行为的描述,如果有的话,可使用与信用证中的描述不矛盾的概括性用语。《关于审核跟单信用证项下单据的国际标准银行实务》中也要求信用证项下提交的单据不得互相矛盾。因此,要根据文件所倡导的"不得相互矛盾"精神,指导"单证一致、单单一致"的审单原则。

2. 主要单据的审核要点

(1)汇票的审核要点。

汇票的审核要点如下。

① 汇票的出票时间和地点必须正确;

② 付款期限必须符合销售合同或信用证的规定;

③ 大小写金额及货币名称和代号必须一致而且规范;在使用信用证时,汇票金额不能超出信用证限额;

④ 出票人、受款人、付款人名称和地址必须填写正确;

⑤ 出票人印章和/或签字不得遗漏;

⑥ 出票条款须填写正确;

⑦ 信用证规定的其他附加条款。

(2) 商业发票的审核要点。

商业发票的审核要点如下。

① 商业发票上的货物描述应该与信用证中的货物描述一致。如果实际发运的货物比信用证规定更详细,则在照抄信用证的内容后,可补充更翔实的信息,但不得与信用证规定相矛盾。

② 唛头是否简洁清晰,一般必须填写的内容是收货人名称、目的地名称和件数,可适当补充有关销售合同或订单号信息,应避免罗列其他内容。如果信用证对唛头做了规定,则必须与信用证中的规定一致。

③ 商业发票一般要由受益人出具,如果信用证中的要求为"Manually signed",则必须由单位主要负责人手签。

④ 在有多品种、规格,但价格又不一样时,要注意审核每种货物金额之和是否与总金额一致。

⑤ 如果在销售合同中有支付佣金或折扣的规定,则必须明确是明佣明折,还是暗佣暗扣,从而确定发票上是否显示。如果信用证中有明确规定,则按规定办理。

⑥ 一般出口商都会在发票上注明信用证号码、开证行名称、启运地和目的地等项目内容,若信用证未要求,可不注明,但当出口商自行打上时,必须确保正确;

⑦ 如果信用证规定将总金额分项表示,即注明成本价、运费、保险费,可能还有佣金等,要注意分项金额之和应与总金额一致;

⑧ 信用证中规定的附加条款在商业发票上有无体现。

(3) 运输单据的审核要点。

运输单据的审核要点如下。

① 运输单据的名称和类别须符合信用证或销售合同的规定。如果信用证或销售合同要求用海运提单,则须审核提供的是否是港至港提单;如果指定为空运,则必须审核航空运单等。

② 托运人一般应为出口商或信用证的受益人。在转让信用证项下,可接受以受让人作为托运人。

③ 提单抬头与背书要求与信用证是否相符。

④ 被通知人的名称和详细地址及通信方式与信用证要求是否一致。有时信用证加列通知开证行,要审查是否照办。

⑤ 审核提单时应注意海运提单是否为"已装船"提单,提单上必须用"装船批注"表明货已装上某一具名船只,该装船批注的日期即视为装运日期,因此它不得迟于信用证的装运期。

⑥ 运输单据对货物描述的要求与商业发票对货物描述的要求不同,在运输单据中,对货物的描述可使用统称,不需要详细列具体规格,但不能与信用证、发票中货物的描述矛盾。

⑦ 提单对运费条款的规定与成交条件是否矛盾。

(4) 保险单据的审核要点。

保险单据的审核要点如下。

① 保险人和保险单据的名称应符合信用证规定。

② 被保险人应按照信用证的规定缮制或为信用证的受益人。

③ 保险标的物一般为货物的总称,应与运输单据相同。

④ 承保风险应符合信用证关于保险险别的规定,包括险别、使用条款、生效日期。

⑤ 保险期限应符合信用证的规定,启运地、目的地、运输工具、航程则必须与运输单据一致。

⑥ 保险金额的大小写必须一致;金额必须符合信用证的要求,信用证未注明金额要求时,应按发票上货物金额的110%投保;投保货币应符合信用证中的规定(有特殊规定的除外)。

⑦ 除非信用证要求注明,保险费一般可不显示,只打"As Arranged"。

⑧ 代理人,即保险公司在目的地的理赔代理人,应有全称和详细地址;理赔地点一般应为目的地。

⑨ 保险单的签发日期不得迟于运输单据的签发日期;承保公司签字与盖章不得遗漏。

⑩ 保险单的背书需按信用证规定办理。

3. 单证不符的处理办法

在实际操作中,如果单证不符已经产生且无法避免,一般可以尝试用以下方法解决。

(1) 与开证申请人协商解决。

开证行拒付并不意味着开证申请人拒付,如果开证申请人最终放弃不符点,尽管开证行并不受开证申请人决定的约束,但一般会配合开证申请人付款。所以开证行拒付后,如果不符点确实成立,应分析与开证申请人之间的关系以及此笔交易的实际情况,以决定怎样与其交涉,说服开证申请人接受不符点并付款。只要货物质量过关,商品市场价格较好,开证申请人一般不会以此为借口拒绝接受单据。

(2) 降价或另寻买主。

如果不符点确实是成立的,且货物质量有缺陷,因市场不佳或客户信誉不好,开证申请人有时会拒绝付款,或为转嫁市场价格波动的风险而提出降价的要求。遇到这种情况,一般可采取三个办法。一是从合作角度考虑,尽量争取开证申请人的让步,并在日后的贸易往来中给以其他优惠,从而避免当笔业务的经济损失。二是在交涉不力的前提下,可答应客户降价的请求。三是可权衡利弊,根据市场情况,积极联系新的买主,如市场情况较好的话,也可以将此作为与客户交涉的策略。就一般情形而言,开证申请人关心的是自身的利润,如果商品市场价格趋升,开证申请人不会冒同时损失利润和客户的风险而坚持拒付。

(3) 退单退货。

在开证行提出实质性不符点、拒付行为又很规范,与客户交涉不力、寻找新买主而不得的情况下,就只有退单退货了。不过在做出此决定之前,一定要仔细核算运回货物所需的费用和货值之间是否有账可算,有利益即迅速安排退运,因为时间拖得越久,费用(港杂、仓储等)就越高;若运回货物得不偿失,则不如将货物放在目的港,任由对方海关处理。

四、能力训练

浙江慧峰医用敷料有限责任公司操作案例

浙江慧峰医用敷料有限责任公司于2019年3月28日向韩国VATK公司出口一批医用敷料,单证员在出货后按照销售合同(见样单8-12)及信用证(见样单8-13)的要求缮制结汇单证。交单之前单证员认真对照制单要求及出货信息对商业发票(见样单8-14)、装箱单(见样单8-15)、检验证书(见样单8-16)、提单(见样单8-17)进行了审核。

样单 8-12　销售合同

Sales Contract
ZHEJIANG HUIFENG SURGICAL DRESSINGS CO.,LTD
Address: No. 288Xiaoshu Road, Hangzhou, Zhejiang, China.
TEL: 0571-85093×× 　　FAX: 0571-85093×××

DATE: JAN. 20. 2019
S/C NO.: HF-DMS0901

VATKKOREA REP. COMPANY LTD.
567-5, DO LUNG-HI, KO DUCK-MYEN, PYUNG TAEK-SI, GYEONG GI-DO, KOREA REP.

We as Seller confirm having sold you as Buyer the following goods on the terms and conditions as stated below and on the back hereof.

QUANTITY	DESCRIPTION	PRICE	SHIPMENT
18 000rolls 54 000rolls 162 000rolls 126 000rolls	130G/M 100％ COTTON ELASTIC BANDAGE 5 cm * 4 m 7.5 cm * 4 m 10 cm * 4 m 15 cm * 4 m	$0.1247 $0.1759 $0.2282 $0.3305	March. 2019

Total Amount: USD90 354.6

General Terms and Conditions

1. F.O.B, SHANGHAI, CHINA
2. PORT OF LOADING: SHANGHAI, CHINA; PORT OF DESTINATION: BUSAN, KOREA REP.
3. MODE OF TRANSPORT: BY SEA
4. DATE OF DELIVERY: MARCH, 30, 2019
5. PACKING: EXPORT PACKING
6. TERMS OF PAYMENT: Documentary L/C (at sight)
7. PRINCIPAL TO PRINCIPAL BASIS: This Contract Recognizes the fact that it is on a principal to principal basis between Seller and Buyer.
8. QUANTITY: Quantity is subject to a variation of zero percent(0％) plus or minus at Seller's option.
9. SHIPMENT: The date of Bill of Lading shall be taken as the conclusive date of shipment. Partial shipment and/or transshipment shall be permitted, unless otherwise stated on the face hereof. Seller shall not be responsible for non-shipment or late shipment in whole or in part by reason of Force Majeure, such as fires, floods, earthquakes, tempests, strikes, lockouts, and other industrial disputes, mobilization, war, threat of war, riots, civil commotion, hostilities, blockade, requisition vessel, and any other contingencies beyond Seller's control.
10. INSPECTION: Inspection performed under the Import manager of VATU KOREA REP. Company LTD. is final respect of quality and/or conditions of the contracted goods, unless otherwise stated on the face hereof.
11. TRADE TERMS: The trade terms used in this contract shall be governed and interpreted by the provisions of INCOTERMS(2000 edition) unless otherwise specifically stated.
12. INFRINGEMENT: Buyer shall hold Seller harmless from liability for any infringement with regard to patent, trade mark, design and/or copyright originated or chosen by Buyer.
13. CLAIM: Any claim by Buyer must be made in writing within fourteen(14) days will be recognized if they are used.

14. ARBITRATION: Any dispute arising from or in connection with the Sales Contract shall be settled through friendly negotiation. In case no settlement can be reached, the dispute shall then be submitted to China International Economic and Trade Arbitration Commission (CIETAC), Suzhou Commission for arbitration in accordance with its rules in effect at the time of applying for arbitration. The arbitral award is final and binding upon both parties.
15. GOVERNING LAW: This Contract shall be governed in all respects by the laws of .
16. This Contract is in two copies effective since being signed and sealed by both parties.

BUYER	SELLER
VATU KOREA REP. COMPANY LTD.	ZHE JIANG HUIFENG SURGICAL DRESSINGS CO., LTD
(Signed)	(Signed)

样单 8-13 信用证

MT S700	ISSUE OF A DOCUMENTARY CREDIT
APPLICATION HEADER	* KOOKMIN BANK
	* SEOUL
	* (HEAD OFFICE)
SEQUENCE OF TOTAL	* 27: 1/1
FORM OF DOC. CREDIT	* 40A: IRREVOCABLE
DOC. CREDIT NUMBER	* 20: M07E1901NS20096
DATE OF ISSUE	31C: 190121
APPLICABLE RULES	* 40E: UCP LATEST VERSION
EXPIRY	* 31D: DATE 190406 PLACE AT NEGOTIATING BANK
APPLICANT	* 50: VATK KOREA REP. COMPANY LTD.
	567-5, DO LUNG-HI, KO DUCK-MYEN, PYUNG TAEK-SI, GYEONG GI-DO, KOREA REP.
BENEFICIARY	* 59: IHEJIANG HUIFENG SURGICAL DRESSINGS CO., LTD
	NO. 288 XIAOSHU ROAD, HANGZHOU, ZHEJIANG, CHINA
AMOUNT	* 32B: CURRENCY USD AMOUNT 90354.60
AVAILABLE WITH/BY	* 41D: ANY BANK
	BY NEGOTIATION
DRAFT AT	42C: AT SIGHT
DRAWEE	42A: * KOOKMIN BANK
	* SEOUL
	* (HEAD OFFICE)
PARTIAL SHIPMENT	43P: ALLOWED
TRANSSHIPMENT	43T: ALLOWED
PORT OF LOADING	44E: SHANGHAI PORT
PORT OF DISCHARGE	44F: BUSAN PORT, KOREA REP KOAEA
LATEST DATE OF SHIP.	44C: 190330
DESCRIPT. OF GOODS	45A: 130G/M100%COTTON ELASTIC BANDAGE DETAILS ARE AS PER SALES CONTRACT ISSUED ON JAN. 20, 2019
	FOB SHANGHAI
	ORIGIN: CHINA
DOCUMENTS REQUIRED	46A:
	+ SIGNED COMMERCIAL INVOICE IN 3 FOLD.
	+ PACKING LIST IN 3 FOLD.

+ FULL SET OF ORIGINAL CLEAN ON BOARD MARINE BILL OF LADING MADE OUT TO ORDER OF KOOKMIN BANK, MARKED FREIGHT COLLECT AND NOTIFY THE APPLICANT.

+ CERTIFICATE OF INSPECTION IN 3 FOLD.

ADDITIONAL COND. 47A:

+ A FEE OF USD 80 IS TO BE DEDUCTED FROM EACH DRAWING FOR THE ACCOUNT OF BENEFICIARY. IF DOCUMENTS ARE PRESENTED WITH DISCREPANCY(IES).

+ ALL DOCUMENTS MUST BEAR NUMBER OF L/C.

DETAILS OF CHARGES 71B: ALL BANKINGCOMMISSIONS AND CHARGES INCLUDING REIMBURSEMENT COMMISSIONS OUTSIDE SOUTH KOREA REP. ARE FOR BENEFICIARY.

PRESENTATION PERIOD 48: DOCUMENTS MUST BE PRESENTED FOR NEGOTIATION WITHIN 21 DAYS AFTER THE DATE OF SHIPMENT BUT WITHIN THE VALIDITY OF THE CREDIT.

CONFIRMATION *49: WITHOUT

INSTRUCTION 78: + PLEASE REIMBURSE YOURSELVES BY PRESENTING BENEFICIARY'S DRAFT TO THE DRAWEE BANK.

+ WACHOVIA BANK HOLDS SPECIAL INSTRUCTION REGARDING DOCUMENTS DISPOSAL AND REIMBURSEMENT OF THIS L/C.

"ADVISE THROUGH" 57A: BANK OF CHINA

* HANGZHOU

*(HANGZHOU BRANCH)

其他附加资料:

SPECIFICATION	ROLLS/CTN	G.W.(KG)	N.W.(KG)
5 cm * 4 m	720ROLLS	@21	@19
7.5 cm * 4 m	480ROLLS	@21	@19
10 cm * 4 m	360ROLLS	@21	@19
15 cm * 4 m	240ROLLS	@21	@19

样单 8-14 商业发票

浙江慧峰医用敷料有限责任公司

ZHEJIANG HUIFENG SURGICAL DRESSINGS CO.,LTD

NO. 288 XIAOSHU ROAD, HANGZHOU, ZHEJIANG, CHINA

TEL: 0571-85093×× FAX: 0571-85093×××

COMMERCIAL INVOICE

TO: VATKKOREA REP. CO.,LTD.
567-5, DO LUNG-HI, KO DUCK-MYEN,
PYUNG TAEK-SI, GYEONG GI-DO, KOREA REP.

INVOICE NO.: HF-DMSI09001
DATE: MAR. 17, 2019
S/C NO.: HF-DWS0901
L/C NO.: M07E1901NS20096

Marks	Commodity Description	Quantity	Unit Price	Amount
N/M	130G/M 100% COTTON ELASTIC BANDAGE			FOB SHANGHAI
	5 cm*4 m	18 000ROLLS	$0.1247	$2 244.60
	7.5 cm*4 m	5 400ROLLS	$0.1759	$9 498.60
	10 cm*4 m	162 000ROLLS	$0.2282	$36 968.40
	15 cm*4 m	126 000ROLLS	$0.3305	$41 643.00
	TOTAL:	360 000ROLLS		$90 354.60

DETAILES ARE AS PER SALES CONTRACT ISSUED ON JAN. 20,2019

浙江慧峰医用敷料有限责任公司
ZHEJIANG HUIFENG SURGICAL DRESSINGS CO.,LTD.

样单8-15 装箱单

浙江慧峰医用敷料有限责任公司
ZHEJIANG HUIFENG SURGICAL DRESSINGS CO.,LTD

NO. 288 XIAOSHU ROAD, HANGZHOU, ZHEJIANG, CHINA
TEL: 0571-85093×× FAX: 0571-85093×××

PACKING LIST

TO: VATKKOREA REP. CO.,LTD.   INVOICE NO.: HF-DMSI09001
567-5, DO LUNG-HI, KO DUCK-MYEN,   DATE: MAR. 17,2019
PYUNG TAEK-SI, GYEONG GI-DO, KOREA REP.   S/C NO.: HF-DMS0901
   L/C NO.: M07E1907NS20096

Marks	Commodity Description	Quantity	Quantity (roll)	Gross Weight	Net Weight
N/M	130G/M 100% COTTON ELASTIC BANDAGE				
	5 cm*4 m	25 CTNS	18 000ROLLS	525KGS	475KGS
	7.5 cm*4 m	112 CTNS	53 760ROLLS	2 352KGS	2 128KGS
	10 cm*4 m	450 CTNS	162 000ROLLS	9 450KGS	8 550KGS
	15 cm*4 m	525 CTNS	126 000ROLLS	11 025KGS	9 975KGS
	75 cm*4 m	1 CTNS	240ROLLS	12KGS	10KGS
		1 113 CTNS	360 000ROLLS	23 364KGS	21 138KGS

TOTAL PACKED IN 1 113 CARTONS
GR. WT: 23 364KGS
NET. WT: 21 138KGS
MEASUREMENT: 118.1CBM
ORIGIN: CHINA

浙江慧峰医用敷料有限责任公司
ZHEJIANG HUIFENG SURGICAL DRESSINGS CO.,LTD.

样单 8-16　检验证书

浙江慧峰医用敷料有限责任公司
ZHEJIANG HUIFENG SURGICAL DRESSINGS CO.,LTD
NO. 288 XIAOSHU ROAD,HANGZHOU,ZHEJIANG,CHINA
TEL：0571-85093×××　　FAX：0571-85093×××

CERTIFICATE OF INSPECTION

TO：VATK KOREA REP. CO.,LTD.　　　　　　　INVOICE NO.：HF-DESI09001
　　567-5, DE LUNG-HI, KO DUCK-MYEN,　　　DATED：MAR. 17, 2019
　　PYUNG TAEK-SI, GYEONG GI-DO, KOREA REP.　S/C NO.：HF-DMS0901
　　　　　　　　　　　　　　　　　　　　　　L/C NO.：M07E1901NS20096

Product Name：100% cotton elastic bandage

Commodity Description	Business Standard	Test Result
5 cm*4 m	1. Length of bandage (fully stretched)：4 m±0.1 m	Qualified
7.5 cm*4 m 10 cm*4 m	2. Width of bandage：5 cm±2 mm,7.5 cm±3 mm,10 cm ±5 mm,15 cm±5 mm	Qualified
15 cm*4 m	3. The elasticity of bandage shall be not less than 180%	≥200%

Examiner Signature：　　　　　　　　　　　　Checker：
Report Date：MAR. 25, 2019

　　　　　　　　　　　浙江慧峰医用敷料有限责任公司
　　　　　　　　　　　ZHEJIANG HUIFENG SURGICAL DRESSINGS CO.,LTD.

样单 8-17　提单

1. Shipper Insert Name, Address and Phone	B/L No. OBSSO0984
ZHEJIANG HUIFENG SURGICAL DRESSINGS CO.,LTD NO. 288 XIAOSHU ROAD,HANGZHOU,ZHEJIANG, CHZNA	 **中远集装箱运输有限公司** **COSCO CONTAINER LINES**
2. Consignee Insert Name, Address and Phone	TLX：33057 COSCO CN
TO ORDER	FAX：0086(021) 6545-8984
	ORIGINAL Port-to-Port or Combined Transport **BILL OF LADING**

3. Notify Party Insert Name, Address and Phone It is agreed that no responsibility shall attach to the Carrier or his agents for failure to notify) VATK KOREA REP. CO.,LTD. 567-5, DO LUNG-HI, KO DUCK-MYEN, PYUNG TAEK-SI, GYEONG GI-DO, KOREA REP.	RECEIVED in external apparent good order and condition except as other-Wise noted. The total number of packages or unites stuffed in the container, The description of the goods and the weights shown in this Bill of Lading are Furnished by the Merchants, and which the carrier has no reasonable means Of checking and is not a part of this Bill of Lading contract. The carrier has Issued the number of Bills of Lading stated below, all of this tenor and date, One of the original Bills of Lading must be surrendered and endorsed or signed against the delivery of the shipment and whereupon any other original Bills of Lading shall be void. The Merchants agree to be bound by the terms And conditions of this Bill of Lading as if each had personally signed this Bill of Lading. SEE clause 4 on the back of this Bill of Lading (Terms continued on the back Hereof, please read carefully). * Applicable Only When Document Used as a Combined Transport Bill of Lading.

4. Combined Transport *	5. Combined Transport *
Pre-carriage by	Place of Receipt
6. Ocean Vessel Voy. No.	7. Port of Loading
GOLDEN COMPANION V. 907N	NINGBD
8. Port of Discharge	9. Combined Transport *
BUSAN PORT, KOREA REP	Place of Delivery

续表

Marks &. Nos. Container/Seal No.	No. of Containers or Packages	Description of Goods (If Dangerous Goods, See Clause 20)	Gross Weight kgs	Measurement
N/M COSU3438253/232645 COSU548582/434448	1113CTNS	SHIPPER LOAD, COUNT &. SEAL 130G/M 100% COTTON ELASTIC BANDAGE 2*40'FCL CY-CY FREIGHT PREPAID	24 364KGS ON BOARD MAR. 28, 2019	118.10CBM
		Description of Contents for Shipper's Use Only (Not part of This B/L Contract)		

10. Total Number of containers and/or packages (in words) SAY ONE THOUSAND ONE HUNDRED AND THIRTEEN CTNS ONLY				
Subject to Clause 7 Limitation				
11. Freight &. Charges	Revenue Tons	Rate	Per	Prepaid	Collect
Declared Value Charge					

Ex. Rate:	Prepaid at	Payable at	Place and date of issue
			SHANGHAI, MAR 28, 2019
	Total Prepaid	No. of Original B(s)/L	Signed for the Carrier, COSCO CONTAINER LINES
		THREE(3)	AS CARRIER
LADEN ON BOARD THE VESSEL			
DATE		BY	

五、岗位拓展

讨论话题：单证出现不符点的处理问题。

浙江慧峰医用敷料有限责任公司出口一批医用绷带到意大利，这笔业务采用信用证结算。出货完成后单证员把整套结汇单证交给议付行，结果银行国际业务部的工作人员在审单后说存在如下不符点：

（1）商业发票条款之一为：MANUALLY SIGNED COMMERCIAL INVOICE IN THREE COPIES.

信用证中要求对商业发票"MANUALLY SIGNED"，而所交的商业发票没有手签，只是盖了法人章。

（2）信用证中规定最迟装运日是2019年5月25日，而提单签发日是2019年5月26日。

（3）受益人证明条款为：BENEFICIARY'S CERTIFICATE STATING THAT ONE SET OF NON-NEGOTIABLE SHIPPING DOCUMENTS HAS BEEN SENT TO THE APPLICANT BY DHL COURIER AFTER SHIPMENT AND THE COURIER RECEIPT SHOULD ACCOMPANY THE DOCUMENTS. 受益人证明条款要求出口商在货物装运后寄装运单据的副本给进口商，并提供快递收据作为结汇单据，而在所交的单据中没有快递收据。

（4）交单时保险单没有进行空白背书。

讨论引导：如何处理这些不符点？

附录一
企业单证实例

Seller:

售货确认书
SALES CONFIRMATION

NO: 301018
DATE: MAR. 31, 2003

BUYER: HUSSAIN TAHER TRADING EST.

SELLER:

兹经买卖双方同意成交下列商品订立条款如下:
The under signed Sellers and Buyers have agreed to close the following transactions according to the terms and conditions stipulated below:

货号 Article Number	品名及规格 Description of Goods	数量 Quantity	单价 Unit Price	金额 Amount
20MM-25MM-30MM	SUPER BRAND BRASS PADLOCK PACKING:50CARDS IN A CARTON	10000 CARDS IN 200CARTONS	C&F C1% DUBAI,U.A.E USD0.86/CARD	US$8600.00 TOTAL:US$8600.00

1. 装运期
   Time of shipment: WITHIN 45 DAYS AFTER RECEIPT OF THE ADVANCE PAYMENT

2. 装运口岸和目的地: 由 至 不准许分批与转船.
   Loading Port & Destination: From CHINA to DUBAI, U.A.E. with transshipment and partial shipments allowed.

3. 保险: □由卖方按发票金额110%投保一切险及战争险, 按1981年1月1日中国人民保险公司条款负责. □由买方自理.
   Insurance: □To be effected by the Sellers for 110% of invoice value against All Risks and War Risks as per C.I.C. dated 01/01/1981. □To be effected by the Buyer.

4. 付款条件:
   Terms of Payment:10% OF THE AMOUNT ADVANCED PAYMENT, THE BALANCE AGAINST THE FAX OF B/L.

5. 品质/数量异议: 如买方提出异议,凡属品质异议须于货到目的口岸之日起30天内提出,凡属数量异议须于货到目的口岸之日起15天内提出,对所装货物所提出任何异议属于保险公司、运输公司其他有关运输机构或邮递机构责任者,售方不负任何责任.
   Quality/Quantity Discrepancy: In case of quality discrepancy, claim should be filed by the Buyer within 30 days after the arrival the goods at port of destination. while for quantity discrepancy claim should be filed by the Buyer within 15 days after the arrival of the goods at port of destination. It is understood that the Seller shall not be liable for any discrepancy of the goods shipped due to causes for which the Insurance Company, Shipping Company and other transportation organization and/or Post Office are liable.

6. 本确认书内所述全部或部分商品,如因人力不可抗拒的原因,以致不能履行或延迟交货,售方概不负责.
   The Seller shall not be held liable for failure or delay in delivery of the entire lot or a part of the goods under this Sales Confirmation in consequence of any Force Majeure incidents.

7. 买方应于收到本售货确认书后5天内答回一份,逾期本确认书须经售方进一步确认,否则无效.
   The Buyer is requested to sign and return one copy of this Sales Confirmation within 5 day after receipt of the same when 5 days are overdue, the confirmation shall be invalid except that it is further confirmed by the sellers.

8. 仲裁: 凡因执行本合同所发生的或与本合同有关的一切争议,应由双方通过友好协商解决,如果协商不能解决,应提交中国国际经济贸易仲裁委员会根据该会现行的仲裁规则进行仲裁,仲裁裁决是终局的,对双方都有约束力.
   Arbitration: All disputes arising from the execution of, or in connection with this contract, shall be settled amicably through friendly negotiation in case no settlement can be reached through negotiation, the case shall then be submitted to China International Economic and Trade Arbitration Commission, for arbitration in accordance with its rules. Chinese law shall governing law of this Sales Confirmation The arbitration in accordance with its rules. Chinese law shall governing law of this Sales Confirmation The arbitral award is final and binding upon both parties.

买方   卖方
Confirmed by:

广州市外经实业贸易有限公司
GUANGZHOU FOREIGN ECONOMIC
ENTERPRISES & TRADING CO.,LTD.

地址：中国广州市人民北路691号金信大厦B座6楼
Add: 6/F. Block B, Jin Xin Bldg.,
691 Renmin Rd. North, Guangzhou China.

电话 Tel: 81080735
电传 Telex:
传真 Fax:81080752
电子邮箱 E-mail: get.company@163.net

成交确认书
SALES CONFIRMATION

买方 Buyers: ORCHARD SUPPLY HARDWARE
地址 Address: 2650 N MACARTHUR DRIVE TRACY, CA 95376
电话 TEL: 电传 TELEX: 传真 FAX:

编号 No.
日期 Date:
订单号码: 5315-A
Order No.

兹经买卖双方同意成交下列商品订立条款如下：
The undersigned Sellers and Buyers have agreed to close the following transactions according to the terms and conditions stipulated below:

包装 Packing	品名规格 DESCRIPTION		数量 Quantity	单价 Unit Price	合计 TOTAL
CARTONS	1001	4'BAMBOO TORCH	10368PCS	$0.215	$2229.12
				合约总值 Total Contract Value:	$2229.12

1. 价格条件
   Price condition:
2. 装运期
   Time of Shipment:
3. 装运口岸至目的地 SHANGHAI 由广州至 TRACY, CA VIA OAKLAND 批与转船．
   Loading Port & Destination: From Guangzhou to _____ withtranshipment and partial shipments allowed
4. 保险 由卖方按发票全部金额110%投保至 _____ 为止的 _____ 险．按中国海洋运输保险条款（1995/1/1）办理．
   Insurance: To be effected by Sellers for 110% of full invoice value covering _____ up to _____ only, subject to C. I. C(1/1/81)
5. 付款条件 买方须于20 年 月 日前开具保兑的、不可撤消、可转让、可分割的即期信用证给卖方．信用证必须具有在装运完成后直到第15天仍有在中国认付的有效期；否则卖方有权取消本售货合约，不另通知，并保留因此而发生的一切损失的索赔权．
   Terms of Payment: By confirmed, irrevocable, transferable and divisible, Letter of Credit to be available by sight draft to reach the Sellers before _____ and to remain valid for negotiation in China until the 15 th day after the date of shipment, failing which the Sellers reserve the right to cancel this Sales Confirmation without further notice and to claim from the Buyer for losses resulting therefrom.
6. 装船标记
   Shipping Mark:

卖方
The Sellers

买方
The Buyers

```
2003DEC25 14:58:36                                    LOGICAL TERMINAL HUP3
MT S700              ISSUE OF A DOCUMENTARY CREDIT         PAGE 00001
                                                           FUNC ZJHU700
MSGACK  DWS7651 AUTH OK, KEY B1031221DB6AA793, BKCHCNBJ FNBB**** RECORD
BASIC HEADER         F-01-BKCHCNBJA92G-1018-820324
APPLICATION HEADER   O 700 1520 031224 FNBBUS33AXXX 8452 391497 031225 0420 N
                              *FLEET NATIONAL BANK
                              *BOSTON, MA
USER HEADER          SERVICE CODE      103:
                     BANK. PRIORITY    113: ZJTR
                     MSG USER REF.     108: 031224033700
                     INFO. FROM CI     115:
SEQUENCE OF TOTAL    *27   : 1 / 1
FORM OF DOC. CREDIT  *40 A : IRREVOCABLE
DOC. CREDIT NUMBER   *20   : 511451607
DATE OF ISSUE        31 C  : 031224
EXPIRY               *31 D : DATE 040318 PLACE COUNTRY OF BENEFICIARY
APPLICANT            *50   : MERC USA INC.
                             41 NEWMAN STREET
                             HACKENSACK,, NJ 07601
BENEFICIARY          *59   : HUZHOU SEVEN FORTUNE IMP AND EXP CO
                             LTD  313 BINHE ROAD HUZHOU
                             ZHEJIANG, CHINA 313000
AMOUNT               *32 B :           CURRENCY USD AMOUNT 71,752,80
POS. / NEG. TOL. (%)  39 A : 05 / 05
AVAILABLE WITH/BY    *41 D : ANY BANK
                             BY NEGOTIATION
DRAFTS AT ...         42 C : DRAFTS AT SIGHT FOR 100 PERCENT OF
                             INVOICE VALUE
DRAWEE                42 D : FLEET NATIONAL BANK
PARTIAL SHIPMENTS     43 P : ALLOWED
TRANSSHIPMENT         43 T : NOT ALLOWED
LOADING IN CHARGE     44 A :
                             CHINA
FOR TRANSPORT TO ...  44 B :
                             NEW YORK
LATEST DATE OF SHIP.  44 C : 040228
DESCRIPT. OF GOODS    45 A :
              100 PERCENT POLYESTER DYED MEN'S GARMENTS
              STYLE 19A56 SHIRTS, 1122 PCS., USD3.85/PC
              STYLE 19356,27656,9456 SHIRTS, 6870 PCS, USD 3.65/PC
              STYLE P0556 PANTS, 7992 PCS, USD 5.30/PC
              TOTAL QTY - 7992 SHIRTS AND 7992 PANTS
              FREE ON BOARD CHINA
DOCUMENTS REQUIRED    46 A :
              DOCUMENTS TO BE PRESENTED (ORIGINALS UNLESS OTHERWISE STATED):
              1- SIGNED COMMERCIAL INVOICE IN ONE ORIGINAL AND THREE COPIES
              2- PACKING LIST IN ONE ORIGINAL AND TWO COPIES
              3- BENEFICIARY SIGNED STATEMENT CERTIFYING THAT ONE COPY OF EACH
              DOCUMENT HAS BEEN FAXED TO MERC USA, INC AT FAX NO. 201-489-7636
              WITHIN 5 DAYS AFTER THE SHIPMENT.
              4- SIGNED CLEAN FULL SET ON BOARD MARINE BILL(S) OF LADING WITH
              ON BOARD NOTATION DATED NOT LATER THAN LATEST SHIPPING DATE,
              EVIDENCING CHINA AS PORT OF LOADING AND NEW YORK AS PORT OF
              DISCHARGE, TO THE ORDER OF FLEET NATIONAL BANK MARKED 'FREIGHT
              COLLECT' SHOWING 'NOTIFY MERC USA INC., 41 NEWMAN STREET,
              HACKENSACK,, NJ 07601'. ALSO NOTIFY STILE ASSOCIATES, LTD., 181
              SOUTH FRANKLIN AVE., 4TH FLOOR VALLEY STREAM, NY 11581, TEL:
              516-394-2100 AND FAX: 516-394-2121.
ADDITIONAL COND.      47 A :
              ALL DOCUMENTS PRESENTED MUST BE IN ENGLISH.
```

```
                                                      LOGICAL TERMINAL HUP3
2003DEC25 14:58:36                                    PAGE 00002
MT S700          ISSUE OF A DOCUMENTARY CREDIT        FUNC ZJHU700
                                                      UMR  16194157
```

IF WE SEND A NOTICE OF DISCREPANCIES TO THE PRESENTOR OR
OTHERWISE REFUSE DOCUMENTS PRESENTED TO US, WE MAY REVOKE OUR
REFUSAL, RETRACT ANY STATEMENT THAT WE HOLD THE DOCUMENTS AT THE
PRESENTOR'S DISPOSAL, AND HONOR THE DOCUMENTS BY TAKING THEM UP
AND PAYING, ACCEPTING, OR INCURRING A DEFERRED PAYMENT
UNDERTAKING FOR THEM, AS THE CASE MAY BE, PROVIDED THAT WE DO SO
BEFORE THE CLOSE OF THE BANKING DAY FOLLOWING THE DAY OF OUR
RECEIPT OF THE PRESENTOR'S DEMAND FOR THEIR RETURN OR OTHER
DISPOSITION.
ALL PARTIES TO THIS LETTER OF CREDIT ARE ADVISED THAT THE U.S.
GOVERNMENT HAS IN PLACE SPECIFIC SANCTIONS AGAINST CERTAIN
COUNTRIES, RELATED ENTITIES AND OTHER INDIVIDUALS. UNDER THESE
SANCTIONS FLEET NATIONAL BANK AND ANY OF ITS AFFILIATES OR
SUBSIDIARIES ARE PROHIBITED FROM ENGAGING IN TRANSACTIONS THAT
ARE SUBJECT TO THESE SANCTIONS.
INSURANCE EFFECTED BY THE BUYER.
WE WILL DEDUCT FROM THE BENEFICIARY 75.00 USD FOR EACH SET OF
DISCREPANT DOCUMENTS IN ADDITION, TELEX EXPENSES, IF ANY,
INCURRED BY US AS A RESULT OF DISCREPANT DOCUMENTS ARE ALSO FOR
THE BENEFICIARY'S ACCOUNT.
THE NUMBER AND DATE OF THE CREDIT AND THE NAME OF OUR BANK MUST
BE QUOTED ON ALL DRAFT(S) REQUIRED.
WE HEREBY AGREE WITH DRAWERS AND/OR BONAFIDE HOLDERS OF DRAFTS
DRAWN UNDER AND IN COMPLIANCE WITH THE TERMS OF THIS CREDIT, THAT
THESE DRAFTS SHALL BE DULY HONORED UPON PRESENTATION TO THE
DRAWEE.
THE AMOUNT OF EACH DRAFT NEGOTIATED UNDER THIS CREDIT MUST BE
ENDORSED ON THE REVERSE OF THIS CREDIT, AND THE PRESENTATION OF
ANY SUCH DRAFT TO US SHALL BE A WARRANTY BY THE PRESENTING BANK
THAT SUCH ENDORSEMENT HAS BEEN MADE.
FORWARD DOCUMENTS AND DRAFTS IN ONE MAILING:
    FLEET NATIONAL BANK
    120 BROADWAY, 10TH FLOOR
    SUITE 1025
    NEW YORK, NY 10271
    ATTN: TRADE SERVICES DEPARTMENT
THE USE OF ANY OTHER MAILING ADDRESS MAY RESULT IN DELIVERY
DELAYS FOR WHICH WE DISCLAIM RESPONSIBILITY.

```
DETAILS OF CHARGES    71 B : ALL BANKING CHARGES OUTSIDE OF
                             FLEET NATIONAL BANK ARE FOR THE
                             BENEFICIARY'S ACCOUNT.
PRESENTATION PERIOD   48   : DOCUMENTS MUST BE PRESENTED WITHIN
                             15 DAYS OF TRANSPORT DOCUMENT
                             SHIPMENT DATE/ FCR RECEIPT DATE AND
                             WITHIN THE L/C VALIDITY.
CONFIRMATION         *49   : WITHOUT
"ADVISE THROUGH"      57 D : BANK OF CHINA
                             NO. 128 RENMIN ROAD, HUZHOU,
                             HUZHOU BRANCH
                             ZHEJIANG, CHINA 313000
SEND. TO REC. INFO.   72   : AC 018090065008 TELEX NO. 373023
                             HUSBR CN, BENE TEL NO.
                             86-572-211-4896
TRAILER                    : ORDER IS <MAC:> <PAC:> <ENC:> <CHK:> <TNC:> <PDE:>
                             MAC: 97446DF9
```

湖州经济技术开发区进出口有限公司
HUZHOU ECONOMIC&TECHNOLOGICAL DEVELOPMENT ZONE IMP. & EXP.CO., LTD.
ADDRESS: 208 LONGXI ROAD, HUZHOU, ZHEJIANG, CHINA
TEL:0086-572-2109120,2101956　　FAX:0086-572-2103937

To: M/S
STRONG INC., LTD.
2-4-4 ARAKAWA, ARAKAWA-KU
TOKYO 116 JAPAN

发 票
INVOICE

发票号码 Invoice No.	23HZ0503
合约号码 S/C No.	22HZ026
日 期 Date	APR.28,2003

装船口岸 From: SHANGHAI　　目的地 To: YOKOHAMA, JAPAN　　信用证号数 L/C No.
开证银行 Issued by:

唛头号码 MARKS& NUMBERS	数量与货品名称 QUANTITIES & DESCRIPTION			单价 UNIT PRICE	总值 AMOUNT
N/M	FOOTWEAR OUTSOLE PLASTIC			CNF YOKOHAMA	
	7355P	30CTNS	900PRS	USD1.250/PR	USD1125.00
	7356YE	20CTNS	600PRS	USD1.250/PR	USD750.00
	7357R	20CTNS	600PRS	USD1.250/PR	USD750.00
	7358B	20CTNS	600PRS	USD1.250/PR	USD750.00
	7359P	10CTNS	300PRS	USD1.250/PR	USD375.00
	7360YE	20CTNS	600PRS	USD1.250/PR	USD750.00
	7361R	10CTNS	300PRS	USD1.250/PR	USD375.00
	7362B	20CTNS	600PRS	USD1.250/PR	USD750.00
	TTL:	150CTNS	4500PRS		TTL: USD5625.00

湖州经济技术开发区进出口有限公司
HUZHOU ECONOMIC & TECHNOLOGICAL DEVELOPMENT ZONE
IMPORT & EXPORT CO., LTD.

湖州　　宠物用品有限公司
HUZHOU　　PET PRODUCTS CO., LTD.
3/F, BLOCK E, FUCHENG BLDG, HUZHOU, ZHEJIANG, CHINA
TEL: 00-86-572-2607088; FAX: 00-86-572-2659990

MARKS & NUMBERS				发票号码 INV. NO.	18MM0113
AS PER INV.NO.	**PACKING LIST**			合约号码 S/C NO.	18MM0113
18MM0113	(WEIGHT & MEASUREMENT LIST)			日　期 DATE	JAN.22,2019

ART. NO.	DESCRIPTION	QUANTITY	PACKAGE	G.W.	N.W.	MEASUREMENTS
	ELECTRIC CANDLE SHAPE 15W	427500PCS	1425CTNS	10085.50KGS	6523.00KGS	63.68CBM
	ELECTRIC ROUND SHAPE 15W	50000PCS	100CTNS	950.00KGS	600.00KGS	6.47CBM
		TTL:	1525CTNS	11035.50KGS	7123.00KGS	70.15CBM

湖州　　宠物用品有限公司
HUZHOU　　PET PRODUCTS CO., LTD.

湖州　　　宠物用品有限公司
HUZHOU　　　PET PRODUCTS CO., LTD.
3/F, BLOCK E, FUCHENG BLDG, HUZHOU, ZHEJIANG, CHINA
TEL: 00-86-572-2607088; FAX: 00-86-572-2659990

TO: M/S MIAN MACHINERY STORES
13-BRANDRETH ROAD, LAHORE
PAKISTAN

INVOICE

发票号码 INV. NO.	18MM0113
合约号码 S/C NO.	18MM0113
日期 DATE	JAN.22,2019

装船口岸 From	目的地 To	信用证号码 Letter of Credit No.
SHANGHAI	KARACHI	

开证银行 Issued by

唛头号码 Marks & Numbers	品名描述 Description	数量 Quantities	单价 Unit Price	总值 Amount
			CNF	KARACHI
LIDO	ELECTRIC CANDLE SHAPE 15W	427500PCS	USD0.07/PC	USD29925.00
MMS	ELECTRIC ROUND SHAPE 15W	50000PCS	USD0.07/PC	USD3500.00
			TTL	USD33425.00

1. AS PER OUR PROFORMA INVOICE NO.18MM0113 Dec.06.2018
2. GOODS ARE OF CHINESE ORIGIN
3. H.S CODE 85392990

湖州　　　宠物用品有限公司
HUZHOU　　　PET PRODUCTS CO., LTD.

FROM : SHANGHAI HUA SHEN   FAX NO. : 00862165352221   APR. 25 2003 10:43AM P. 3

(12)

上海华申进出口有限公司
SHANGHAI HUA SHEN IMPORT AND EXPORT CO.,LTD.
694 HUI MIN ROAD SHANGHAI,CHINA TEL: 35100638

MARK & NOS:
JCC
HAMBURG
ORDER:9902962
STYLE:086/101
AVA2954942
C/NO.
MADE IN CHINA

装 箱 单
PACKING LIST
WEIGHT LIST
MEASUREMENT LIST

发票号：
INVOICE NO.   HC03055545
合同号
CONTRACT NO. 03PG5545
日期：
DATE: APR 25,2003

ORDER NO.9902962 LEATHER JACKET

C/NO.	48	50	52	54	56	58	TOTAL (CM)	G.W: N.W:
1-19	10						190PCS 88X67X13	19KGS 15KGS
20	9						9PCS	"
21-59		10					390PCS	"
60		8					8PCS	"
61-99			10				390PCS	"
100			8				8PCS	"
101-139				10			390PCS 92X73X13	"
140				8			8PCS	"
141-159					10		190PCS	"
160					9		9PCS	"
161-179						10	190PCS	"
180						9	9PCS	"

TOTAL PACKED IN 180 CTNS ONLY
GROSS WEIGHT:3420KGS
NET WEIGHT:2700KGS
MEASUREMENT:14.65M3

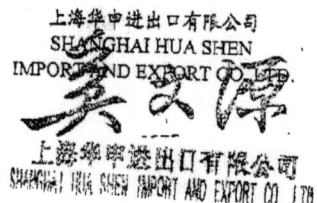

ORIGINAL

1. Goods consigned from (Exporter's business name, address, country) HUZHOU BAIYE INDUSTRY CO., LTD. 19TH FLOOR, MEIXIN BUILDING, HUZHOU, ZHEJIANG, CHINA	Reference No. G183308005680192 **GENERALIZED SYSTEM OF PREFERENCES** **CERTIFICATE OF ORIGIN** (Combined declaration and certificate) **FORM A**
2. Goods consigned to (Consignee's name, address, country) THE WILLIAMS BROTHERS CORP. STRIKE FIRST CORP. 777-781 TAPSCOTT ROAD STRIKE FIRST RECEIVING SCARBOROUGH ONTARIO M1X 1A2 (CANADA) TEL:001-416-299-7767 FAX:001-416-299-8039 MR.BILL WILLIAMS	Issued in **THE PEOPLE'S REPUBLIC OF CHINA** (Country) See notes overleaf
3. Means of transport and route (as far as known) FROM NINGBO, CHINA TO TORONTO, CANADA BY SEA	4. For official use ISSUED RETROSPECTIVELY

5. Item number	6. Marks and numbers of packages	7. Number and kind of packages, description of goods	8. Origin criterion (see notes overleaf)	9. Gross weight or other quantity	10. Number and date of invoices
1		THREE (3) PALLETS OF EMPTY FIRE EXTINGUISHER *** *** *** *** *** DELEI FIRE (PRODUCT'S NAME) QTY.: C/NO.	"P"	2024PCS	18BY802 NOV. 22, 2018

11. Certification It is hereby certified, on the basis of control carried out, that the declaration by the exporter is correct. Hangzhou, China, NOV. 29, 2018 Place and date, signature and stamp of certifying authority	12. Declaration by the exporter The undersigned hereby declares that the above details and statements are correct; that all the goods were produced in **CHINA** (country) and that they comply with the origin requirements specified for those goods in the Generalized System of Preferences for goods exported to CANADA (importing country) HUZHOU BAIYE INDUSTRY CO., LTD. Hangzhou, China, NOV. 29, 2018 Place and date, signature of authorized signatory

186043273

ORIGINAL

1. Exporter HUZHOU BAIYE INDUSTRY CO.,LTD 19TH FLOOR,MEIXIN BUILDING, HUZHOU,ZHEJIANG,CHINA TEL:0086 572 2031878/2612688 FAX:0086 572 2035922/2612000	Serial No. CCPIT342 1800102046 Certificate No. 18C3305A0256/00004
2. Consignee NAFFCO JEBEL ALI FREE ZONE DUBAI-U.A.E P.O. BOX17014 TEL:00971-4-8815653 FAX:00971-4-8816229	**CERTIFICATE OF ORIGIN** **OF** **THE PEOPLE'S REPUBLIC OF CHINA**
3. Means of transport and route FROM SHANGHAI CHINA TO DUBAI UNITED ARAB EMIRATES BY SEA	5. For certifying authority use only
4. Country / region of destination UNITED ARAB EMIRATES	VERIFY URL:HTTP://CHECK.CCPITECO.NET/

6. Marks and numbers	7. Number and kind of packages; description of goods	8. H.S.Code	9. Quantity	10. Number and date of invoices
NF (PRODUCT'S NAME) P/I NO. 2017NF47 P/O N106854 QTY. C/NO. ***	FIVE (5) PALLETS OF FIRE FIGHTING EQUIPMENT PARTS	8424.9010	11000PCS	18BY022 JAN.08,2018

11. Declaration by the exporter The undersigned hereby declares that the above details and statements are correct, that all the goods were produced in China and that they comply with the Rules of Origin of the People's Republic of China. 湖州佰业进出口有限公司 HUZHOU BAIYE INDUSTRY CO., LTD HUZHOU JAN.08,2018 Place and date, signature and stamp of authorized signatory	12. Certification It is hereby certified that the declaration by the exporter is correct. CHINA COUNCIL FOR THE PROMOTION OF INTERNATIONAL TRADE ADDRESS:4F SOUTHERN BUILDING,INTERNATIONAL TRADE BUILDING,NO.137 PENGHUANG ROAD,HUZHOU CITY,ZHEJIANG PROVINCE FAX:0086-572-2176783 TEL:0086-572-2103972 HUZHOU JAN.08,2018 Place and date, signature and stamp of certifying authority

ORIGINAL

1. Exporter's Name and Address, Country HUZHOU　　　PET PRODUCTS CO., LTD. 3/F BLOCK E, FUCHENG BLDG, HUZHOU, ZHEJIANG, CHINA TEL: 00-86-572-260　　, FAX: 00-86-572-265	CERTIFICATE NO. P193308026970003 **CERTIFICATE OF ORIGIN** **CHINA-PAKISTAN FTA** (Combined Declaration and Certificate)
2. Consignee's Name and Address, Country MACHINERY STORES 13-BRANDRETH ROAD, LAHORE PAKISTAN TEL: 00-92-42-3763 FAX: 00-92-21-3241	Issued in　THE PEOPLE'S REPUBLIC OF CHINA 　　　　　　(Country) See Instructions Overleaf
3. Producer's Name and Address, Country HUZHOU　　　PET PRODUCTS CO., LTD. 3/F BLOCK E, FUCHENG BLDG, HUZHOU, ZHEJIANG, CHINA TEL: 00-86-572-260　　FAX: 00-86-572-265	
4. Means of transport and route (as far as known) Departure Date　JAN. 28, 2019 Vessel /Flight/Train/Vehicle No.　YM EFFICIENCY 119W Port of loading　SHANGHAI, CHINA Port of discharge　KARACHI, PAKISTAN FROM SHANGHAI CHINA TO KARACHI PAKISTAN BY SEA	5. For Official Use Only ☐ Preferential Treatment Given Under China-Pakistan FTA Free Trade Area Preferential Tariff ☐ Preferential Treatment Not Given (Please state reason/s) Signature of Authorized Signatory of the importing Country

6. Item number	7. Marks and numbers on packages; Number and kind of packages; description of goods; HS code of the importing country	8. Origin Criterion	9. Gross Weight, Quantity and FOB value	10. Number and date of invoices	11. Remarks
1	ONE THOUSAND FOUR HUNDRED AND TWENTY FIVE (1425) CTNS OF ELECTRIC CANDLE SHAPE 15W H.S. CODE: 8539.29	"P"	427500PCS USD: 29267	18MM0113 JAN. 22, 2019	**********
2	ONE HUNDRED (100) CTNS OF ELECTRIC ROUND SHAPE 15W H.S. CODE: 8539.29	"P"	50000PCS USD: 3433		
	*** *** *** *** *** Marks and numbers on packages: LIDO MMS				

12. Declaration by the exporter	13. Certification
The undersigned hereby declares that the above details and statement are correct; that all the goods were produced in 湖州　　　宠物用品有限公司 HUZHOU　　　PET PRODUCTS CO., LTD. 　　　　　　　(Country) and that they comply with the origin requirements specified for these goods in the China-Pakistan Free Trade Area Preferential Tariff for the goods exported to PAKISTAN (Importing country) Place and date, signature of stamp of authorized signatory	It is hereby certified, on the basis of control carried out, that the declaration by the exporter is correct. [HANGZHOU CUSTOMS seal – THE PEOPLE'S REPUBLIC OF CHINA 杭州海关] Place and date, signature and stamp of certifying authority

中华人民共和国海关出口货物报关单

预录入编号：E20190000179970731　　海关编号：223120190000573309　（洋山市内）　　页码/页数：1/1

境内发货人	(913305231472690)　安吉县 敷料有限责任公司	出境关别 (2248)　洋山港区	出口日期	申报日期 2019-02-18	备案号
境外收货人 RAFFIN MEDICAL		运输方式 (2)　水路运输	运输工具名称及航次号 COSCO DENMARK/027W	提运单号 CNSH105586	
生产销售单位	(91330523147269)　安吉县 敷料有限责任公司	监管方式 (0110)　一般贸易	征免性质 (101)　一般征税	许可证号	
合同协议号 AC-1810-01401		贸易国（地区）(FRA) 法国	运抵国（地区）(FRA) 法国	指运港 (FRA000) 法国	离境口岸 (311002) 洋山港
包装种类 (22)　纸制或纤维板制盒/箱		件数 1668	毛重（千克） 9626	净重（千克） 6054	成交方式 (3) FOB	运费 //	保费 //	杂费 //
随附单证号 随附单证1：　　随附单证2：					
标记唛码及备注 备注：指运港 FOS　集装箱箱标箱数及号码：2；GCNU4778615					

项号	商品编号	商品名称及规格型号	数量及单位	单价/总价/币制	原产国（地区）	最终目的国（地区）	境内货源地	征免
1	30059010	弹性绷带 3|0|医疗，外科用|棉纱，涤棉，涤纶丝|零售包装|RAFFIN|无型号 |0.0182KGX200ROLLS/CTN	6054.90000千克 6054.90000千克	35.8311 216953.62 人民币	中国 (142)	法国 (305)	(33059)湖州	照章征税 (1)

特殊关系确认 否	价格影响确认 否	支付特许权使用费确认 否		
报关人 员 QJDF	报关人员证号	电话	兹声明对以上内容承担如实申报、依法纳税之法律责任	海关批注及签章
申报单位 (913101097687673722)　上海前锦国际货运有限公司			申报单位（签章）	

免责声明：本单证仅供阅览，不承担任何法律责任。格式依据：中国国际贸易单一窗口。

中国人民财产保险股份有限公司
PICC PROPERTY AND CASUALTY COMPANY LIMITED

总公司设于北京　一九四九年创立
Head Office Beijing　Established in 1949

本保单限于2011年12月31日前填开使用有效

货物运输保险单
CARGO TRANSPORTATION INSURANCE POLICY

发票号(INVOICE NO.): 10BY187
合同号(CONTRACT NO.):
信用证号(L/C NO.):

保单号次 POLICY NO. HW38Z/ PYIE201033050200001094

被保险人 INSURED: HUZHOU FIRE INDUSTRY CO., LTD.

中国人民财产保险股份有限公司(以下简称本公司)根据被保险人的要求,由被保险人向本公司缴付约定的保险费,按照本保险单承保险别和背面所载条款与下列特款承保下述货物运输保险,特立本保险单。
THIS POLICY OF INSURANCE WITNESSES THAT PICC PROPERTY AND CASUALTY COMPANY LIMITED (HEREINAFTER CALLED "THE COMPANY") AT THE REQUEST OF THE INSURED AND IN CONSIDERATION OF THE AGREED PREMIUM PAID TO THE COMPANY BY THE INSURED, UNDERTAKES TO INSURE THE UNDERMENTIONED GOODS IN TRANSPORTATION SUBJECT TO THE CONDITIONS OF THIS POLICY AS PER THE CLAUSES PRINTED OVERLEAF AND OTHER SPECIAL CLAUSES ATTACHED HEREON.

标记 MARKS & NOS.	包装及数量 QUANTITY	保险货物项目 DESCRIPTION OF GOODS	保险金额 AMOUNT INSURED
AS PER INVOICE NO. 10BY187	3115CTNS	FIRE FIGHTING EQUIPMENT PARTS	GBP54705.51

总保险金额 TOTAL AMOUNT INSURED: GBP FIFTY FOUR THOUSAND SEVEN HUNDRED AND FIVE AND CENTS FIFTY ONE ONLY

保费 PREMIUM: AS ARRANGED
启运日期 DATE OF COMMENCEMENT: AS PER B/L
装载运输工具 PER CONVEYANCE: PRAGUE EXPRESS 02W17

自 FROM: SHANGHAI
经 VIA:
至 TO: SOUTHAMPTON

承保险别 CONDITIONS: COVERING TRANSPORT INSURANCE FROM PLACE OF DISPATCH TO PLACE DESTINATION INCLUDING
CARGO CLAUSES (A)
WAR CLAUSES (CARGO)
STRIKE CLAUSES (CARGO)

所保货物,如发生保险单项下可能引起索赔的损失或损坏,应立即通知本公司下述代理人查勘。如有索赔,应向本公司提交保单正本(本保险单共有___份正本)及有关文件。如一份正本已用于索赔,其余正本自动失效。
IN THE EVENT OF LOSS OR DAMAGE WHICH MAY RESULT IN A CLAIM UNDER THIS POLICY, IMMEDIATE NOTICE MUST BE GIVEN TO THE COMPANY'S AGENT AS MENTIONED HEREUNDER. CLAIMS, IF ANY, ONE OF THE ORIGINAL POLICY WHICH HAS BEEN ISSUED IN **TWO** ORIGINAL(S) TOGETHER WITH THE RELEVANT DOCUMENTS SHALL BE SURRENDERED TO THE COMPANY. IF ONE OF THE ORIGINAL POLICY HAS BEEN ACCOMPLISHED, THE OTHERS TO BE VOID.

SURVEY TO BE CARRIED OUT BY A LOCAL COMPETENT SURVEYOR. CLAIM DOCUMENTS TO BE MAILED TO THE UNDERWRITER, WE SHALL EFFECT PAYMENT BY REMITTANCE TO THE CLAIMANT.

中国人民财产保险股份有限公司 湖州市分公司
PICC Property and Casualty Company Limited, Huzhou Branch

ORIGINAL

			B/L NO. 8NGBGOA3AJ91...
1. Shipper SHENZHEN CHANGXINGYUAN INDUSTRIAL DEVELOPMENT CO.,LTD.		中海集装箱运输(香港)有限公司 CHINA SHIPPING CONTAINER LINES (HONG KONG) CO., LTD.	
2. Consignee YONG DA DI HU SHAO GAN VIA BRAMANTE 9 20156 MILANO IT TEL:0039-023494466 CELL:3385253887		Cable : CSHKAC Telex : 87986 CSHKAHX Port-to-Port or Combined Transport **BILL OF LADING** RECEIVED in external apparent good order and condition. Except otherwise noted, the total number of containers or other packages or units shown in this Bill of Lading receipt, said by the shipper to contain the goods described above. Which description the carrier has no reasonable means of checking and is not part of the Bill of Lading. One original Bill of Lading should be surrendered, except clause 22 paragraph 5, in exchange for delivery of the shipment. Signed by the consigned or duly endorsed by the holder in due course. Whereupon the other original(s) issued shall be void. In accepting this Bill of Lading, The Merchants agree to be bound by all the terms on the face and back hereof as if each had personally signed this Bill of Lading. WHEN the Place of Receipt of the Goods an inland point and is so named herein, any notation of "ON BOARD" "SHIPPED ON BOARD" or words to like effect on this Bill of Lading shall be deemed to mean on board the truck, trail car, air craft or other inland conveyance (as the case may be), performing carriage from the Place of Receipt of the Goods to the Port of Loading. SEE clause 4 on the back of this Bill of Lading (Terms continued on the back hereof Read Carefully)	
3. Notify Party (Carrier not to be responsible for failure to notify) SAME AS CONSIGNEE			
4. Pre-carriage by	**5. Place of Receipt**		
6. Ocean Vessel CSCL NINGBO **Voy.No** 0037 W	**7. Port of Loading** NINGBO	**ORIGINAL**	
8. Port of discharge GENOVA	**9. Place of Delivery** GENOVA	**10. Final Destination** (of the goods-not the ship)	
11. Marks & Nos. container seal No. N/M	**12. No. of containers or P'kgs.** 1147 CARTONS	**13. kind of Packages : Description of Goods** SHIPPER'S LOAD, COUNT & SEAL SAID TO CONTAIN SLIPPER SCARF	**14. Gross Weight kgs** 23000 KGS **15. Measurement** 68 CBM 1X40'HC CY-CY FREIGHT PREPAID
CCLU6070542/731085/40'HC			
		16. Description of Contents for Shipper's Use Only (CARRIER NOT RESPONSIBLE)	
17. TOTAL NO. CONTAINERS OR PACKAGES (IN WORDS)	SAY ONE THOUSAND ONE HUNDRED FORTY SEVEN(1147)CARTONS ONLY		
18. FREIGHT & CHARGES CHINA SHIPPING (ITALY) AGENCY CO.S.R.L(Head Office) ADDRESS: P.ZZA G.ALESSI 2/9 16128 GENOVA - ITALY TEL:0039 010 56071 FAX:0039 010 5607670	**19. Revenue Tons**	**20. Rate** **21. Per**	**22. Prepaid** Collect
		CSCL(ZHEJIANG)	GENERAL MANAGER AS AGENT FOR THE CARRIER CHINA SHIPPING CONTAINER LINES(HONG KONG) CO., LTD.
24. Ex. Rate:	**25. Prepaid at**	**26. Payable at**	**27. Place and Date of Issue** NINGBO MAR 09,2007
	28. Total prepaid in	**29. No. of Original B(s)/L** THREE	Signed for the Carrier
DATE MAR 09,2007		BY	
			CHINA SHIPPING CONTAINER LINES (HONG KONG) CO., LTD. STANDARD FORM 9701 * Applicable Only When Document Use as a Combined Transport Bill of Lading

NO.600476726

Shipper/ Exporter (complete name and address)		Bill of Lading No.
ZHEJIANG FUERJIA WOODEN CO LTD TANGNAN VILLAGE JIUGUAN TOWN HUZHOU ZHEJIANG CHINA TEL:0086-572-3517107 FAX:0086-572-3511111		SHANYCB10336

BILL OF LADING

TOPOCEAN CONSOLIDATION SERVICE (LOS ANGELES) INC.

OTI License # 14097 N

Consignee (complete name and address)
CON-BAMERICA 28210 OLD 41 RD UNIT 311 BONITA SPRINGS FL 34135 TEL:1 239 949 6653 FAX:1 239 949 6781

RECEIVED by the Carrier the Goods as specified above in apparent good order and condition unless otherwise stated, to be transported to such place as agreed, authorized or permitted herein and subject to all the terms and conditions appearing on the front and reverse of this Bill of Lading to which the Merchant agrees by accepting this Bill of Lading, any local privileges and customs notwithstanding.

The particulars given above as stated by this shipper and the weight, measure, quantity, condition, contents and value of the Goods are unknown to the Carrier.

Notify party (complete name and address)
1)SAME AS CONSIGNEE 2)BAMERICA CORPORATION 2016 NW 82ND AVE MIAMI,FL 33122 PH#(305)477-1910 FAX:(305)477-4029

In WITNESS whereof one (1) original Bill of Lading has been signed if not otherwise stated above, the same being accomplished the other(s), if any, to be void. If required by the Carrier one (1) original Bill of Lading must be surrendered duly endorsed in exchange for the Goods or delivery order.

Where applicable law requires and not otherwise, one original BILL OF LADING must be surrendered, duly endorsed, in exchange for the GOODS or CONTAINER(S) or other PACKAGE(S), the others to stand void. If a "Non-Negotiable" BILL OF LADING is issued, neither an original nor a copy need be surrendered in exchange for delivery unless applicable law so requires.

Place of receipt	Port of Loading
SHANGHAI	SHANGHAI,CHINA
Vessel / Voyage	
MSC SILVANA	O1101A
Port of discharge	Place of delivery
LOS ANGELES,CA	LA PORTE,TX (DOOR)

Final destination (for the Merchant's reference)

PARTICULARS FURNISHED BY SHIPPER

MKS & NOS/ CONTAINER NOS	NO. OF PKGS.	DESCRIPTION OF PACKAGES AND GOODS	GROSS WEIGHT	MEASUREMENT
MSKU6721930 / 40DRY / SEAL# CN8062954		FREIGHT COLLECT FCL/FCL 755 CTNS	19,500.00 KGS	27.620 CBM
MSKU6721930/CN8062954 PO#8545	1 CNTR(S)	S.T.C.:755 CTNS SOLID HARDWOOD FLOORING SHIPPER'S LOAD AND COUNT THIS SHIPMENT CONTAINS NO SOLID WOOD PACKING MATERIALS	755 CTNS 19,500.00 KGS	27.620 CBM

SAY TOTAL ONE (1*40DRY) CONTAINER(S) ONLY

ON BOARD DATE: JAN 9, 2011

09 JAN 2011

TELEX RELEASE

Excess Value Declaration: Refer to Clause 6(4)(B) + (C) on reverse side			
Freight and charges:	Prepaid	Collect	FOR DELIVERY OF GOODS PLEASE APPLY TO: TOPOCEAN CONSOLIDATION SERVICE(NYC) INC 247 MERRICK ROAD, SUITE 104 LYNBROOK, NY 11563 TEL:1-516-791-0112 FAX:1-516-791-0121
OCF & DDC COLLECT AS ARRANGED			
			09 JAN 2011
GRAND TOTAL			PLACE AND DATE OF ISSUE CHINA (MAINLAND) JAN 9, 2011
Number of Original B (s)/L	Shipper - reference S/O No. 105370		**TOPOCEAN** CONSOLIDATION SERVICE (LOS ANGELES) INC.

Jurisdiction: All disputes in any way related to the Bill of Lading shall be determined by the United States District Court for the Central District of California to the exclusion of the jurisdiction of any other courts in the United States or the courts of any other country PROVIDED ALWAYS that the carrier may in its absolute and sole discretion invoke or voluntarily submit to the jurisdiction of any other court which, but for the terms of this Bill of Lading, could properly assume jurisdiction to hear and determine such disputes, but such shall not constitute a waiver of this provision in any other instance.

TOPOCEAN CONSOLIDATION SERVICE LOS ANGELES INC
AS CARRIER

COPY & NON NEGOTIABLE

AS AGENT FOR THE CARRIER

附录二
常用外贸单证术语

All Risks, A. R.	一切险
Accountee	开证人
Accreditor	开证人（委托开证人）
Actual Gross Weight	实际毛重
Advanced B/L	预借提单
Advising Bank	通知行
Aflatoxin Risk	黄曲霉素险
Agreement	协议
Airway Bill	空运货单
Airport of Departure	始发站
Airway Bill, AWB	航空运单
Amount Insured	保险金额
Amount of Credit	信用证金额
Anticipatory L/C	预支信用证
Anti-dated B/L	倒签提单
Applicant	开证人（申请开证人）
Application for Letter of Credit	开证申请书
Application for Transportation Insurance	海运出口货物投保单或运输险投保申请单
At the Request of	应（某人）请求
Available by Drafts at Sight	凭即期汇票付款
Both Days Inclusive, B. D. I.	包括头尾两天
B/C Bill for Collection	托收汇票
B/D Bill Discount	贴现汇票
Back to Back L/C	背对背信用证
Balance, Bal.	余额
Bank Receipt	结汇水单
Bearer B/L	不记名提单
Beneficiary	受益人

Beneficiary's Certificate/Declaration/Statement	受益人证明书
Beneficiary's Certified Copy of Telex(fax)	受益人签字证明的电传(传真)副本
Bank Identification Code, BIC	国际银行代号(即 SWIFT CODE)
Bill of Exchange	汇票
Bill of Lading	提单
Black List Certificate	黑名单证明
Blank Endorsed	空白背书
Breakage of Packing Risk	包装破裂险
Buyer's Name and Address	买方名称和地址
by T.T	电汇
Carbon Copy, C.C.	抄送
Combined Certificate of Value and Origin, C.C.V.O.	价值、产地联合证明书(海关发票)
Certificate of Origin, C/O	原产地证书
Cargo Receipt	承运货物收据
Carrier	承运人
China Council for the Promotion of International Trade, CCPIT	中国国际贸易促进委员会
Certificate of Chinese Origin/Certificate of Origin of China	中国原产地证书
Certificate of Measurement &./or Weight	衡量证书
Certificate of Origin "Form A"	"格式 A"原产地证书
Certificate of Value	价值证明书
Certificate of Origin under the Bangkok Agreement	《曼谷协定》优惠原产地证书
Certified Cheque	保付支票
Chargeable Weight	收费重量
Charter Party B/L	租船提单
Check/Cheque	支票
Cheque Payable to Bearer	不记名支票或空白支票
Cheque Payable to Order	记名支票
Claim Payable at	赔款偿付地点
Clash and Breakage	破损、破碎险
Clean B/L	清洁提单
Clean Draft	光票
Clean L/C	光票信用证
Combined Certificate	联合凭证

Combined Transport Documents, C. T. D.	多式联运单据
Commercial Invoice	商业发票
Conference Line Certificate	班轮公会船只证明
Confirmation	确认书
Confirmed L/C	保兑信用证
Confirming Bank	保兑行
Consignee	收货人
Consular Invoice	领事发票
Container Booking Note	集装箱货物托运单
Container Ship Certificate	集装箱船只证明
Contract	合同
Copy	副本
Courier Receipt	快递底单
Credit Note	贷记通知
Crossed Cheque	划线支票
Customs Declaration/Customs Manifest	报关单
Customs Invoice	海关发票
Documents against Acceptance, D/A	承兑交单
Demand Draft, D/D	票汇
Documents against Payment, D/P	付款交单
Dock Receipt, D/R	场站收据
Date and Place	出票日期和地点
Date for Presentation of Documents	交单期
Date of Shipment	装船期
Debit Note	借记通知
Declaration and Other Contents	声明文句及其他内容
Declaration of No-wood Packing Material	非木质包装声明
Declaration of Origin	产地证明书(产地声明)
Deferred Payment L/C	延付信用证
Description of Goods	品名及货物描述
Dispatch	发送
Direct B/L	直运提单
Documentary Draft	跟单汇票
Documentary L/C	跟单信用证
Documents Required	单据要求
Documents to Accompany Air Waybill	货运单所附文件
Draft	汇票
Draft ×× Days after B/L Date	提单日后××天付款

Draft ×× Days after Date	出票日后××天付款
Draft ×× Days after Sight	见票后××天付款
Draft at Sight	即期汇票
Drawee	受票人、付款人
Drawer	出票人
Errors and Omissions Excepted, E. & O. E.	有错当查
Endorsement	批单
Establishing Bank	开证行
Expiry(Expiring) Date	有效期
Export Contract	出口合同
Export License	出口许可证
Exporter's Name and Address	出口商名称和地址
Free from Particular Average, F. P. A.	平安险
Failure to Deliver Risk	交货不到险
Favor in Yourselves	以你本人为受益人
For Account of	付(某人)账
Form E	中国-东盟自由贸易区优惠原产地证书
Freight Prepaid B/L	运费预付提单
Freight to Collect B/L	运费到付提单
Freight Note/Voucher	运费收据
Fresh Water and/or Rain Damage	淡水雨淋险
From... to...	起讫地点
Generalized System of Preferences Certificate of Origin Form A, G. S. P.	普惠制原产地证书
Gross Weight(Per Package/Total)	毛重(单件/合计)
HS Code	商品 HS 编码
HAWB, House Air Waybill	航空分运单
Holder	持有人
Hook Damage Risk	钩损险
House B/L	运输代理行提单
Import Contract	进口合同
Import Duty Risk	进口关税险
In Duplicate	一式两份
In Favor of/In One's Favor	以(某人)为受益人
In Triplicate	一式三份
Indivisible L/C	不可分割信用证
Inspection Certificate for Bow Silk Classification & Condition Weight	生丝品级及公量检验证书
Inspection Certificate of Weight or Quantity	重量或数量检验证书

Inspection Certificate of Disinfections or Sterilization	消毒检验证书
Inspection Certificate of Fumigation	熏蒸检验证书
Inspection Certificate of Hold/Tank	船舱检验证书
Inspection Certificate of Packing	包装检验证书
Inspection Certificate of Quality	品质检验证书,质量检验证书
Inspection Certificate of Temperature	温度检验证书
Inspection Certificate on Container	集装箱检验证书
Insurance Declaration	保险声明书
Insurance Policy	保险单
International Multi-modal Transport	国际多式联运
Irrevocable L/C	不可撤销信用证
International Standard Banking Practice for the Examination of Documents under Documentary credit, ISBP	关于审核跟单信用证项下单据的国际标准银行实务
Issued by	出单人
Issued Retrospectively	后发证书
Issuing Bank	开证行
Itinerary Certificate	航程证明
L/C No. and Contract No.	信用证号码及合同号码
L/C with T/T Reimbursement Clause	带电汇条款信用证
Latest Date of Shipment	最迟装运日期
Letter of Credit	信用证
Liner B/L	班轮提单
Long Form B/L	全式提单
M/T Mail Transfer	信汇
Marine/Ocean Bill of Lading	海运提单
Marks & No.	唛头及件数
Mate's Receipt, M/R	大副收据
Master Air Waybill, MAWB	航空主运单
Means of Transportation and Route	运输工具和航线
Measurement List	尺码单
Memorandum	备忘录
Minimum B/L	最低运费提单
No Marks, N/M	无唛头
Name of Commodity & Specification	品名和规格
Name Survey Agent	保险人在货运目的地的检验代理人
Nature and Quantity of Goods	货物名称及数量
Negotiation	议付

Negotiating Bank	议付行
Net Weight(Per Package/Total)	净重(单件/合计)
No. /Invoice No.	编号或商业发票编号
Notify Party	被通知人
Notifying Bank	通知行
Number Kind of Packages	件数和包装方式
Open Account,O/A	赊销
Ocean Marine Cargo War Risk	海运战争险
Ocean Vessel,Voyage No.	船名、航次
On Behalf of	代表某人
On Board B/L, Shipped B/L	已装船提单
On Deck B/L	甲板提单
On Deck Risk	舱面险
Open Policy/Cover Note	预约保单
Opener	开证人
Opening Bank	开证行
Order B/L	指示提单
Original	正本
Original Documents	正本单据
Proforma Invoice,P/I	形式发票
Packing Documents	包装单据
Packing List/Packing Slip	装箱单
Parcel Post Receipt	邮包收据
Partial Shipments	分批装运
Payee	收款人
Payer	付款人
Paying Bank	付款行
Per Conveyance	装载运输工具
Place and Date of Issue	出单地点和日期
Place of Clearance	报关口岸
Place of Delivery	交货地
Place of Receipt	收货地
Policy No.	保单编号
Premium Paid	保费已付
Principal	开证人(委托开证人)
Processing with Customers' Materials	来料加工
Promissory Note	本票
Purchase Contract	购买合同
Quantity	数量
Railway Bill	铁路运单

Rate/Charge	费率
Received for Shipment B/L	备运提单
Reciprocal L/C	对开信用证
Reimbursement	索偿
Reimbursing Bank	偿付行
Rejection Risk	拒收险
Revocable L/C	可撤销信用证
Revolving L/C	循环信用证
Risk of Intermixture and Contamination	混杂、玷污险
Risk of Leakage	渗漏险
Risk of Odors	串味险
Risk of Rust	锈损险
Risk of Shortage in Weight	短量险
Shipping Order, S/O	装货单
Sales Contract	销售合同
Sanitary Inspection Certificate	卫生检验证书
See Attachment	见附页
Seller's Contingent Risk	卖方利益险
Ship's Nationality Certificate	船籍证明
Ship's Age Certificate	船龄证明
Ship's Classification Certificate	船级证明
Shipper	托运人
Shipper's Declared Value	托运人申明的价值
Shipper's Letter of Instruction	国际货物托运书
Shipping Advice	装运通知
Shipping Marks and Nos.	唛头及编号
Shipping Note, S/N	订舱委托书
Shipping Order, S/O	装货单
Short Form B/L or Simple B/L	略式提单
Sight Drafts	即期汇票
Sight L/C	即期信用证
Signature	签章
Signature and Others	受益人签章及其他
Signature of Shipper	托运人签字
Sinosure	中国出口信用保险公司
Slg. On or Abt.	开航日期
Stale B/L	过期提单
Straight B/L	记名提单
Strike Risk	罢工险
Sweating and Heating Risk	受潮受热险

Theft Pilferage and Non-delivery, T. P. N. D.	偷窃、提货不着险
Telegraphic Transfer, T/T	电汇
Tax Refund	退税
Telex Released/Surrendered B/L	电放提单
Through B/L	联运提单
Time Drafts	远期汇票
To Whom It May Concern	致有关当事人(中性抬头)
Total Amount Insured	总保险金额
Transferable L/C	可转让信用证
Transferee	受让人
Transshipment	转运
Transshipment B/L	转运提单
Traveller's L/C	旅行信用证
UCP600	跟单信用证统一惯例600号出版物
Unclean B/L	不清洁提单
Unconfirmed L/C	不保兑信用证
Unit Price and Amount	单价与总金额
Un-transferable L/C	不可转让信用证
Usance L/C	远期信用证
Veterinary Inspection Certificate	兽医检验证书
With Average or With Particular Average, W. A. or W. P. A.	水渍险
Weight List/Weight Note	磅码单/重量单
With Recourse L/C	有追索权信用证
Without Recourse L/C	无追索权信用证

参考文献

[1] 姬文桂,林继玲. 外贸单证实务[M]. 北京：机械工业出版社,2019.

[2] 傅利利. 外贸单证实务[M]. 北京：中国人民大学出版社,2019.

[3] 章安平. 外贸单证操作：第5版[M]. 北京：高等教育出版社,2019.

[4] 李贺,李纲,季彬,郭爽. 外贸单证实务——应用·技能·案例·实训：第3版[M]. 上海：上海财经大学出版社,2019.

[5] 李继宏. 外贸单证实务[M]. 北京：机械工业出版社,2014.

[6] 林榕,吕亚君. 外贸单证实务[M]. 北京：人民邮电出版社,2019.

[7] 国际商会中国国家委员会. ICC跟单信用证统一惯例(UCP600)[M]. 北京：中国民主法制出版社,2006.

[8] 中国商业企业管理协会. 国际商务单证教程[M]. 北京：科学技术文献出版社,2011.

[9] 屈韬,何秉毅. 外贸单证实务[M]. 上海：上海财经大学出版社,2011.

[10] 中华人民共和国海关总署 http://www.customs.gov.cn/

[11] 中国自由贸易区服务网 http://fta.mofcom.gov.cn/

[12] 福步外贸论坛 http://bbs.fobshanghai.com/

[13] 海关律帅网 http://www.customslawyer.cn/